LEISURE HOUR SERIES

JOSEPH NOIREL'S REVENGE

BY

VICTOR CHERBULIEZ

Translated from the French

BY

WM. F. WEST, A. M.

(Reprinted from The Week)

NEW YORK
HOLT & WILLIAMS
1872

CONTENTS.

JOSEPH NOIREL'S REVENGE.

CHAPTER I.

MON-PLAISIR AND ITS INMATES.

ALTHOUGH perfect happiness is not of this world, something very like it was to be found, a few years ago, in a country house two or three miles from Geneva, on the main road from that city to Saint-Julien. This house, which its inmates had christened *Mon-Plaisir*, is approached by means of a long avenue of pear-trees, and presents an agreeable picture to the passer-by. Standing on the summit of a grassy slope, surrounded by masses of verdure and a garden of roses, it overlooks an orchard on the west and a terraced vineyard on the east. This vineyard is bordered by a brook and a row of willows.

The proprietor of this smiling domain was a citizen of Geneva, M. Thomas Mirion, a furniture manufacturer and dealer, a man who understood his business, and who had been made rich by it. This fortunate man could not conceal his happiness; it beamed forth in his honest face, in his round and rosy cheeks, in his bright and confident glance, and in his smile, which indicated an amiable good-nature, a trait of character that had never proved injurious to his business. It must be admitted that, though Heaven had helped him, this broad-shouldered, strong-backed man had nobly helped himself. Constantly at work, always contented, he had that perseverance that conquers all things, that good nature that simplifies all difficulties, that care and circumspection that avoids all false steps. Although he had always wished to live well and cut a figure in the world, he had never allowed his expenses to exceed his income. Dieting his vanity, so to speak, he had never taken from his business more than could well be spared from it. Finally some important orders which he turned to good profit, made him rich. An association which had built several large hotels on the shores of Lake Leman, made a contract with him to furnish them. He realized a large sum by this contract, and that too without violating his conscience. He was not a man to supply a poor article ; but managed so well that the buyer was well pleased, and the seller even more so. Profitable investments and fortunate speculations tripled and quadrupled his gain ; he became a man of means. As his property increased, he satisfied, one by one, all those desires which had for a long time been silently brooding in his breast, which had so often been repressed by his wise and prudent policy. He bought, piece by piece, a tract of land of which he had first obtained the refusal, built a small summer-house upon it, where the family passed their Sundays and holidays, and finally replaced the summer-house by an elegant and costly dwelling. A year later he had a stable, two horses, and a carriage. He had at last arrived at the summit of his desires. It is proper to add that M. Mirion had none of those disagreeable ways that render a *parvenu* so insupportable. Although he could easily have proved how wealthy he was, he did not assume the airs of a Marquis of Carabas, and did not delight in bullying his neighbors or in spattering them with mud from his high station. He continued to work and kept his shop open as before. Caring little to rise above his former position, to *grimpionner*, as they say at Geneva, he did not try to associate himself with people of high rank, and remained faithful to all his old friendships. We may say further that his house did not in any respect resemble a castle, that his carriage was handsome but unpretentious, and his two horses were honest nags that trotted well, but never mistook their place, nor put on airs with those passing by.

Plutarch tells us that those envious of Sylla called him "the fortunate," and that the great man was not offended by it, but spoke of Fortune as having aided him, and congratulated himself on having so good a friend. Like Sylla, M. Mirion had his envious acquaintances who said to him, "You are extremely fortunate, Mirion; you have had wonderful opportunities during your whole life." M. Mirion, without being at all provoked, would answer them, "My friends, you are right; I was born under a lucky star. Nature has done well by me; she has given me an iron constitution, a good stomach, arms and legs that are fond of work, and a certain share of common sense to guide me. I admit that I have had opportunities. It is not less true that I commenced in a small way, and, if I have had success, I believe that I have done something toward obtaining it." While speaking thus, he would cast a fond glance on his house and stable, his vineyard, and his pear-trees. "The best of it is," he would add, "it has all been honestly acquired. I am not like some people that we know. I am a man of principle. I can place my hand upon my breast and feel that my conscience does not reproach me." M. Mirion loved to talk of his conscience and his principles; it is a peculiarity which a few of his countrymen share with him.

If M. Mirion was a happy man, Mme. Mirion was surely a happy woman. She had not, however, the clear good sense and easy temper of her husband. Her happiness was noisy, demonstrative, and somewhat lyrical. Small and plump, with a well-rounded form and face, she spun round quickly like a top, while her eyes and tongue moved as nimbly as her limbs. She ran to and fro, turned about, and went away, chatting all the time; she was always out of breath, and her two chief pleasures were to get excited and to talk. To tell the truth, she was not altogether free from that fault which the English have termed snobbishness. She exhibited a somewhat exaggerated admiration for her home and every thing it contained, including the ducks and canaries. Her pear-trees were the finest in the world, the roses in her garden had a sweetness which was elsewhere unknown, the water from her pump had a slight nutty taste which was incomparable, her hens laid four times as many eggs as her neighbors', and these eggs from some unknown cause, always had a double yelk. In short, Mon-Plaisir was a remarkable place, under the especial blessing of Heaven, where every thing happened that was desired, where the grass grew thicker than in any other spot, where the rain always fell as it was wanted; a true paradise lighted by a sun which was not the ordinary sun that every body saw, but a sun assigned to the especial service of M. and Mme. Mirion. The innocent fancies of his wife often made our furniture dealer smile. Sometimes even he teased her a little. "My good Marianne," he would say, "there are some things which you have a perfect right to believe, but it's better not to speak of them, for fear of making other people laugh." "I don't care, let them laugh," she would reply; "it's only because they envy us." She would then reproach him for not gaining all the advantage that he could from his new position, for not making enough show and parade. She thought that rejoicing and noisy gayety were the necessary accompaniments of happiness, that they were the sign to be placed before the door. Her secret ambition was to have a large marble fountain, with its Tritons, beneath her windows, to plant an allegorical statue before her gate, to replace the good Savoyard girl who waited on the table with a fashionable waiter wearing a white cravat, and to give each week a fête, when rockets should be sent up from the lawn—Mme. Mirion had a weakness for rockets. Unfortunately allegories, white cravats, and fire-works had no attractions for M. Mirion. He was fond of ease and comfort, but he thought that vanity was expensive and not particularly profitable. These slight differences of opinion, however, did not lead to any serious conflicts in the household. Mme. Mirion adored her husband, whom she looked upon as a great man, and she resigned herself to his refusal as dictated by a wisdom superior to her own. On his side, M. Mirion took pleasure in giving his wife credit for all her good qualities, and for all the help which her habits of system and order had been to him. She attended to her household duties with indefatigable care and vigilance, having an eye everywhere, in the cellar and the garret, in the pantry and the kitchen. Her faithfulness and ability were more than an offset to her unfortunate passion for Tritons.

The happiness of these worthy people was contagious; they delighted in seeing every thing about them joyful and contented. Cats, dogs, and chickens, every thing at Mon-Plaisir lived in luxury and tasted the pleasures of a quiet and peaceful life under a merciful and paternal rule. The most petted of the domestic animals that had found shelter and food at Mon-Plaisir, were two old maids, relatives of M. Mirion, who boarded them at a very moderate charge. The one, Mlle. Baillet, was his aunt on his mother's side. She was usually spoken of as Aunt Amaranth, because that was her favorite color, as could be seen by her bonnet-strings, the trimmings of her dress, and her beautiful purple stockings. In spite of her seventy years, this worthy lady was marvelously well preserved. Always neat and dressed with care, having a somewhat affected air and voice, with shoulders drawn in and chin raised, she stood as straight as a wax candle, and when seated, her back never touched the chair. She had read a little, and had seen something of the world. Having spent ten years in the service of a noble family of Mecklenburg, she had there learned a number of maxims and aphorisms, and a complete code of social and moral ethics. When I said that she knew something of the world, I meant her world, the world of Mecklenburg. According to her account, there was nothing to be compared to the court of Schwerin, the most elegant of all the German courts. So dazzled had she been by the splendor which she had there seen, that she no longer deemed a country respectable, unless it had an equestrian order and was governed by a prince who had his foot soldiers and couriers always about him. She knew every letter in the *Almanach de Gotha*, could recite all the genealogies of the duchy, and abounded in anecdotes, more or less apocryphal, concerning the reigning grand duchess and her mother. She had once had the honor of being present at a court ball. This ball was the great event of her life; she had described it a hundred times, she was always ready to describe it again. M. Mirion stopped his ears when she began, but Mme. Mirion was more and more pleased with each repetition of this wonderful story. Proud of having beneath her roof one who had seen real princes in flesh and blood, it seemed to her that, thanks to Aunt Amaranth, she was in some way related to the Grand Duke of Mecklenburg.

Very different was Mlle. Grillet, M. Mirion's first cousin, a puny little woman, who seemed scarcely to have strength enough to move about. Somewhat deformed, her body being out of shape and one shoulder larger than the other, she looked very little like a person of romantic imagination. Nevertheless she had once had her romance which had ended unfortunately. She had fallen madly in love with a gay deceiver, who had amused himself by making sport of her, and it was some time before the innocent creature understood that he was only trifling. This unhappy experience had made her very suspicious and extremely timid; the world seemed to her to be full of thorns, making it necessary to look carefully before her at every step. A scalded cat fears cold water; she was afraid of ridicule, of the opinions and perfidies of men. At every new occurrence, she asked herself, "What will people say?" and from fear that something would be said, she was very reticent, keeping her thoughts entirely to herself. Mme. Mirion accused her of being narrow-minded, and was a little provoked because she agreed with her husband in the matter of the Tritons. Her opinion having been asked by her cousin, Mlle. Grillet had stated, in her usual drawling tone, that naked Tritons were not a proper ornament for a respectable gentleman's grounds, and that all the neighbors would surely talk about them. Mme. Mirion, however, was forced to acknowledge that she was a very useful person. If she had never been in Mecklenburg, nor seen the mother of the grand duchess, she knew well what the garden contained and put up the most excellent brandied plums.

In every concert a false note will sometimes occur, and in the crowd which surrounds the conqueror's triumphal car, there is usually some ill-tempered person ready to remind him of the mutability of fortune. It was M. Mirion's elder brother, generally known as Uncle Benjamin, who, at Mon-Plaisir, served as the false note and monitor. His visits there were long and frequent, and Mme. Mirion plied him with attentions and crammed him with sweetmeats, in vain attempts to soften his cynical temper; for, although he was one of the best men in the world at heart, he found more or less fault with every thing. Perhaps there was a little envy in his disposition. The father of MM. Thomas and Benjamin Mirion, an honest carpenter, had concluded in his great wisdom, that his son Thomas would never be a man of genius, and had taken him from school at an early age to place the plane and chisel in his hands. At the same time he had conceived the highest opinion of Benjamin's talents, and had spared no expense in his education. "Our fine lad," he would complacently remark, "our fine lad will be the genius of the family." After having carried him successfully through his classes and taken all the prizes, Benjamin's precocious genius was suddenly arrested, and all the care that had been spent upon him served to produce only a very ordinary teacher of mathematics, who went through life just managing to support himself, while the despised Thomas, constantly rising, finally inscribed his name in the golden book of the Genevan millionaires. Benjamin had the best wishes possible toward his brother, but it seemed to him that fortune had bestowed her favors in a capricious manner. "Why is Mon-Plaisir his instead of mine?" he kept asking himself. This thought was with him when he went to sleep, and came to him as soon as he awoke; it did not, however, prevent him from becoming very angry with other envious people who spoke slightingly of his brother. "He has been both able and honest," he would say to them in a surly tone. "Why don't you follow his example?" Uncle Benjamin was like those mothers who keep picking at their children, but will not let any one else interfere with them.

Two hours never passed at Mon-Plaisir without his saying something to wound the vanity of his too sensitive sister-in-law. He had a geometrical eye, and took pleasure in criticising the lines in which her fruit trees and rose bushes were arranged. He maintained that the walls were not plumb, that the squares of the floor were not of equal size, and that the stairs were not in good proportion. When contradicted, he armed himself with a plumb-line, rule, and square, and in a calm but determined manner, compelled the angry Mme. Mirion to listen till he had finished his demonstration — he planted his compasses in her heart. What was yet worse, he pretended that Mon-Plaisir was not the most healthy place in the world, that the exhalations from the brook which bounded the property on the east were injurious to throats that were at all delicate. Regularly, at the breakfast table, he was seized with a long and violent fit of coughing. "What's the matter, Benjamin?" his brother would ask with a little impatience in his tone. "It's no use," he would reply, "I can't come here without catching cold." At this Mme. Mirion would grow very excited. In her heart she looked upon her brother-in-law as an evil genius, as a tantalizing and disagreeable person; before the world, she spoke of him in the highest terms, as a very superior man, who was an honor to his country. Her family pride rose into heroism.

CHAPTER II.

MARGUERITE MIRION.

Notwithstanding what Uncle Benjamin said, I believe that Mon-Plaisir was a healthy place enough; I also believe, without having seen them, that Mme. Mirion's rose-bushes were a credit to her. She had, however, another cause for the most heartfelt joy and satisfaction. The loveliest rose of her garden, the most precious ornament of her house, the feast of her eyes, her highest pride and glory was her daughter. Certain it is that Mlle. Marguerite Mirion was beautiful; all Geneva, if called upon, would bear witness to the fact. She was tall, slender, exquisitely graceful, with beautifully rounded throat and arms, having the hands and feet of a duchess, light wavy hair drawn back from her brow, handsome brown eyes soft as velvet, a dazzling complexion, and a smile the charm of which was enhanced by an expression of indescribable simplicity and frankness. As she walked, free from thought or care, up and down the avenue of pear-trees leading to the road, those passing by stopped before the gate to look at her, saying to themselves, "What a lovely flower!" These words came naturally to the lips on seeing her. She had come up like a flower; nature had done all for her. Although Mlle. Marguerite Mirion was aware of the fact that she was beautiful, although she was not displeased when others gazed upon her, there was not the slightest grain of coquetry in her disposition, and in her simplicity, she ignored all those little affectations and allurements which often form the stock in trade of a pretty girl. She could do without these, she could afford to leave them to those who were somewhat doubtful concerning their beauty; hers was not to be disputed. When, on Sunday, she accompanied her mother to church, their entrance always caused a great sensation; all eyes were turned toward them, and a hum of admiration, very grateful to the heart of Mme. Mirion, was heard. This admiration was pleasing also to M. Mirion; he idolized his daughter, and as he gazed upon her, he always seemed to grow taller. Even Uncle Benjamin laid down his arms before Marguerite. He was very attentive to her, supplying her with candies and reciting madrigals to her; all his savings and all his poetry went in that direction. Sometimes, taking her by the chin, he would say, "What a pretty girl you are! Where on earth did you come from? Your father's eyes are like a frog's, your mother is short and dumpy: how could they have produced a masterpiece like you? If they were to tell the truth, they would confess that they found you under a cabbage leaf."

A handsome girl, especially if she be an only child, is usually spoiled. Although M. and Mme. Mirion had tried their best to spoil their daughter, they had not succeeded in so doing. Her generous nature had not been injured by the excessive kindness which had been bestowed upon her. All who knew her could say that she was neither proud nor haughty. Aunt Amaranth and Mlle. Grillet could both testify that she had an even and gentle temper, and that she was thoughtful of others, treating them with kindness and delicate attention. What chiefly distinguished her was the purity of her sentiments and the nobility of her character. She was above all sordid calculations, all low thoughts and feelings; she did not need to fight against them, she was free from their attacks through her perfect ignorance of evil. Vanity sometimes has its uses. If Marguerite had always lived at home, she would, I fear, have become dull and stupid; she would have contracted some incorrigible faults. Fortunately, her lady mother had decided to give her what she called a first-class education, and to accomplish this, had the courage to send her from home to a celebrated and aristocratic boarding-school in the canton of Vaud. Marguerite found herself associated there with young ladies of high birth. In this noble company she cut but a poor figure; notwithstanding her handsome eyes, the furniture dealer's daughter was put in the background. She had no partiality shown her; she received her due, but was never courted. At this school, she learned to make comparisons which helped to form her judgment. She also learned to control her actions and her words, which is the true foundation of a first-class education. Fortunately, however, she did not lose her light-heartedness and gayety, but took them home with her just at the close of her seventeenth year. She also carried back a confused mass of scribblings, of studies, some well, some ill digested, a dim knowledge of many things, and a fair musical education. The evening of her arrival, in spite of all that M. Mirion and the timorous Mlle. Grillet could say, the house was illuminated from garret to cellar, and the terrace lighted *à giorno* with transparencies and fireworks.

Mon-Plaisir was a new acquaintance for Marguerite ; it had been bought during her absence. A very pleasant room, exquisitely decorated and furnished, had been prepared for her. In it were rich ornaments and moldings, tables of ebony and mosaic, a Persian carpet, and curtains of white cashmere, while pretty trifles and flowers were scattered all about. Marguerite was in love with her little room. She spent whole hours there alone, flitting like a bird about her flower-stands, opening a book, reading a little and stopping in the middle of a sentence, or leaning on her window-sill and casting a happy glance over the orchard, the road, the hills, the Jura, joyful in life and youth, having no care,with the spring-time in her cheek, with content and cheerfulness in her heart. The bell would ring for breakfast. She would go down to the dining-room, kiss Aunt Amaranth and say to her, " Is it as pleasant as this in Mecklenburg?" Afterwards she would throw her arm round Cousin Grillet's waist and draw her into the garden, saying, " Let's see how our rose-bushes are coming on." On the way she would pluck a flower and put it in her hair. Returning to the house, she would sit down at the piano, and play a barcarolle, or sing a love song in a full, clear voice, paying attention wholly to the music and caring little for the words, which she thought she understood, but which, in reality, were Hebrew to her. In the evening, she would embroider, talk about her school, or nestling in an arm-chair, receive the attentions of her uncle

Benjamin, if he were there, and laugh loud and long at his compliments and madrigals. The family separated at ten o'clock. She would then go directly to her room, and sometimes would open her window to look upon the moon; but no confidences passed between them, they had nothing of importance to say to each other. When half undressed, she would kneel down, and, her head resting against her flower-stand, would breathe this silent prayer to her kind Father: "Thou art good and wise, thou knowest what is needful for me; if it be possible, let all my life be like to-day." Then she would fall into a calm, deep, and dreamless slumber, awaking to rejoice that the sun was again shining, and that Life, standing by her bedside, was awaiting her.

It will readily be believed that Mme. Mirion's thoughts pierced farther into the future than those of Marguerite. Her maternal vanity was at work, and in her mental orisons, she was not satisfied to ask, "May to-morrow be like to-day." Her prayer was, "Thou knowest what I desire; when will he come? Grant, O Lord! that he may be like a fairy prince!" What she read most and understood best in the New Testament, was the parable of the talents and the sacred duty which is imposed upon us, of obtaining all the interest that we can, as we shall one day be called upon to render up an account. Heaven had placed a treasure in her hands; the investment of this treasure was the chief aim of her life. She would often sit quietly by the hour, plunged in deep reveries; then starting suddenly, she would ask her husband: "Do you want to know what I'm thinking of?" "Oh dear!" he would reply stroking his chin, "I can guess without any trouble. Your head is full of sons-in-law, stout and lean, little and big; I care little for them. What do all these dreams amount to? Let's enjoy the present and take the future as it comes." Mme. Mirion had sense enough not to make her daughter acquainted with her plans and wishes, and Marguerite was very far from guessing them. The pastor of their parish, a wise man in his way, said of her, "She is a tranquil lake; guard her from storms." Like her father, she enjoyed the present, dreaming neither of marriage nor of husbands. She was so ill-informed on certain points, she paid no attention to the fact that the son of a rich linen-draper was in the habit of coming every Sunday to Mon-Plaisir, under the pretext of playing billiards with M. Mirion, but really for the sake of seeing her. The indifference of his fair charmer prevented him from declaring his suit in person; he, however, engaged a third party to speak for him. M. Mirion was tempted to say yes; Mme. Mirion cried out against the proposition, declaring that the gentleman was not worthy of her daughter, and did not figure in her collection. He was dismissed and nothing was said to Marguerite. If she had been consulted, what answer would she have given? Like all natures swayed rather by affection than by passion, she had something of weakness and indecision in her character. Moreover, she had thought little on these matters; she would have said: "Dear me! if it seems best... I will do just as you wish."

CHAPTER III.

JOSEPH NOIREL.

In this happy household, however, there was one unhappy person. No one was to blame for this. Always welcome, loved by every one, treated, though a stranger, like one of the family, his lot seemed an envious one. But there are many causes of suffering here below: sorrow has many aspects, sadness many mysteries, and, ofttimes, if the question were put to us, "Why do you complain, have you not every thing you wish?" we should have a perfect right to answer, "What do you know about it?" The discontented person of whom I speak was one of M. Mirion's workmen, a youth of twenty-five, named Joseph Noirel. He had dark brown hair, was of medium height, and of slight but muscular frame; he had a strong will, and with his ten fingers he accomplished wonders. His face was very intelligent and somewhat pale; occasionally a sudden glow would flush his cheeks. To tell the truth, this face was not very regular; the mouth and nose were both too large. The clear gray eyes, however, like the eyes of certain greyhounds, like the limpid water of certain streams, were full of light and motion; their glance was both deep and penetrating. Sometimes they disclosed a whole history, and that history by no means a cheerful one.

The poor boy had been reared by wretched parents. His father had been a jack at all trades who accomplished nothing. He tried his hand at almost every thing, but finally gave himself over entirely to idleness and dissipation. With want gnawing him like an incurable leprosy, a stranger to every sentiment of honor, delighting in strong drink, hugging his poverty, scarcely would he have worked a week, before he would desert his employer, dive into some out-of-the-way kennel, and there drink up his wages; after all was gone, he would return home, with an empty pocket, a dull eye, and a thick tongue, and say to his wife with a maudlin laugh, "Well! what of it? I've been on a spree."

"You'd better go on another," she would reply; "there's not enough in the house to feed a spider."

"You lie!" he would answer; "the young rascal must have brought in something."

The truth is, it was the young rascal, that is Joseph, who in these days of misery was compelled to provide for them. He set out every morning, according to orders, with a crust of dry bread in his pocket and a basket on his arm, selling matches and begging from door to door. Woe to him if his returns were scanty: the blows rained upon his head like hail. One day, weary of climbing stairs and having his ears boxed for his trouble, he ran away; he was caught and beaten so cruelly that it took away from him all desire of repeating the experiment. Sometimes his mother would treat him very harshly; then in a fit of tenderness, in order to console him for the sufferings he had undergone, she would take him to spend the evening at a coffee-house, where, with eyes and ears wide open, he would listen for hours to the gushing notes of Mlle. Zephyrine, the prima donna of the Eldorado at Lyons. These were his holidays, his intermittent Paradise. The next day, he would start on his route again, asking from house to house for a little help, crying to move the sympathies of the kind gentlemen and ladies, a sad trade, to which, thank Heaven, he could never reconcile himself; he followed it unwillingly, looking for all the world like a whipped cur. There was something within him, I know not what, which protested against his work; a kind of native pride, which he must, I think, have inherited from some remote ancestor. When his story was disbelieved or he was called a beggar, he would straighten himself up and sing in a loud voice some strain which he had caught from Mlle. Zephyrine. Freaks of this kind did not serve to improve his trade; each day the number of houses which he dared not approach increased. Each day, also, the hovel which he knew as home became more forlorn and uninhabitable; in order to obtain food, the furniture and even the bedclothes were disposed of. His father had an attack of *delirium tremens;* thenceforth he was unable to do any work. Fearful quarrels occurred between him and his wife: they caught each other by the hair, exhausting the Billingsgate vocabulary in their rage. The child, pale and shuddering, was a witness of these stormy scenes. Fortunately Noirel had a second attack; he was taken to the hospital, where he died; and ten months later his widow was laid up with sciatic gout, which entirely deprived her of the use of her limbs.

The parish pastor found a place for the invalid in an alms-house, and looked about for a home for the helpless orphan. He spoke of him to M. Mirion, and recommended him warmly to his charity. Joseph was then thirteen years old. M. Mirion sent for him and questioned him. After some deliberation, he agreed to take charge of the boy, to give him food and shelter, and to receive him as an apprentice. As often happens, this good deed afterward had its reward; but the young rascal at first gave his employer much anxiety and trouble. In his former occupation, he had contracted some very bad habits; he had learned to hate all rule and discipline, to run about the streets, and had acquired a stock of vagabond and blackguard wit, which escaped him at the slightest provocation. Although a tight rein was held upon him, he would sometimes escape and stay away whole days at a time. M. Mirion talked with him in his important manner, delivered before him wise and lengthy moral essays which floated away upon the wind, and gave him whippings, which he seemed to care little for, having a tough skin and a pride which the rod could not break. What finally influenced him more strongly than the lectures or any thing else, was an almost passionate love of work which suddenly came upon him. We always like to do what we can do well; one fine morning Joseph found his vocation, and from that moment he became another man; he went to work with a will, his arms became more active while his legs enjoyed a rest. This change at first revealed itself in the love which he manifested for his tools: he handled them with the greatest respect; a speck of rust troubled him, and he gladly devoted his leisure hours to sharpening his planes, chisels, and saws. Seeing this, M. Mirion took a liking to his protege ; he considered that a love of tools was a certain indication of ability. He was astonished also by his manual skill and his inventive powers, and prophesied that he would make his mark. He had him instructed in geometry and drawing. This did not satisfy Joseph ; he studied trigonometry and perspective without a teacher, and became an able draughtsman and designer. At the age of twenty-five he was a master joiner, by far the best workman in M. Mirion's employ, and devoted his attention to fine cabinet work, at the same time giving his advice in all other matters. Although he was really a foreman, he did not have that title ; he was simply M. Mirion's adviser, working for him and receiving fair wages for his work. Inasmuch as he boarded and lodged with his employer, he was enabled to save some money ; he used it to pay his mother's board. She was still a helpless invalid, but clung obstinately to life. As soon as he could, he took her from the alms-house, and found a home for her with some country people. Thanks to him, she was no longer dependent on public charity, and in this particular Joseph's pride was satisfied.

It appears that after all Joseph Noirel had no reason to complain. The little vagabond had been fortunate : it is not every one that meets a M. Mirion on life's highway. Well lodged and fed, without any present trouble, or any great anxiety for the future, loving his work and respected by all about him, what had he to complain of? A secret sorrow : his position was a false one, and a false position is intolerable to a proud nature. He led two modes of life, and both were unpleasant to him : at the same time a workman and his employer's intimate companion, neither he nor his comrades knew exactly where he stood ; a wall seemed built between him and them. Every morning they saw him riding in with M. Mirion from the country ; often during the day, the latter would seek him at his bench, and talk with him in a low and confidential tone. When the clock struck twelve he would call him into his private office, where they would lunch together ; in the evening the carriage would return for them. In vain was Joseph the truest of comrades, in vain at every meeting did he assert before *his brethren, the workingmen,* that he was one of them and wished to be nothing else ; there was in his manner, his cultivated tone, and his precise language, a certain mark of superiority and self-respect which kept them at a distance. They were suspicious of him, regarding him as a doubtful character, the favorite of their employer, almost a gentleman. Some of them even looked upon him as a spy, but were very careful what they said about him. Although he was of slender form, and his small and delicate hands had caused him to be nicknamed the young lady, Joseph had proved on more than one occasion that he could take his own part, and that his fists could do good service. He was therefore treated respectfully, but every one seemed to avoid speaking before him ; a conspiracy was formed to maintain in the shop that silence which keeps a man in quarantine.

At Mon-Plaisir it was very different. The family, which had in a certain sense adopted him, treated him with the greatest confidence. At the table or elsewhere, M. and Mme. Mirion discussed before him all their little affairs and family secrets. When we look for poison we find it everywhere. Joseph was a Genevese, that is he was sensitive and moody, attaching great weight to little things. He was provoked by the confidential way in which he was treated. He thought, "Mme. Mirion would not have spoken as she did before me, if I were a person whose opinion she cared any thing about." Again he would say, "How kind they all are to me ! Kindness is not friendship though, it is a very different affair." Moreover, there were many little things which showed him he was not the equal of those with whom he sat at table ; the servants were particular, as they always are, to make him understand this. The girl who waited on the table, after saying to M. Mirion in a respectful tone, "Can I help you to any thing, sir ?" would suddenly turn to Joseph with, "Will you have some beef ?" This *will you have some beef* and the manner in which it was said were insupportable ; it seemed to say to him, "My dear friend, you are out of place." He dreaded above all the dinner parties which M. Mirion occasionally gave to his friends. He had requested to have his meals sent to his room on such occasions, but M. Mirion had answered him, "Why do you ask that, my boy? Are you not one of the family?" He felt himself out of place in the society of these merry tradespeople, who treated him in a familiar manner which did not entirely conceal their sense of superiority. At one of these parties, he overheard Mme. Mirion say to one of her friends, "Are you surprised that he's so much attached to us? Does he not owe us every thing?" These words were constantly ringing in his ears; he often repeated them aloud, while the bread that he ate seemed very bitter. No one in the house had the least suspicion of his secret troubles. The worthy M. Mirion could not have understood his feelings; I know not whether he would have been sad or angry if he had learned that his workman was not the happiest Joseph in the world. He loved to be with him, and to gaze upon him, not only because he was so useful to him, but also because he recalled the best action of his life, an action which would gain him a sure entrance into Paradise. "He is a lucky fellow," he would mutter to himself; "if it had not been for me, he would have died, like his father, in the hospital, or perhaps in the penitentiary. He owes a big candle to Providence and me. Show me another workman, if you can, who lives so comfortably with his employer, forming his character in the society of honest people!" Thanks to Joseph, M. Mirion's conscience was always easy. In the morning, he would slap Joseph smartly on the back, saying, "Have you slept well, you lucky dog?" He never could have believed that this lucky dog would have slept better in an empty garret, and that on his bed of down, he sometimes had bad dreams, in which he found himself alone in the midst of a vast desert.

It was unfortunate for Joseph that he had none of that independence of character which is called ingratitude. Certain it is, that ingratitude greatly simplifies such difficulties, but not every one, who wishes to be ungrateful, can be so. Joseph knew better than any one how much he owed to M. Mirion, and, knowing it so well, he did not like to be reminded of it. He had not tried to forget the condition in which M. Mirion had found him. All the scenes of his childhood were indelibly impressed upon his mind. When he recalled them, he found himself in the sixth story, in a dirty garret, the walls of which had that frightful look which disorder lends to poverty; he saw in one corner his father buried in a drunken stupor, while his mother stood before him, her face distorted with anger, heaping a torrent of reproaches on the drunkard, and shaking her clenched fists in the face of fortune. He recalled also his mortification, his heart sickness, and all the evil thoughts that kept passing through his brain when he went from door to door, with his basket on his arm, covered by an old green rag, out at the elbows, which had formerly been a curtain, and wearing an old pair of pantaloons, through the holes in which his ragged shirt was visible. He saw himself lolling out his tongue at one porter after another, as they drove him from their doors, or sitting on a step to count in his cold, blue fingers the pennies which he had received, and to think of the blows which the evening had in store for him, or, in order to forget his misery, dragging his worn-out shoes through the gutter, while he talked familiarly with the sewer, his best friend. When he compared his early days, what he might have been, with what he now was, it seemed to him that the thread of his life had been broken, that he had been born a second time. Whence had come this love of work which had been his salvation, this pride which had kept him firm and true, this honor which had made him despise all that was mean and vulgar? How far it seemed from his father's kennel to this family of good and worthy people who had received him, to this hospitable home where his shipwrecked bark had found a haven, to this beautiful attic-room in which he lived, from the vine-embowered window of which could be seen the lawn, and a grove of oak trees where the nightingales sang sweetly every spring. No, he had never thought of repudiating his debt; but he had hoped that he might, at some time, repay it by one supreme effort, and then say to his benefactors, "Our accounts are settled, now we can start clear again." As this time did not come, his gratitude turned to bitterness and pain, and, as often happens, he visited on society his ill-humor and discontent. He argued that the world was badly made, and that it would be doing mankind a service to re-make it. He had secretly read several works on socialism. There was no necessity for reading them; certain ideas are found everywhere to-day; we breathe them in the very air. Joseph's theories were very confused; he would have found some trouble in putting them into practice. He had some good sense, however, and neither accepted Communism, nor railed at capital. On the contrary, he considered capital the best thing in the world, the only difficulty being that it did not do its duty, and was too careful of itself; he thought that an industrious workman ought always to be able to borrow enough to start a shop and begin work on his own account. Sometimes when he stood at his bench, his plane gliding rapidly beneath his hand, his thoughts flew still more swiftly. He would begin to hum a tune, and as he did so, would see the old world swept away in flames, while from its smoldering ashes rose another world, where every thing was new, where there was plenty of air and room for all, where the proud were perfectly at ease, where no one bore upon his shoulders that heavy burden of gratitude which weighs down like a mountain; in short, an ideal and perfect world, where the Joseph Noirels were on an equal footing with the Thomas Mirions. What wonders accompany the humming of a tune! We can not always sing, however, and when the sound of their voices no longer soothes them, the Josephs awake and find that there has been no change at all, either in themselves or their surroundings.

CHAPTER IV.

JOSEPH IN LOVE.

I have not yet mentioned the greatest of Joseph's griefs, the one which gave form and reality to all the others. He had conceived and secretly cherished a passion which had overpowered him, and was constantly preying on his heart. This passion was hopeless ; he might as well have loved a star. He was twenty-two years old, when one day there appeared at Mon-Plaisir a beautiful young girl, who had just returned from boarding-school. He had taken very little notice of her in her younger days, he had not seen her for a long time ; she now appeared in ripened bloom. She seemed beautiful as a dream to him, and scarcely had he been two minutes in her society, before he felt a tightening of the chain that bound him, and knew that Mon-Plaisir was now a prison, from which he could never have the courage to escape.

The fact is, that the first week succeeding Marguerite's return, he experienced for her only a profound admiration, mingled with the intensest curiosity. He felt that he could never be any thing to her, that she was beyond his reach, that her silky tresses, her fair face, her soft and gentle glances, her clear voice and ringing laugh were not at his disposal. He was like a little beggar girl, standing before the window of a toy store, staring at one of those handsome dolls that speak and move their eyes ; she very well knows that the doll is not for such as she, but she feels a sense of ownership in looking at it, and even poverty has eyes, thank God ! Little by little, Joseph discovered that Marguerite was as good as she was beautiful, that she had a heart as pure as gold, that she exhibited none of the follies peculiar to her class, and that she had lost none of her natural charm under the influence of her doting mother and her teachers. He grew bolder and occasionally spoke to her ; he questioned her, but with a timid and bashful air. He wanted to know what the doll was made of, what there was inside of it. His investigations proved very entertaining, and Mon-Plaisir now appeared like a new place to him. In the evening, returning from his work, he would say to himself, "Now I shall hear her laugh and sing!" It seemed to him that henceforth there was some little happiness in store for him.

It is right to tell children that they may look at, but must not touch the things about them. It happened on the morning of a certain holiday, that Joseph was in one corner of the grounds, working on an arbor which he had planned: he amused himself in this way in his leisure hours. Marguerite had risen early the same morning, and had gone forth to greet the dawn. Wearing morocco slippers ornamented with red rosettes, holding in her hand, like a marchioness of the olden time, a light, gold-headed cane which her uncle Benjamin had given her, she undertook to make a trip round her domain. As she passed before the arbor, she spied Joseph and stopped to see him work. Suddenly a few large drops of rain fell near them. "I must run," she cried; "if my dress gets wet it will be spoiled." She took the most direct route home, going across a field that had just been ploughed. At the third step she took, one of her slippers was buried in the soft ground. Standing on one foot, leaning on her cane as well as she could, she called for help, laughing all the time. The rain fell faster. Joseph ran to her; a sudden boldness seized him. "You can never get across the field alone," he said; "shall I carry you?" She assented without any hesitation. He threw off his coat, and wrapped it round her to protect her dress; then lifted her, scarcely knowing what he did; and when, at last, he knew that he was indeed holding her within his arms and pressing her against his breast, a thrill of delight ran through his frame, he stumbled as though overcome with joy. He began to run, jumping across the furrows; it seemed as though his precious burden belonged to him, as though he could carry it with him where he pleased. Once when Marguerite moved, her hair brushed against his cheek. He stopped suddenly, trembling with passion; but his glance fell upon two wondering eyes, in whose clear, tranquil depths dwelt only innocence. These eyes brought him to himself again, and he proceeded on his way. At last he put her down at the entrance to the house. "Where is my slipper?" she said. "How careless I am!" he answered; "I must have dropped it." He did not tell the truth; he pretended to hunt for it, while all the time it was safe in his pocket, where he had placed it when he picked her up. A slipper is easily forgotten. Little did any one think that Joseph had carefully hidden it away. When he drew it forth and held it in his hands, it told him a story, always the same, which he never grew tired of, and yet by which he never was deceived. I have said that he had good common sense; he knew very well that if he had not been a simple workman, Mlle. Mirion would never have permitted him to carry her. But what of that? He had met with an adventure in a ploughed field, and this adventure would henceforth be the brightest spot in his whole life.

From that day, Joseph had one fixed idea, and this idea was a constant source of anguish to him. He had sufficient self-control not to betray himself, to conceal his secret from all eyes. His room was directly over that of Mlle. Mirion. Little did any one suspect that every evening he threw himself upon the floor, pressing his ear close against it. The floor was thick and impenetrable to every sound; he could hear nothing, but he believed he heard. He experienced an indescribable agitation as he thought, "She is there; her life and mine are separated only by the thickness of a plank." When he closed his eyes, it seemed to him that the floor became transparent, that he saw her moving busily about, like a bee among the flowers. Sometimes he fell asleep in this position and had the most delightful dreams, waking the next morning to curse the inexorable reality which drove away these charming visions.

Marguerite was far from suspecting what was passing in the workman's mind; if she had been informed of it, it would have overwhelmed her with astonishment. She thought little of Joseph, except when he was present. He simply inspired her with feelings of good will and respect. Her father often praised him to her. "You see, Margot," he would say, "the boy is a perfect treasure. I don't tell him so, of course, for fear that it will spoil him; but he can make any thing he pleases with those hands of his. And then the good judgment that he shows. Even I have to consult him sometimes on important matters. Good deeds have their reward; from the very day that he came into my house, my business has prospered." Not only was Marguerite disposed to think well of Joseph on her father's recommendation, but she also liked to talk with him herself. What he said did not resemble at all the gossip that she heard about her; it pierced through the conventionalisms of the society in which she lived, with a boldness of thought that pleased her, she knew not exactly why. The citizen has a fondness for closed doors, not only because they shut out draughts, but also because an open door makes him uneasy; there may enter something unpleasant: an idea, for instance, or a revolution. The workman, on the other hand, holds his wide open, to get the air and to allow the future to come in. Often nothing but misconceptions and frightful errors enter by it; yet how many live on fallacies! In short, it seemed to Marguerite that, when her father invited his friends to dinner, there was something almost stifling in the conversation, while in the little that Joseph Noirel said, there was a certain freshness that made one breathe with perfect freedom, an indescribable something that came from the soul, making known the man. It was a confused impression which she did not try to clearly comprehend: her roses and canaries took up too much of her time. If Joseph had set out for Australia, she would have wished him a pleasant journey, and would occasionally have asked if any news had been received from him: that would have been all.

Though we may have good common sense, we sometimes believe in the impossible; of what use else is hope, that daughter of folly? There were times when Joseph thought, Why should it not happen? He took to reading novels; he searched with avidity for adventures that resembled his own. Shepherds marrying princesses he often met with, especially in fairy tales ; but, in the end, his reason would take a terrible revenge, completely overwhelming him. What likelihood was there that his wild passion would ever be returned? And if this miracle should take place, would the result not be that he would simply dash his head against a wall? He pictured to himself Mme. Mirion's indignation and cry of horror, on learning that from the depth of his obscurity, Joseph Noirel had dared to raise his eyes to her daughter and her idol. The good lady was so far from believing such an enormity possible, that more than once she introduced her favorite subject in Joseph's presence. One evening, when he had remained in the drawing-room later than usual, reading the paper by the fire, she suddenly turned toward her husband who was dozing in his arm-chair, saying, "You men are so strange, you never care to think about the future."

"Why! what's the matter?" said he, waking with a start. "Is the house on fire?"

"The matter is that a father owes certain duties to his child, and you care little enough about them."

"I'm neglecting my duties, because I'm taking a nap by the fire, I suppose. What bee has stung you now, Madame Marianne Mirion?"

"When any one is fortunate enough to have a daughter like our Marguerite," she replied in an impressive manner, "his first duty is to find a husband worthy of her."

"There come the everlasting sons-in-law again." He rose from his chair as he continued, "Would you like to have me take the first train, to offer my daughter to Prince Charming?"

"I can't understand how any one can jest on such a subject. I tell you we don't see enough society; we do wrong to spend the winter in the country, like so many wolves. It might do well enough if we could give a few parties ...."

"And have some fireworks," he interrupted.

"Your jokes will drive me mad," she answered, in a pet. "To hear you, Thomas, any one would think that you were light and trifling."

"Oh! I'm not light by any means," he said, taking with his

hands the measure of his portly paunch. "Don't be angry, my good wife. I've often told you there was no need of any trouble in this matter. Next St. Martin's day our chick will be only twenty; and, besides, you're so difficult to suit. Upon my word, you ought to have a son-in-law made to order. Why don't you ask Aunt Amaranth to write a line to her noble friend, the Duke of Mecklenburg? Perhaps he has a cousin, not yet provided for, who would serve our purpose."

He saw that she was now getting angry in earnest, and added, as he chucked her under the chin, "Be a good little woman, and don't get excited. Your dear husband has discovered that we don't often, in this world, find what we're hunting for, but we sometimes find what's even better."

At the first words of this conversation, Joseph started as though he had received an electric shock, and let his paper fall from his hands. He picked it up again, folded it as well as he could, left the room, and did not close his eyes all night. From that day a deep gloom settled on him. He ate scarcely any thing; if asked what was the matter, he replied that he was not hungry, and this answer seemed satisfactory. He kept fiercely at work, but sang no more. He dreamed none the less, however. He prayed silently for storms: he besought them to come quickly, there was urgent need; next St. Martin's day, Marguerite would be twenty, and Madame Mirion might any day secure a son-in-law. He cried in frenzy and despair for that great overturning which was to level all distinctions, to overthrow the proud and haughty, to raise the victims of oppression and of scorn, and to prepare the way for that ideal world, in which Madame Mirion would seek out Joseph Noirel, and say to him, "Marguerite loves you—she is yours."

CHAPTER V.

AN UNEXPECTED VISITOR.

On the 31st of July, 1869, at two o'clock in the afternoon, M. Mirion was busy in his office, proving his accounts. When he had finished, he put his pen behind his ear, and went up to the second story, where the work-rooms were, to give some orders. On coming down into the store again, he found there a stranger, who had a decidedly military air. His face impressed M. Mirion at once. He was a man of about forty-five, of medium height, and aristocratic appearance; he had a well-bronzed skin, a black mustache, hair a little gray, a nose somewhat bent, deep-set and piercing eyes, and the keen glance of a hawk. His face betokened intelligence and will; its expression would have been harsh and almost threatening, had it not been relieved by a smile which sometimes was very pleasing. He had come in to examine a collection of cabinets of the style prevalent in the reign of Louis XIII., which M. Mirion had obtained from a convent at Valais, and had had restored by Joseph, who excelled in this kind of work. He looked over all these antiquated articles without finding any thing that pleased him; but finally selected a small portable desk, a piece of Venetian work, of very neat design. He drew from his pocket-book a card, on which he wrote his address, requesting M. Mirion to send the purchase to his hotel as soon as possible, as he wished to send it, the same evening, to his home in Burgundy. His card read: Count Roger D'Ornis, late Captain in the Third Zouaves.

"The choicest articles of my collection are not here," said M. Mirion, after directing one of his clerks to carefully pack the desk. "My daughter, like you, has a passion for old-fashioned furniture; she has ransacked my shop. In spite of all that I could do, the most handsome things have been carried off to Mon-Plaisir."

"Mon-Plaisir? where is that?" asked M. D'Ornis.

"Mon-Plaisir is my country house," responded M. Mirion, somewhat astonished by the question. "I have there two old tables covered with moldings, grooves, and the queerest little figures. It would make your mouth water to look at them. My wife would be glad enough to get rid of these tables; she complains that they collect the dust, and that it makes the servants sick to clean the copper on them. What my daughter says is law, however, so I keep my tables. If you would like to see them, I shall be glad to have you visit Mon-Plaisir."

M. D'Ornis thanked him coldly, excusing himself by saying that he had to start the next day on a trip to Chamouni; he then took up his hat, which he had placed upon a chair. At the same moment, the door of the large and gloomy store was thrown wide open, and Mlle. Marguerite Mirion, dressed in pink from head to foot, entered like a sunbeam. "Father, dear," she said, "I came to tell you that I'm going shopping and have forgotten my money; I'll take some of yours instead." So saying, she fumbled for a moment in his vest pocket, and, taking out a napoleon, stowed it away inside her glove.

"Didn't I tell you that they robbed me?" cried M. Mirion turning toward M. D'Ornis, who, half hidden in the shadow of a large side-board, had his fierce glance fixed on Marguerite. She now noticed, for the first time, that there was a stranger present, and bowed, at the same time coloring slightly. "Since I've been caught so nicely," she said, "I can do nothing better than to run away." And with another graceful nod, she started toward the door.

"The carriage will be here at six o'clock precisely," said her father. "Are you going to keep us waiting as you did the other day?"

"You know I'm always doing something wrong," she answered as she left them.

M. D'Ornis walked up and down the floor once or twice, as though buried in deep thought; then said to M. Mirion:

"Your tables keep running in my head. I so much wish to see them that I will put off my trip; when shall I call at your house?"

"To-morrow will be Sunday," answered M. Mirion. "I'll be at Mon-Plaisir all day, and we'll esteem it a great honor to receive you. You mustn't expect to see a castle though. It's a very plain and ordinary kind of house. We common people, you know ...."

M. D'Ornis did not wait for him to finish. "I will be there, to-morrow," he said, and went away.

At six o'clock, as M. Mirion was getting into the carriage, where his daughter was already seated, he noticed M. D'Ornis, who was reading a placard further down the street. As the carriage passed, he turned round and bowed.

"Who is that gentleman?" asked Marguerite.

"A count, my dear; he's coming to Mon-Plaisir to-morrow, to see my tables. Don't say any thing to your mother about it, though. The thought of receiving such a distinguished person would be too much for her brain; she wouldn't sleep all night, and I don't know—the Lord forgive me—but she might even hang the house with flags."

"Dear me!" she said, "a count is just like other men."

"Well said, Miss Philosophy!" he answered, giving her a tap on the cheek.

The next day, Count Roger D'Ornis arrived at Mon-Plaisir at precisely two o'clock. M. Mirion was alone, his wife and daughter having gone to call upon a neighbor. He exerted himself to please his guest, and in the first place took him to look at the tables, which he described with the minutest detail, not omitting an ovolo or quarter-round. M. D'Ornis looked and admired, but was not enthusiastic over them; every time the door opened he turned round quickly, and seemed disappointed that some one he expected did not appear. When the subject of the tables was exhausted, M. Mirion proposed that they should look at the house, and took his guest from cellar to garret, from poultry-yard to garden, saying in a tone of pretended humility, "It's hardly worth looking at; my house is not a castle; it's not a bad one of its kind, though." M. D'Ornis followed him about, listening, saying little, yawning perhaps, but not going away. They passed through the billiard-room on their return. M. Mirion proposed to the Count that they should have a game. He consented. He played remarkably well, making several fine runs. As they were finishing their second game, Mme. Mirion appeared, accompanied by her daughter. M. Mirion introduced the stranger to her. She stared and changed color. Her agitation increased when, her husband having asked M. D'Ornis to stay to dinner, the latter accepted the invitation, without waiting to be urged at all. She took M. Mirion one side, and scolded him well for not having told her about his visitor. The idea of offering a count nothing better than pot-luck!

"Don't get excited," he replied; "for heaven's sake, don't get excited. Our guest is a man who can get along without partridges and truffles."

He could not calm her, however. She ran in haste to inform Mlle. Baillet of the great event, to beg her to put on her finest ribbons, and to have her best wits about her, in order that she might entertain their guest. Mlle. Baillet had moved in the best society; she must know how to talk to a count. Then she went down to the kitchen, where she held a conversation with her cook, stopping every minute to cry out, "No fish, no fowls, no game! I'm the most unlucky woman in the world." However, as she was a woman of resources, she soon became mistress of the situation, and putting on a large brown linen apron, set to work to make a highly seasoned dish of her own invention, and to prepare some cream fritters, which even Uncle Benjamin declared could not be beaten. Meanwhile, Aunt Amaranth, while dressing her hair, had prepared herself to furnish her part of the entertainment. When she descended to the drawing-room, more amaranthine than ever, with her head full of witty and agreeable remarks, she was surprised to find Marguerite getting ready to play billiards with Count D'Ornis. She had admitted that she sometimes played with her father, and he had asked permission to test her skill. She had consented with that gentle grace, that amiable simplicity which was so natural to her. He told her that she would play a good game, if she were better acquainted with its principles.

"Principles!" she answered, laughing; "ask my aunt if I'm not well acquainted with them."

"Fortunately, they're easily acquired," he said as a slight smile curled his lip, and he commenced giving her a lesson. At the end of half an hour he told her that she had improved wonderfully. Mlle. Baillet did not say a word; this game of billiards did not please her. She had not relished their joking about principles. At Schwerin, principles and rules of conduct are very plentiful; Mlle. Baillet had brought many of them away with her, and when she prepared to ventilate them, she always assumed an air of great importance. There are some things too sacred to joke about.

They sat down to dinner at seven o'clock. Mme. Mirion considered it necessary to apologize to her guest. He had taken her by surprise, and that too on Sunday, when they made as little preparation as possible at Mon-Plaisir, in order that the cook might not have to work. These excuses were entirely uncalled for: at Mon-Plaisir the ordinary fare was excellent, and, on this occasion, the special dishes were delicious. Moreover, M. D'Ornis seemed to pay little attention to his plate; he ate sparingly and talked scarcely at all; he kept looking about him and taking observations. Mlle. Baillet tried to keep the conversation moving; it seemed ready to die away every minute. By a series of laborious transitions, she at last arrived at Mecklenburg, and began the story of the famous court ball, which had been the great event of her life. M. D'Ornis did not seem particularly interested; he cared as little for both the Mecklenburgs together as he did for what was passing in the moon. When his turn came, Uncle Benjamin mounted the breach, and began to talk about the wines of Burgundy. He asked M. D'Ornis if his vineyards were nearer Beaune than Nuits. M. D'Ornis replied that he had no vineyards, that there was not one within ten leagues of him, as he lived in Upper Burgundy, a grazing and wooded country. It was Marguerite who finally broke the spell. She had seen by M. D'Ornis's card that he had served in the Third Zouaves. She asked him about his army life. He suddenly became animated. He had fought in Mexico ; he told the story of the taking of Puebla, where he had received two wounds which fortunately had not been serious. He spoke earnestly, without referring to himself, and his eloquence produced a deep impression on his hearers. Mme. Mirion fairly drank in his words. Now and then she nudged Mlle. Grillet who sat next to her, saying in a low tone, "How well he talks ! just listen to him."

Puebla being taken, however, he relapsed into his former gloomy silence. He looked straight before him twisting the ends of his mustache. In vain, after they had gone into the drawing-room, did Marguerite assail him with new questions ; he answered her only in monosyllables. At ten o'clock he rose, said good-night, refused their offered carriage, lit a cigar, and started off on foot. When he had reached the end of the avenue, he sat down on a large stone and remained there a long time, his hat pushed forward and his cigar between his teeth, gazing sometimes at the stars, sometimes at the dusty road. What was he thinking of ? His revery would have lasted until dawn perhaps, if a large dog that was prowling about the road, and to whom this dreamer seemed a suspicious character, had not rushed at him, barking furiously. Enraged at being thus disturbed, he rose, picked up a stone, and threw it with all his might at the offender, who ran off howling. After this performance he started toward Geneva, where he arrived in the early hours of the morning. While this was taking place, there were many comments and criticisms exchanged at Mon-Plaisir. Scarcely had M. D'Ornis left the room, when Mme. Mirion approached her husband, and patting him softly on the cheek, said, "What a dear, good man you are, Mirion, to bring that gentleman here ! That's the kind of man to know, so elegant and distinguished ! What a noble air, what noble manners ! You would know he was a count, just to see him get up and sit down again. Then that story he told us. . . . . How my heart beat! I thought I heard the cannon, the grape-shot, and the trumpets. It seemed as though I was in Mexico."

Her enthusiasm was so intense that no one dared to say a word, always excepting Uncle Benjamin, who never neglected an opportunity to take down (as he expressed it) his dear sister-in-law. "If your Count," he said in his sarcastic way, "knows how to talk, he knows how to hold his tongue too. As soon as he had finished taking Puebla, he sat a whole hour without opening his mouth. It was nothing but pride, if I'm not mistaken. Confound it! he said to himself, I won't exert myself for such common people. I noticed too that your table didn't please him. He ate scarcely any thing at all. You ought to have had truffles for the gentleman. I believe now he's laughing to himself over his dinner, his host, and the whole concern, in fact."

"You've got a quick tongue, Benjamin," she answered sharply. "We can't have any pleasure here, without your crawling over it like a caterpillar, and whenever we eat any thing in this house, we always get some of your hairs in it. Count D'Ornis, himself, told your humble servant he thought her fritters were excellent. If he didn't eat much, it was probably because his wounds have affected his appetite, and if he said nothing, it was because he preferred to let those talk, who are all the time saying silly things that no one cares any thing about."

Delighted at having put his sister-in-law in a passion, Uncle Benjamin was about to pursue his point; but M. Mirion, as usual, interfered and separated the combatants. "You know well enough, Puss," he said to his wife, "that Benjamin loves to tease, you can't prevent it; besides, in well-constituted governments, there always is an opposition party. Uncle Benjamin is the Left of the House; he is a loyal Left though, I can tell you."

CHAPTER VI.

M. D'ORNIS CALLS AGAIN.

Mme. Mirion retired to her room at an early hour; she felt that she must be alone. While Count D'Ornis sat motionless on the stone, she was no less quiet in her arm-chair. Although the Count had not during the evening addressed a single compliment to her daughter, Mme. Mirion had more than once caught him casting side-glances at Marguerite. "Could such a thing happen?" she thought. "No, it would be too good; it was not possible." She did not sleep well, she was dreaming through the whole night that a white mouse was scratching at the door, which partly opened now and then. The mouse was just coming in, when a gust of wind blew the door quickly to. This dream was symbolical. The white mouse represented a rash idea which was moving about Mme. Mirion's brain, scratching and trying to get in; but her good sense, that stern guardian, drove it away, in spite of all that she could do.

The next day, the other members of the household were all occupied with their daily duties, thinking no more of Count D'Ornis; Mme. Mirion, however, had him constantly in her mind. During the morning, she felt a presentiment which was afterward realized, showing conclusively that she had good reason to trust her own sagacity. After lunch, she said to her daughter, who was in morning costume, "You're not going to keep on that shabby gray dress, are you, Marguerite?"

"Why, mamma, you know we never have any calls on Monday."

"Something tells me that we'll have one to-day,' she answered. "Dress yourself up, my pet; it's best to be on the safe side."

Marguerite good-naturedly went up to her room to do as her mother had requested. She soon came down again, this time handsomely dressed. Making a low courtesy, she said, "How do I look now?"

"You look lovely, my dear. A young lady of your age always ought to be prepared. Here, put this rose in your hair; you know flowers are very becoming to you."

"O dear! I should think you expected an emperor or a king to-day," she answered with a laugh.

"Do as I tell you. I love to see you looking well. You've one fault though, you laugh too much. If you're not careful, it will spoil your mouth. It's very easy to make a pretty mouth; all you have to do is to say *pomme* once in a while...... Try it; say *pomme.* You'll see....."

"*Pomme, pomme,*" said Marguerite looking in the glass. "Yes, it's very pretty; but I would rather sing, I think."

She sat down at the piano and began a song. Mme. Mirion, who was sitting by the window, engaged in fancy work, now and then raised her eyes from her embroidery to look out. Suddenly she was seized with a strange trembling; she had just noticed, at the turn of the road, a black spot approaching Mon-Plaisir. She kept her eyes fastened on it, while gradually her face grew brighter; it came nearer and nearer, and finally turned into the avenue. She said nothing to Marguerite, who was still singing, her back turned toward the door, so that she did not see M. D'Ornis enter. The Count waved his hand toward Mme. Mirion, and stood silent, waiting for the song to be finished. Marguerite sang it through, then shut the piano, and turning round, perceived the enemy. She colored a little and seemed embarrassed for a moment, looking handsomer than if she had said *pomme* a dozen times.

"That's the way she sings every day," cried Mme. Mirion, "without practicing at all."

"What would you say, sir," added Marguerite raising her hands in a comical way, "if you should hear my Sunday singing!"

"I prefer what I heard just now," he answered bowing. "It pleased me very much." This was the first compliment he ever paid her; it also was the last.

Mme. Mirion proposed to the Count that they should take a walk about the grounds. She wished to exhibit Marguerite in the open air and in the sun, to prove that her beauty was not afraid of the severest test. She also wished to show him the whole of Mon-Plaisir. M. D'Ornis evidently was prepared for whatever might be required of him. On the way, they picked up Mlle. Baillet in the garden ; her anecdotes this time proved more successful than before. M. D'Ornis, who had made a firm resolve to be agreeable, listened without winking, to the long catalogue of virtues of the grand duchess's mother, which polite attention raised him very high in the estimation of the former associate of the aristocracy. Mme. Mirion, for the first time in her life, thought that Aunt Amaranth talked too much of Mecklenburg. She kept constantly interrupting her in order to bring her daughter forward. She said in a loud voice, " Marguerite, you understand botany ; what is the name of that little lilac flower ? Marguerite, you understand astronomy ; what quarter is the moon in now ?" " I must tell you, Count," she added, " that my daughter is running over with science. The education of young ladies, nowadays, is carried to such perfection, especially in this country ! She has been for five years at a boarding-school, where they learn every thing, positively every thing. All the professors there are first-class men. Marguerite was associated with young ladies of high birth, and was very intimate with them ; but she left all these fine people to come back to her old mother. She has a remarkably good disposition ; she is easily pleased and is happy everywhere. I say to her sometimes, Do try to have one fault ; I don't like to have you too perfect ".... Then stopping a moment to pick up a small white stone from the gravel walk, she continued, " Marguerite, you understand mineralogy, what is the name of this pebble ?" " I call it a pebble;" answered Marguerite. " That's all I learned about it from my ten first-class professors." Poor Marguerite knew not what to do, to avoid this flood of compliments and questions which her mother rolled upon her. She finally began to laugh heartily, and her glance met that of Count D'Ornis, who, in spite of his usual gravity, also laughed.

This interchange of merriment did more to make them understand each other, than a long conversation on astronomy could possibly have done.

As they were thus talking, they finished their walk around the grounds, without the time seeming at all long to M. D'Ornis. When he took leave, Mme. Mirion asked him if she should not have the pleasure and honor of seeing him again. He answered that he should start for Chamouni the next morning, should stay there several days, and on his return would come to say farewell to Mon-Plaisir. Mme. Mirion stood gazing after him until he reached the end of the avenue ; then, imitating the voice and accent of Uncle Benjamin, "You may rest assured, sister-in-law," she cried, "that this gentlemen is laughing to himself at his host and the whole concern, in fact ..... What a disagreeable creature that Benjamin is. How I should like to see him now ; how I would give it to him !" Fortunately for him, Uncle Benjamin did not come home to dinner ; he very prudently kept away. By some instinct he was always warned of any good fortune that befell his sister-in-law. The very days when Mme. Mirion calmly awaited the moment of her triumph over him, the loyal opposition would not appear at Mon-Plaisir ; it would be impossible to give it to him. M. D'Ornis's second call left Mme. Mirion in a state of nervous excitement that began to tell upon her health. This time the door had opened, the white mouse had gone in. What had yesterday appeared absurd to her, now seemed likely enough to happen. When she considered the facts, and reflected that some day this great event might take place, that some day, perhaps, she could publish the news through the city, the villages, and the country houses round about, she was seized with nervous tremblings and twitchings, while her brain kept constantly in a whirl. She was like a fisherman, whose highest ambition it is to take a perch or carp, and who sees an immense trout, a real salmon-trout, approaching his net ; he begins to tremble, his breath comes short and quick. Great hopes are always accompanied by great apprehensions ; Mme. Mirion dared not yet believe in her good fortune. Her manner changed. She became taciturn ; no one seemed, to her mind, worthy to be made the confidant of her dreams, her impatient wishes, and her fears. A week passed. What had become of M. D'Ornis? Nothing had been heard of him. The good old lady felt her hopes grow smaller day by day. She was cross and fidgety ; she scolded every body, not excepting her daughter, who, in her happy heart, cared little whether Count D'Ornis were alive or not. M. Mirion asked his wife, "What's the matter with you?" She answered him, "If you don't know, there's no use in telling you."

CHAPTER VII.

A PROPOSAL OF MARRIAGE.

It was about ten days after M. D'Ornis had set out for Chamouni, when one afternoon, toward four o'clock—it was the thirteenth of the month and a Friday—M. Mirion, taking the fresh air on his door-step, saw his man suddenly appear a little way down the street. M. D'Ornis, walking directly up to him, asked with a grave face, for a few moments' private conversation. M. Mirion took him at once into his office. His first thought was that M. D'Ornis wanted to borrow some money of him! "Ah! my fine fellow," he said to himself, "I'm not taken in so easy as you think, perhaps. All hands on deck, and stand ready to receive the enemy." Imagine then his stupefaction, when the Count, taking a seat, said directly, in a clear, calm voice, "M. Mirion, I have come to ask your daughter's hand."

M. Mirion gave a start and clung to his chair to keep from falling. All the furniture in the store seemed to be dancing a hop-waltz around him.

"What was that, Count?" he asked with a scared look.

"I repeat, M. Mirion, that I have come to ask your daughter's hand."

There was a short silence, during which M. Mirion tried in vain to collect his thoughts. He kept saying to himself, "Is he joking? Is he trying to make a fool of me?" This proposal astounded him, and almost took away his breath.

M. D'Ornis grew tired of waiting for his answer. "Listen," he said, "I will explain myself. Mlle. Mirion is too attractive for you to be surprised that, from the first moment I saw her, her grace and beauty should have made a deep impression on me. I am a man of forty-five, however, and am not likely to do a foolish thing; at my age one reasons and calculates; I have taken time for reflection, you see. For some years I have been tired of my lonely bachelor's life ; I wish to taste domestic happiness, as I understand it, and I believe your daughter will make me happy as my wife. In the first place, she is a Protestant, and I have always been determined that I would marry no one but a Protestant; I have a holy horror of confessors and confessionals. I want my wife to tell me every thing, and to say nothing about my affairs to any one else. In Catholic countries they pretend that Protestant women are wanting in grace and softness, that they are affected, reserved, and independent. Seeing your daughter has convinced me to the contrary. She is so charming, she has such grace of manner, such cheerfulness, such good taste, and yet is so simple and so modest, that I'm delighted with her. She has every womanly grace and virtue; I should be proud and happy if she were my wife, and I have returned from Chamouni to tell you so."

"Really, Count,' answered M. Mirion, "I feel highly honored .... I don't know.... I didn't expect .... I must talk with my wife about it .... Are you sure it's so ? .... Perhaps you may be mistaken .... It's true my business has prospered .... Perhaps .... Yes, I'm afraid the dowry ...."

"The dowry !" interrupted M. D'Ornis. "I don't wish any. That's another of my ideas. I think a woman should belong solely to her husband, and, for this reason, should receive every thing from him. The patrimony of the Counts D'Ornis has greatly diminished since the beginning of the present century; the Revolution made sad havoc with it; but even now, in interest and rents, I have an income of twenty-five thousand francs. That is more than is really necessary to make a man happy, if he has simple tastes, like myself, and wastes nothing for the sake of vanity. If you wish it, I will put you in communication with my lawyer, who will give you any information you may desire on this subject. Monsieur Mirion, I will make a settlement on my wife, which shall be hers during my life and after my death; but no dowry, either large or small, if you please !"

Rising as he spoke, he continued, "Do as I have done, my dear sir, take time for reflection. Above all, I beg of you, let your daughter make her own free choice. I start to-morrow for the Oberland; a week from now I shall be at Zurich. Write me there at the Baur Hotel."

With these words, he bowed and moved toward the door, followed by the astounded M. Mirion, who, in his confusion, had put his handkerchief on his head, and was wiping his face with his velvet cap. "What will Marianne say?" he cried at last,

This was his first thought, and the first sentence that he had been able to complete. He immediately sent an order to his coachman to have the carriage ready, then called to Joseph, "Come, young man, hurry up! I've a tremendous appetite. Confound the business! Let's go to dinner."

Joseph noticed that his employer's manner was very strange; he seemed excited, like a general who had just carried a Malakoff and Redan. During the whole route, M. Mirion kept constantly grumbling at the slow gait of his horse. "Drive faster," he cried to the coachman. "If your horse has got only three legs, why don't you say so?"

Joseph did not understand this feverish haste.

Jumping from the carriage, M. Mirion ran to the drawing-room, where his wife sat alone. He approached her with a jaunty air, caught her by the waist, and spun her twice around. Then, looking her straight in the eyes, he said, "I'll give you a hundred, a thousand chances. Guess it if you dare."

She grew very red, but did not try to guess. "What is it?" she asked. "What's the matter?"

"The strangest, most extraordinary, most unheard of thing!"

"Don't keep me waiting; out with it! quick!"

He told her at last. At the first words, she grew very pale, uttered a cry, and sank into an arm-chair. M. Mirion was about to throw some water in her face, but she made a sign to him to stop, to give her time to recover herself. When she had regained her power of speech, she broke out in a torrent of questions, mingled with exclamations which prevented her from hearing his replies. M. Mirion finally placed both his hands over her mouth, saying, "Let me talk now, you can have your say after I've finished."

After he had explained every thing, going into all the details, after she had twenty times cried out, "This is worth living for, Mirion; we have drawn a prize!" he said to her, "We're not through yet, Puss. I must speak to Margot. She must have time to think about it, for I promised she should be free to choose; she must say yes or no just as she wishes."

He had already left the room, when she caught him by the coat.

"What are you going to do?" she cried. "You men have such a rough way of saying things. I know better than you do, how to prepare our pet."

With these words, she ran quickly up the stairs that led to Marguerite's room, opened the door, pushed it to again with her foot, threw out her arms, and cried, "Come and kiss your mother, Countess D'Ornis." Thus she understood the great art of oratorical preparation.

Marguerite was busy putting her room in order. She would allow no one else to do this, for fear that some of her treasures might be broken. She turned round and looked at her mother, her arms swinging, a feather-duster in her hand. She wondered what all this meant, she thought her mother was only joking. "Kiss me, Margot," repeated Mme. Mirion. "He loves you, he adores you, he came himself, to ask your hand." Then snatching the duster from her, she continued, "What are you doing? Don't you know that dusting will spoil your hands?" Drawing her daughter to the window, she gazed upon her for a moment; then kissing her eyes, those beautiful, brown eyes that worked such miracles, she said, "I guessed right. You love him, don't you, darling? How glad I am, that it is so!"

"Love whom?" asked Marguerite, who had not yet recovered from her first surprise.

"Why, Count D'Ornis, to be sure."

"Is it true? Did the Count? ...."

"Of course it's true .... Poor darling! you ought to have told me; I knew you loved him though."

"How can I love him? I hardly know him."

"That's a fine reason!" answered Mme. Mirion, growing angry. "Love always comes suddenly. When I was your age, I one day saw your father from my window crossing the Fusterie, and I fell in love with him at once."

Marguerite could not help laughing. "I'm not so tender-hearted," she answered. "I don't think I could ever love a gentleman I didn't know."

"Perhaps," her mother said, raising her voice, "perhaps you think Count D'Ornis is homely and awkward . . . ."

"I didn't say so."

"Perhaps he's deformed, hump-backed, bandy-legged . . . ."

"Good heavens! Must I marry all the men that are not hump-backed . . . ."

"Perhaps you don't like his manners. . . ."

"Oh! yes I do; I think he's very elegant."

"Then it's the way he speaks that you don't like. He can't express himself, he stammers. . . ."

"Not at all."

"That story of the battle he told us. . . ."

"Interested me very much."

"Those two wounds he received at the taking of Puebla. . . ."

"I'm sorry he received them, and I wish he could forget them altogether."

"There, I knew you loved him!" said Mme. Mirion. Then turning toward her husband who had just entered the room, she cried, "She loves him, she loves him; it's all settled! I'm the happiest mother in the world."

"Ta, ta, ta," said M. Mirion, who had at last recovered his self-possession. "There's no hurry, and Marguerite has plenty of time to think about it, and make up her mind whether she loves him or not. To start with, I'm going to call a family council to-night. My father used to do this on all important occasions, and he always found it a good thing. Benjamin will be here to dinner, every body will be on hand, and we all can freely speak our minds. Two heads are better than one, you know."

CHAPTER VIII.

THE FAMILY COUNCIL AND ITS RESULT.

This idea of a parliamentary discussion did not suit Mme. Mirion at all; but, her husband insisting on it, she finally consented; she would, at all events, she thought, have an opportunity, that very evening, of hearing her wonderful story told to the whole family. What would her brother-in-law say to it? How he would stare! The members of the privy-council were notified that immediately after dinner there would be a session with closed doors, in the drawing-room, for the discussion of an important subject. The dinner was dull, solemn even. All present felt in the air itself the approach of some great event. The discreet Joseph, to whom nothing had been said, suspected that something was brewing, and was troubled. As soon as he had finished his coffee, seeing that he was in the way, he retired to his room.

Then they all took their places; they formed a circle round the president, who stood before the fire-place, awaiting his words in the midst of a religious silence. Marguerite sat a little to one side, near the light, her eyes fixed on her embroidery. Her face revealed nothing; but more than once she broke her thread. After an impressive exordium, M. Mirion told his story, which produced a startling effect upon his hearers. Glances of astonishment were exchanged and a confused murmur passed through the group. Mme. Mirion, red as a poppy, drank in their surprise as a connoisseur in wines sips a delicious nectar. She had succeeded in producing a sensation.

"My dear friends," said M. Mirion in conclusion, "we did not think it right to make a decision without first consulting you. It is the happiness of my daughter, whom you all love, that is concerned. I hope you will all say freely and conscientiously what you think. My cousin, Mlle. Grillet, has the floor."

Cousin Grillet, whose timidity almost choked her, begged earnestly to be excused from the unexpected honor; but they all urged her so strongly, that she was compelled to speak. Changing color with each word, she stated that her feelings, her surprise.... in short, she could not exactly express her meaning, but they could easily see what joy so wonderful an event had caused her. She had her share, her small and modest share in the glory thus shed on all the family. Still, if they would excuse the liberty she took, there was one shadow resting on her happiness; she feared the slanders and criticisms of the envious. Tall trees attract the lightning; great good fortune excites remark. Would not M. Mirion be accused of not understanding his position, of forgetting the rank from which he had sprung? The world is so malicious! One other thought troubled her: was not M. D'Ornis a Catholic? That was a matter to be considered. What would their pastor, who had instructed Marguerite in religious things, think of it? What would his wife, who insisted so on every question of the catechism, think of it? ...."

"What would his maid-servant, his ox, and his ass think of it?" interrupted Mme. Mirion, who was boiling over with impatience. "Let them think just what they please! I guess we're able to answer for ourselves."

This interruption and the fierce eyes that were glaring at her, threw Mlle. Grillet into utter confusion; she stopped short, and when at last she found her voice, made no more objections, but expressed in advance and without any reservation, her approval of whatever her worthy cousin and his excellent wife, in their great wisdom, should decide upon.

Aunt Amaranth then took the floor, and resolutely maintained that Mme. Mirion was right, that it was impossible to please every body; that it would be a shame to change their plans on account of what envious and foolish people might say. It surely was Providence that, by so extraordinary an event, had procured for Marguerite a home so worthy of herself, her beauty, her grace, her angelic disposition, and her desire to do good to every body. She was born to move in good society, she could not but be successful in it; with a little experience, she would not be out of place in any circle, even in the court of Schwerin. Moreover, M. D'Ornis seemed to her to possess all those qualities which ought to make a woman happy; he was not frivolous and trifling like most of his countrymen. A single glance proved that he was a man of thought and great good sense, full of judgment and experience, rich in all domestic and social virtues. Finally, it would be folly to permit such an opportunity and such a providential husband to escape them; if they should do so, they would never afterward cease to repent it.

"That's the way to talk!" cried Mme. Mirion, jumping from her chair and throwing her arms around Aunt Amaranth.

When Uncle Benjamin's turn came, he sang a very different tune. "Since you do me the honor to consult me," he said, "I am decidedly opposed to the projected marriage."

"Hadn't you better get your rule, so that you can demonstrate it more correctly?" sharply cried his sister-in-law.

He did not allow himself to be put out by this interruption, but went on as follows: "Vanity is an evil counsellor. I understand very well, sister-in-law, how delightful it would be to say, 'the Countess, my daughter,' or 'my daughter the Countess.' It sounds well, and makes the gossips stare; the devil take it, though; it's your daughter's happiness that's concerned; don't make that a sacrifice to your paltry vanity. When Margot becomes a countess, will she have a better form or lighter heart? I fear that, on the contrary, she will lose that charming gayety and sprightliness which, if I may so express it, are the sunshine of this house. As certainly as the three angles of a triangle are equal to two right-angles, so sure is it that we can not be happy except among people of our own class, and in the midst of that society in which we have been reared, and to which we have become accustomed. Where the kid is tied there it must browse; if it run away, Heaven save it from the wolf! Believe me, it's not in a castle of Burgundy that Margot will find peace of heart and happiness. How do you know but that these D'Ornis, the devil take 'em! will look down upon her, will try all the time to make her feel that she's not a fit associate for them? I can see them now, treating her with disdain, asking her in a sarcastic way about her father, the carpenter, and her dear mother, who spent her younger days in measuring linen in a store on the Fusterie. Even her husband .... I grant you, he may love her better than the apple of his eye; but love soon tires, and he will see that he has married beneath him, and will revenge himself by treating her with contempt and scorn. Remember what Sancho Panza said on leaving his island, and finding his ass again: 'Nothing becomes a man so well as the employment he was born for.' And he added, 'Here will I leave the wings of vanity that raised me aloft, to be pecked at by martlets and other small birds.' Sister-in-law, marry your daughter to some good tradesman who is like ourselves and doesn't think that he has sprung from the thigh of Jupiter; to a worthy man who will not despise his wife, nor his wife's mother, and to whom you can say as Mme. Jourdain did, 'Sit down and take dinner with me, Son-in-law.'"

Thus spake Uncle Benjamin, rudely, harshly, perhaps with some good sense. Marguerite stopped her work a moment, and slyly putting out her hand, tapped her uncle on the shoulder in token of her friendliness and approbation. Fortunately, Mme. Mirion did not perceive this by-play. "Don't talk to me about your professors of mathematics!" she cried. "They get a knowledge of the world by logogriphs." Mme. Mirion confused logogriphs with logarithms.

"I'm not through yet," continued Uncle Benjamin. "Who is this Count D'Ornis that you're all so infatuated with? Do you know him? Not a bit of it. He is to you an unknown quantity, an x. Are you even sure that he's a count? Remember what has occurred in other cases at Geneva, and take warning. May it not be that this pretended count is only an adventurer, a knave? I'll bet my eyes there's not a Castle D'Ornis in the whole of France. Besides all this, I can read faces pretty well; his does not please me. There is something in his eyes that betokens no good. Perhaps you will object that he doesn't wish the dowry. That's just what looks suspicious to me. There's something singular in such disinterestedness. Real counts don't marry below their rank without a dowry. This gentleman asks for nothing that he may have all; he'll worry your last cent out of you .... Look out for the whole tribe of D'Ornis and their castles in Burgundy, and may Heaven protect the innocent! That's all I've got to say."

Uncle Benjamin's peroration threw cold water on the meeting. With the exception of Mme. Mirion, who wished her brother in the infernal regions, every one thought: Sure enough, there's neither count nor castle here; this would have been a most unfortunate marriage. In spite of the way in which his wife shrugged her shoulders, M. Mirion could not help admitting that there was some reason in what his brother said, and spoke as follows:

"That is true. We must get more information. We must be careful and keep the reins in our own hands. M. D'Ornis proposed to put me in communication with his lawyer; but he didn't tell me this lawyer's name, and, stupidly enough, I didn't think to ask it. That confounded man goes like a locomotive .... Quick! quick! I've come to ask your daughter's hand. Quick! quick! I'm going to the Oberland .... Now, where can I find him? Where can I write him? Bah! We can get along without him and his lawyer. We don't want to know, within a thousand francs, what our man's fortune is. All we care for is to be sure that he's a count, that he has a castle and estate, and that his reputation is good in his own country. The best diplomacy is secret. We will send forth an emissary, a trusty agent .... Wait, I have it. There is in this very house a good lad who is devoted to us, and who, besides, although a workman, is very discreet and very shrewd. He will go for us, and, without appearing to be doing so, will get all the information. On his return, Joseph Noirel will tell us whether my brother's doubts or Mme. Mirion's shrugs are most to be depended on."

Full of this idea, M. Mirion ran at once to tell Joseph Noirel about it. He found him in his room, where he was sitting without a light.

"Hallo! my boy," he cried," "what are you doing in the dark? Are you asleep?"

"I guess I was," he answered in a voice that did not sound at all like that of a sleepy man.

He quickly lighted his lamp. His employer sat down in front of him, resting his elbows on the table. "You are a good lad, Joseph," he said, "and I have every confidence in you. You know I keep no secrets from you, and have always looked on you as one of my family. Great events are now taking place with us, and you can render us a very important service, in a very delicate matter. You have great good sense, you are very prudent, I know that I can count upon you."

Thereupon he told him the whole story. Joseph trembled beneath the unexpected blow.

"What's the matter, Josephin?" cried M. Mirion. "How pale you are! Where did you get your white face from? I've noticed for some time you were not well. You don't eat any thing, your cheeks are hollow, your eyes dull. A little rest and the fresh air of Burgundy will set you right. You lucky dog! you're going to travel for three or four days. If the news is good, I give you leave, on your return, to stop at Beaune, and empty a bottle or two to Marguerite's health and mine; but don't drink on your way there. A secret diplomatic agent ought to have his wits about him, and his tongue under his control."

Stunning as was the blow, Joseph's pride rose under it. "You can depend on me," he said; "I will do this for you." There was a single question he was burning to ask M. Mirion; but his courage failed him. He talked about almost every other subject; and, finally, in an affectedly careless tone, inquired, "Does she love him?"

"How do I know?" answered M. Mirion. "No one can tell. Before dinner, I heard her through the door, saying to her mother, 'I don't know him!' That's sensible enough. Pshaw! all depends on the news you bring us. Don't worry, she'll love him, if we want her to. She's got such a good disposition."

CHAPTER IX.

JOSEPH VISITS BURGUNDY.

While walking through the grounds with M. D'Ornis, Mme. Mirion had questioned him about his castle, and, although he was not fond of questions, she had learned from him that it was situated three or four miles from Arnay-le-Duc, the chief town of the canton of Côte-d'Or. Joseph's orders were to take the Paris train, stop at Beaune, and pass the night there. At the inn where he slept, no one knew any thing about Ornis. This was a good beginning, and his first night was a peaceful one.

He took the diligence for Arnay the next morning. It was his first journey. His acquaintance with the world had heretofore been limited to Geneva, its lake, and its valley inclosed on all sides by high mountains. The country that he now saw astonished him. He enjoyed leaving the vehicle and climbing the steep slope that separates the vineyards from the highlands. He gazed intently on the vast rolling plain which he was leaving, the gradually rising hills which lay before him, and the distant line of the horizon. Either the novelty of the scene, or the pleasure of moving about and breathing another air, caused every thing to appear to him in glowing colors ; he was in one of those happy moods in which the soul is contented with the world, lending it charms which are quite fictitious.

He reached Arnay about noon and first took time to eat a little lunch. His appetite was soon spoiled, however, for the first person passing by, on being questioned, told him where Ornis was, and pointed out the road leading to it. Joseph thanked him with a surly air, and started on his way. He consoled himself by the reflection that though the village was genuine enough, it was not yet certain about the Count.

Every road does not lead to Ornis. I know not whether Joseph intended it, but he turned off to the right, and was soon lost in the woods. A peasant that he met set him right again. It was already evening, when from the crest of a hill, he saw on the banks of a little stream, a village, and on the rising ground beyond it, a terrace shaded by two magnificent elms. In the foreground of this terrace was a church; behind the church appeared a vaulted passage leading to a gate, which opened on a large court. Beyond this court was an immense castle with battlements and turrets, behind which could be seen a park, so thickly wooded that it seemed almost black. At the sight of this genuine castle, Joseph began to believe in Count D'Ornis, and his brow darkened. It was with a heavy heart that he entered the *White-Horse* Inn, situated at one end of the village, and called for supper.

After finishing his meal, he went into the kitchen, and entered into conversation with Mme. Guibaud, the hostess, a stout Burgundian woman with a jovial face, who had been a widow for three years, and was very desirous of marrying again. She was trying to put a broken coffee-mill in order.

"You don't know how to do it!" said Joseph to her, and taking it from her hands, he set to work to mend it. This pleased the woman, and made her his friend at once. She inquired where he came from. He replied that he was a workman who had had some words with his employer, and was going to look for something to do at Dijon or thereabouts; he was in no hurry though, as he had some money on hand and wanted to see the country.

"You live in a pretty place," he added. "Who does that castle on the hill belong to?"

"What a question! To Count D'Ornis, of course."

"A tall, light-complexioned man, that I saw riding in a carriage a little while ago?"

"No, he isn't light or tall, and he never rides; he is the greatest walker in the country. I don't know who you met; they say the Count is traveling in Switzerland."

There could be no longer any doubt: the Count was as real

as the castle. Joseph was silent for a moment, and then asked, " What kind of a looking man is the Count ?"

" He's got a mouth, a nose, and two eyes in his head. What do you want to know for ?"

" I just now met two men on the road who were talking about him. I heard one of them say, Count D'Ornis is an ugly fellow, he makes his wife very unhappy."

" You heard wrong. The Count hasn't got a wife. The only Countess D'Ornis is the Count's mother, who lives with him. It isn't likely he will ever get married. He's forty-five years old, and don't seem to care much for the ladies. He thinks a good deal more of his dogs and gun."

" He's eccentric, then."

" I suppose so. The fact is, some people like him, and some don't. Another thing about him is, he's more careful of his words than of his money. You might meet him in the village twenty times, without hearing him speak."

" I don't like people who don't talk," said Joseph. " I always think that they're concealing something."

As he spoke these words, a man in a blue blouse leaned toward the fire to light his pipe, and said to Joseph, " You're right, my boy. And those men who told you that the Count made his wife unhappy were right too."

" How can that be, if he hasn't got any ?" asked Mme. Guibaud.

" What difference does that make ?" replied the other in an angry tone. " He might have one, and, if he did—good Lord ! how I should pity her."

" Do you think he'd beat her ?" asked Joseph.

" Within an inch of her life, by thunder !"

" Poor woman ! a real *Geneviève de Brabant !*" said the hostess with a loud laugh that displayed all her teeth.

The man in the blouse was in no laughing humor. " He's a savage," he continued, " and I'd like to see any one who'll say the contrary. It was in Mexico that he changed so. Last winter, a boy happened to hit him with a snowball ; he flew at him like a wild beast, and almost killed him on the spot."

" He was mad, Father Chazet ; any body else might do the

same," answered Mme. Guibaud. "Generally, he's very kind to every body."

"Pshaw! that was before he went to Mexico," said the other firing up. "Mexico's the place to change a man for you. He came back as furious as a wild boar. We'll settle accounts with him some day. If the wheel ever turns ...."

He did not finish his sentence, but started off smoking his pipe and humming the air of the *Ça Ira.*

Joseph had devoured Father Chazet with his eyes, every one of his words was engraved on his memory. The hostess now addressed him, saying, "You ought to know that Father Chazet is a Red, who used to poach on the Count's grounds. He warned him twice; the third time he was caught in the act, arrested, and punished."

"I don't care for that," said Joseph; "he seemed to me a very sensible man."

"Father Chazet is a dotard," said a little old man with a shaking head, who had drawn near the fire to warm his legs, for, summer and winter, he was always cold. He was the school-teacher, M. Machillard. "Count D'Ornis," he continued, "is a good man, God bless him! He isn't proud at all, and treats every one alike. You won't find another such count in the whole world. There's only one thing I blame him for: he will not marry, he will leave no children. He has given the people a fountain and a laundry; he ought to present them besides with twenty little D'Ornis to preserve the breed."

"Twenty little D'Ornis, M. Machillard! Wouldn't that be too many?" asked Mme. Guibaud, who always seemed disposed to take a medium course.

"Make it ten then, and don't bother me," answered M. Machillard with a cough.

"Why don't your Count get married?" Joseph asked. "Hasn't he ever thought about it?"

"Oh, yes! he used to have some idea of it; but for two years .... You know, since the accident, the murder ...."

"Don't bring up those horrible stories again," said Mme. Guibaud. "They've kept me awake many a night already."

"What murder?" said Joseph, laying the coffee-mill down upon the table.

"Don't you know about it? Where have you been?" asked the old man glancing compassionately at him.

"I came from Lyons," answered Joseph. "We heard nothing about it there."

M. Machillard drew his snuff-box from his pocket, took a pinch of snuff between his thumb and finger, and spoke as follows: "These are the facts, young man: Count D'Ornis had an intimate friend, who lived near here at Riviers, the Marquis de Raoux. They always were walking, hunting, and dining together; one couldn't live without the other. They were like Orestes and Pylades. Now it happened ...."

"I'm going to leave you," said the hostess. "How can you tell that dreadful story?"

"It happened in this way," continued M. Machillard in a dogmatic tone. "The Marquis had come, as usual, to take dinner and spend the evening with Count D'Ornis. It was the 26th of February, 1867. It was terribly cold that day, and the wind blew hard enough to tear the cattle's horns off. And now, young man, I'll show you what presentiments are. It's my habit always to go to bed at exactly ten o'clock. I often tell Mme. Machillard that regular habits are what preserve a man; I say the same to you, and hope you'll profit by it. Well! somehow that evening I couldn't make up my mind to go to bed. I had an uneasy feeling in my stomach and my limbs .... It seemed exactly as though something was going to happen. Suddenly the clock struck twelve ...."

"And you heard a shot?" interrupted Joseph.

"Nonsense, young man! Do knives shoot? That's all .... you're too young to listen.... As I was saying, at twelve o'clock the two friends parted. The Marquis went away, crossing the park. When he had reached the little bridge that leads to the wood lying between here and Riviers..... Are you listening now? .... When he had crossed this little bridge, a man, who had been hid behind an oak, sprang upon him and buried a knife in his heart. He fell, stone dead! There's a lesson for you! There was an elegant young man, who had just been to dinner, a good dinner too, and who was feeling very merry, for in those times they drank good wine at the castle .... There he was, stone dead, just as I told you. The body was not found till morning, and then the news was carried to M. D'Ornis. You ought to have seen him. He tore his hair, and caught his friend's body in his arms, as though he would call him back again to life. Such despair I never saw? It was heart-rending. The whole village will tell you so."

"Was the murderer discovered?" inquired Joseph.

"Good gracious! what a hurry you're in. I can't tell you every thing at once. Yes, the murderer was discovered, and held for trial. He was a tramp, a kind of gypsy; he was arrested about twenty-four hours afterward. He denied every thing to the very end, the villain; he defended himself with the greatest obstinacy. Unfortunately for him, there were spots of blood on his blouse, and the Marquis's watch and pocket-book were in his pocket. Will you believe it, the poor, innocent fellow maintained that he had picked them up at the foot of an oak. Does justice listen to such tales as that? Is it likely that a pocket-book and watch would go out walking in the woods alone? A knife was found on him besides. It is true, an expert pretended that this knife had a loose handle, and that it could not possibly have killed a man; but it was proved, as clear as day, that the villain had loosened it after he struck the blow."

"Didn't they ascertain," said Joseph, "whether the knife fitted the wound?"

"Do you pretend to doubt the infallibility of justice, young man? Judges are in the world to judge. If we suppose that they can make a mistake, where will it lead us to? As I was going to say, they guillotined the villain—he didn't manage to escape."

At this point, M. Machillard took his pinch of snuff and cried, "You can come back now, Madame Guibaud, I've finished my story."

"I'm glad to hear it," she answered, entering the room.

"In conclusion," he continued, "since the Marquis's death, Count D'Ornis has been another man. Before that time, he used to seek amusements, and was fond of play.... He played a great deal, and sometimes with high stakes. After his friend's death, there was a change. No more pleasure, no more cards. For eighteen months, he didn't speak more than twenty words. Thin and sad, always dressed in black, he moved slowly about looking like a funeral. He scarcely ever left the house. He passed whole weeks shut up in his room, with his doors and windows hermetically sealed, as though he wanted to make the house a tomb ; he let the grass grow in the court, and the nettles in the garden. It's only during the last six months that he has returned to life ; he has begun to walk and talk again, and last of all has gone to Switzerland, to pass away the time in climbing mountains. Notwithstanding this, as long as he lives, he'll not forget his friend, the Marquis, which goes to prove that he has a heart of gold, and that Father Chazet is a malicious fellow and a gossip-monger."

With these words, M. Machillard returned his snuff-box to his pocket, bowed to the pot-hooks and the saucepans, and went away. "I hope it's true about his having a heart of gold," said the hostess to Joseph ; "but you ought to know that M. Machillard is under obligations to the Count, who once gave bonds for ten thousand francs for him."

"From which I conclude," said Joseph, "that the man and his story are both to be regarded with suspicion...... There's your mill mended," he added. "Good-night to all."

CHAPTER X.

JOSEPH'S ADVENTURES AT CASTLE D'ORNIS.

The clock was striking ten. Joseph walked along with his hands in his pockets, climbed to the church, and pushed on to the castle gate. It was closed and locked. Following the directions which M. Machillard had given him, he turned back and followed the road, until he reached a path leading to a little wood, that lay upon his right. He entered this wood, and soon reached a small rustic bridge spanning a narrow stream, the banks of which were high and steep. Although Joseph was courageous, he could not repress a shudder as his eyes fell on the scene before him. The full moon shone brightly on the spot where the murder had been committed. It seemed to mark the place, to say, 'Tis here. The trees surrounding it appeared like sad and silent witnesses of the crime. Joseph at last decided to cross the bridge which was closed at the other end by a gate. He climbed over this barrier without difficulty, and entered the park; he had not yet lost his former taste for scaling walls, and entering other people's grounds without permission. Notwithstanding the bright moonlight, he could not find a path, the grass grew so thickly and the trees were so close together. More than once he tripped against a stump, more than once his hat was caught in the branches of an oak. Finding he could make no progress, he started to go back again. As he was about climbing the gate a second time, his eyes fell upon a man standing at the other end of the bridge. This man, whose back was turned toward him, had a thick rattan in his right hand, while with his left he held an immense dog by a chain. He was leaning over the rail of the bridge, looking at the flowing water. Soon he muttered in a low tone, "Be still, old fellow! What is done can't be helped." Was he speaking to the Marquis's ghost or to his dog? The latter took the liberty of answering him with a mournful howl; perhaps he had scented Noirel. The man broke into a volley of oaths, looked carefully about him, and seeing no one, silenced the dog by threatening him with his stick, after which they both silently went away. Joseph waited a little for them to disappear, then crossed the bridge, and went back to the inn. He did not sleep well at all, and kept tossing about during the whole night. A traveling salesman, who slept in the next room, heard him cry out twice, "No, you can't have her. She is mine ...."

He awoke early the next morning, with a headache. After breakfast, he decided that before leaving, he would again visit the castle and the park, so as to be able to answer the innumerable questions which Mme. Mirion would be sure to ask him. This time he found the gate open, crossed the large court without meeting any one, and descended by a spiral staircase to the garden, where he found a few wall-flowers, and here and there some faded roses. When he had crossed this garden, he turned round to look at the face of the castle. He was struck by the sad and gloomy appearance of this vast Gothic structure, which was large enough for ten families to live in, yet served as the home of only one man. A projecting portion of the building was all that was in repair, and seemed to be the only part inhabited; the rest had been given up to the rats and spiders. It seemed like an immense body struck with paralysis and living only by the brain and heart. Turning his eyes from the flowerless garden to the gray old walls, Joseph muttered to himself, "What would become of her gay spirits here?" He penetrated into the park, which was funnel-shaped, and turned his steps toward a pond surrounded by weeping-willows. The ground was covered with dead wood, and the trees formed dense and impenetrable thickets. Joseph, with great difficulty, forced his way through to the stagnant pool, which had formerly been a fish pond, but was now inhabited only by frogs. The bending willows hung their mournful branches in the water, entirely concealing the sky from view.

In the centre of a lawn on the border of this pond, stood the marble statue of an officer, with sword in hand. This statue had lost its nose in the battle of the centuries. Its pedestal bore this inscription: "James D'Ornis, Field-Marshal and Commander of the Order of the Holy Ghost, born in 1635, killed in the battle of Nerwinde in 1693."

Joseph turned back toward the castle. He approached the inhabited portion, the doors and windows of which were open. Ascending a flight of steps, he saw before him a large drawing-room, furnished luxuriously, but showing signs of age. An upholsterer with two assistants was engaged in refitting some portions of the room. An old woman, seated in an arm-chair, with a short crutch at her side, was watching them at their work, talking at the same time to a tall, awkward fellow who was standing in front of her, sucking the ivory handle of his cane. This old woman had a very important air, a harsh and crafty face, a pointed chin, thin, compressed lips, projecting eyes that looked like agate marbles, and a sharp glance that was expressive of any thing but goodness, and that accorded well with her shrill voice.

"I tell you again, my dear Du Rozan," she said, "my son is an ungrateful fellow. He has written me only twice since he went away, and then such letters! They were just like telegrams; you know the style of them: 'Arrived at Geneva, bought a watch; arrived at Fribourg, heard the organs; arrived at Berne, saw the bears; arrived at Zurich, took a sail on the lake; the weather is pleasant; I am well, and hope you are the same.' That's all there is to them. Well, well, you know my weakness; I've always adored this monster, and suppose I'll continue to do so to my dying day."

At this moment she perceived Joseph standing by the door. "Who are you?" she cried. "What do you want?"

"I'm a poor workman traveling through France," answered Joseph in a whining tone, such as he had assumed in his younger days, "and if you could help me...."

"Get out!" she cried in an angry tone. "This is no place for tramps and beggars."

"Tramps! believe me, madam...."

She raised her crutch: "My dear Marquis, put that man out!" she said.

"I am out now, don't let the Marquis trouble himself," answered Joseph, changing his tone and beating a retreat.

As he crossed the stone-paved court, he perceived the mysterious stranger, whom he had seen on the bridge the night before. He was talking with a servant dressed in livery. This individual, who had a large parrot nose red as a beet, bushy side-whiskers, also of a beautiful red color, and the airs and manners of a bully, was saying to the servant, "So your master isn't in, eh?"

"He's in Switzerland, I tell you, Monsieur Bertrand, and we don't expect him home for several weeks."

"The devil! that doesn't suit me," he answered striking the pavement fiercely with his stick. "Can't you give me his address?"

"How can I if he doesn't write?.... The Count will no doubt be sorry"....he added with a deferential air; "but he could not have expected.... Generally you visit Ornis in the spring."

"It seems to me I can come whenever I please," answered the other in a surly tone; "besides he ought to have let me know."

"Certainly, certainly," said the servant trying to appease him; "but you know it isn't my fault. Won't you step in and take some refreshments, Monsieur Bertrand. The Countess is at home, and will be glad to see you."

"The devil take your old Countess! She'd let me stand two hours without offering me a chair or a glass of wine."

During this time, the large dog, an ugly-looking animal, after moving about Joseph for a moment, began to bark furiously, and crouched as though to spring at him. Fortunately, Joseph forestalled his attack by giving him a kick that lifted him completely from the ground. "Who are you, I'd like to know?" cried M. Bertrand turning toward Noirel. "Don't hurt my dog!"

"I won t, if he'll leave my pantaloons alone," replied Joseph.

"None of your insolence," answered M. Bertrand. "My little friend, I think I'll have to give you a flogging."

Joseph, whose blood was up, rolled up his sleeves, and marched straight upon the enemy with clenched fists and a defiant air. So confident was his manner that M. Bertrand fell back a step. The servant stepped between them.

"What are you doing here?" he said to Joseph in a haughty tone.

"I found the gate open," he answered, "and walked in to look about; your castle is such a hospitable place though, I don't think I'll trouble you again."

So saying he rolled down his sleeves and quietly walked away, followed by the howlings of the dog, who was careful, however, to keep at a respectful distance. He soon reached the inn, where he proceeded to settle his bill at once.

"You've been to the castle?" asked the hostess in a pleasant tone.

"Your castle is a pretty place!" he answered. "It's as cheerful as a jail, and there's a complete assortment of agreeable creatures there, from the dog that snaps at your legs to the old woman who's as attractive as an angry porcupine."

"Pshaw!" said she, "when the Countess is out of humor .... She's a woman who does a great deal of good, though."

"Heaven help those she assists. She must be very good to them.... By the way," he added, "who is M. Bertrand?"

"Is M. Bertrand here? He must have arrived this morning then. He's a dealer in *bric-à-brac*, as they call it, who now and then comes into Burgundy to buy old iron, furniture, and clocks...."

"He makes himself at home at the castle, anyhow."

"The Count seems to like him very well. He has some old things he sells him, I believe. But what makes you so curious about all these people?"

He answered quickly, "My good woman, I've always hated castles and every thing inside of them."

"You're a Red, then, like Father Chazet?" she said in a reproachful tone.

"As red as I can be," he answered, "and for good reasons, too."

Notwithstanding this profession of faith which she disliked, it was with regret that Mme. Guibaud saw Joseph depart. She was greatly pleased with him, and asked him if he would not visit Ornis again. He answered with a bitter smile, "It isn't likely, unless I take a notion to drown myself some day; I saw a pond over there that would be just the place for it."

"What's the matter, my boy?" she cried. "Does any thing trouble you?"

"How can any thing trouble me? My old master used to tell me every morning that I was a lucky dog, and of course it must be so."

And then, angry at having so nearly betrayed himself, he assumed a reckless, jovial manner, which was by no means natural, caught Mme. Guibaud round the waist, and kissed her on both cheeks. She struggled some, but evidently was not displeased. Joseph turned suddenly and ran away. Standing on the door-step, she watched him moving off, shaking her finger at him when he turned to look at her. She little thought that as he left her he wiped his lips, although, all things considered, Mme. Guibaud was rather an attractive woman. This adventure put her in a pensive mood for several hours, and when Father Chazet came in during the afternoon to empty a bottle or two, she said to him, "Did you notice the little sunburnt fellow who was sitting yesterday by this table? He's the kind of workman for you. He's as genteel and well-bred as any gentleman."

As soon as he reached the crest of the hill, from which he had the day before first looked on Ornis, Joseph threw himself down upon the grass, leaning back against a rock. It was a quiet spot; the clock had just struck twelve, and now all was still. Joseph heard nothing but the distant hum of a mill, and the occasional tinkling of a bell belonging to a solitary cow that was browsing in the woods. Opposite him, on the other side of the valley, rose another hill, on the summit of which stood a dead oak, the mournful outline of which was clearly marked against a smoky sky. On the right, something glittered in the sun above the trees; it was a vane on one of the towers of the castle. Joseph angrily turned away his eyes. That castle was his enemy, an enemy that threatened to deprive him of all he held most dear, to rob him of the treasure of his dreams.

His stern good sense did not allow him to deceive himself. "They will not be influenced by what I tell them," he thought; "they are governed by vanity rather than affection. What do they care for their daughter's happiness? As soon as they find out that this man is really a count, and that in his park there's a statue of one of his ancestors, who was a field-marshal and commander of the Holy Ghost, their foolish heads will all be turned." His only hope, for hope never dies, was that perhaps Marguerite would make some resistance. "I know well enough," he said to himself, "that if she had been with me this morning, that park, pond, and castle, that old witch who threatened me with her crutch, that bridge where the murder was committed—all those things would have made her heart-sick, and Ornis would have seemed to her a sad place, where it would be impossible to smile. If she ask me, I'll tell her just what I think, in spite of every body." His hope, however, was very slight. It had all happened so quickly. The very rapidity with which his misfortune had come upon him terrified him; he saw something fatal in it. "And yet," he thought, "it might have happened otherwise." He shut his eyes and began to dream. He saw himself standing at his bench; near him was seated his wife, gazing on him with fond eyes, and these eyes belonged to him: he had the right to shower kisses on them. He thought "She is mine and mine alone!" His heart was melting in his breast. He gloried in his fate, his trade, his hard work, his poverty which she shared with him, the brown bread which they broke together, and the garret that concealed their happiness; life appeared as bright to him as the summer sky, as sweet as those mysterious, entrancing notes which the nightingale utters to the moon in the gentle nights of spring. There was something, however, in his dream that jarred on his imagination. Marguerite's beauty was not of the type that is usually hidden in a garret, her hands were too white and delicate to wash the dishes or mend the clothes, and her queenly grace would ill become a mechanic's wife. The idea of clothing that symmetrical and charming form in calico or coarse cloth! The idea of imprisoning in a hood those wavy tresses, with which the sun and wind loved to sport! No matter how often Joseph began his dream, it fell to pieces every time, like a house of cards.

"No, she can not be a workman's wife," he thought. "Where can a man be found who is worthy of her, even in her own class. She does not belong to the society in which she lives; she is far superior to those about her; she is like a swan shut up in a poultry-yard. She can not stoop to me, she will not let me rise to her! If the stupid conventionalities that govern society had not placed a barrier between us, she would have taken the trouble to find out that I had a heart worthy of her, and, strong in our love, we would have helped each other to bear the world's scorn. I have always been treated in her presence, however, as a person of no consequence, and although we have lived under the same roof for two years, she has never once thought seriously of her wretched companion, nor known whether he had a heart.... Why did I ever meet her? Why has cruel fate opened to me the garden in which grew this beauteous flower, and condemned me to look at it, to become intoxicated with its perfume, and then said to me, "Touch it not, another must pluck it before your eyes!" Then he began to find fault with fickle fortune, to reproach it for its favors more cruel than its hardships. "You have placed a man's heart within my breast," he cried, "and will not allow me to follow the yearnings of that heart." He opened his eyes; his elbows were resting on his knees, his chin was supported in his hands. He gazed for a long time at the dead oak in front of him. It seemed to have been struck by lightning; it was still standing, but there was no life in it. Joseph thought, "Shall I be able to keep from falling, too?" He rose. Frantic with rage, he picked up an enormous stone, and threw it against the rock with such force that it flew to pieces. Two children were passing along the path, singing,

> Bourguignon salé,
> L'épée au coté,
> La barbe au menton,
> Saute, Bourguignon.

They saw Joseph; the expression of his face was so ferocious that, thinking him a raging madman, they fled into the woods, shrieking with terror. Their cries brought Joseph to himself. He picked up his cap and knapsack, and started on again. He reached Arnay just in time to catch the coach for Beaune, where he passed the night. The next afternoon, he was in Geneva.

He arrived at Mon-Plaisir about two o'clock. Mme. Mirion, whose eyes were sweeping the road like a field battery, saw him in the distance. She ran down to the gate, pale with emotion and out of breath, crying out, "Is he a count?" He nodded his head. She asked no more, but ran at full speed up the avenue, swinging her arms like an old-fashioned telegraph, and shouting so loud as to be heard all over the neighborhood, "Just as I told you! he is a count, a real count!"

CHAPTER XI.

MARGUERITE PROVES THE AMIABILITY OF HER DISPOSITION.

Joseph Noirel had judged rightly concerning the effect his story would produce. As soon as he reached the house, he was taken to an inner room, where he had an interview of two hours with M. and Mme. Mirion. He told them all that he had seen and heard. Mme. Mirion was provoked that he laid so much weight on certain details, which she thought unworthy of notice. What did she care for Chazet? He was a poacher and a drunkard. Were those the kind of people to listen to? The satirical portrait which Joseph drew of the old Countess brought to her lips a smile of pity. "You don't know what you're talking about," she said. "What seems like pride to you is simply a noble grace and majestic manner, which sets well on great people." Only one thing made a disagreeable impression on her, that was the bridge where the murder had been committed. Fortunately, the murderer was not living. She promised herself that when she became intimate with her son-in-law, she would persuade him to take away the bridge and put up another a little further down the stream.

When Joseph had concluded, M. Mirion said to him, "Well done, my son! You have accomplished your mission like the intelligent lad that you are. Now give me your opinion. You are not ungrateful, you love us, and you want Marguerite to be happy as much as we do. I've often consulted you on important matters; this is of the greatest consequence. I won't promise to agree with you, but I'd like to know what you think."

"Why, Thomas, you're out of your mind!" cried Mme. Mirion. "If you're going to consult every body...."

"Joseph isn't every body," he answered, interrupting her. "I've always considered him as one of the family."

"What do you care about what I think?" inquired Joseph.

" I care enough about it to ask you for your candid opinion. Are you for or against this marriage? You must have some idea about it."

" My opinion, then, since you desire it," answered Joseph, " is that Count D'Ornis is an eccentric person, as my good hostess of the *White-Horse* expressed it. He has lately met with some misfortunes which have greatly troubled him. He is trying to forget them, and he thinks that getting married will help him to accomplish this. Chance threw your daughter in his way, and he was pleased with her. This doesn't surprise me, for I believe that he wishes to marry a tradesman's daughter. He thinks that he can mould her to his will, and accustom her to his habits and mode of life, which are different from those of ordinary mortals. Can he make her happy? Neither you nor I can tell, and perhaps it would be well to inquire further into the subject. Otherwise, it's nothing but a lottery."

" Suppose it is a lottery," cried Mme. Mirion in her shrillest tone. " Isn't every marriage a lottery, I'd like to know? When I married you, Mirion, did I know who you were, or whether you would make me happy or not?"

" You are exaggerating," he replied. " The Mirions were well known here. And, besides, my face was a sufficient guarantee. . . ."

" While Count D'Ornis," she answered, " looks like a Blue-Beard, I suppose. Did you see any claws on his hands?"

"Ah! madam," said Joseph, "such people, if they have claws, don't show them to every body. They keep them in their pockets, and only take them out on great occasions."

Mme. Mirion bounced upon her chair; her patience was entirely exhausted by this last remark. She stretched out her hand toward Joseph with a tragic air, and said, " You are our enemy! You have sworn to defeat this marriage. I believe you are bribed by my brother Benjamin."

At these offensive words, Joseph started to his feet, pale with anger. He was about to speak, when M. Mirion interposed. "You don't mean that, Marianne," he said to his wife in a coaxing tone. "Joseph our enemy! Have we not brought him up? If it had not been for us, would he not be lying now in the dirt where his father died? He knows well enough it's so, and he loves us all, you and me, every thing here, even to the dogs and chickens.... I asked him to speak. He won't say any thing more. You shall have your own way about it. My father used to say that mothers ought to marry off their daughters."

Mme. Mirion was pacified at once. "We mustn't forget," she said, "that Marguerite is to decide for herself. I know where to find her, and will give her all the information she desires, without exerting the least influence upon her; but I know, beforehand, that she will be of my opinion. I must request you, Joseph," she added dryly, "not to have any private conversation with her; it would not be proper."

"There's no necessity for saying that," remarked M. Mirion as he patted Joseph on the head. "Noirel never speaks without good cause. He's both grateful and discreet."

Mme. Mirion went into the garden to look for her daughter; she found her arranging a basket of flowers for the dining-room. Marguerite was not ignorant of the fact that the secret agent had returned, and I should not dare to say that she was not agitated a little. However that might be, she turned toward her mother, saying in a sprightly way, "Well! what news?"

Her mother made her sit down beside her on a bench. "My dear child," she said in a trembling voice, "Joseph has returned from Ornis, where he has talked with a great many people, among others with the hostess of the *White-Horse*, a very repectable woman, who is far superior to her position. The report which he has just given your father and myself surpasses our expectations. In the first place, notwithstanding all the tirades of your uncle Benjamin, there is an Ornis. I knew well enough there was. It's a beautiful village, situated in a very fertile valley, and inhabited by excellent people. There you will find magnificent trees, delightful scenery, mountains, sparkling streams, a clear sky...."

"Except when it rains," interposed Marguerite.

"Don't pick me up so," answered Mme. Mirion, a little nettled. "I don't deny that it occasionally rains at Ornis. Did I say it never rained there? As regards the Count, he is a real count; the origin of his family is lost in the night of time. His park is full of statues of his ancestors. One of them, James D'Ornis, was a commander of the order of the Holy Ghost. Do you understand, a commander? He covered himself with glory in the crusades. He died somewhere, I don't remember the place, in 1693."

"According to that," said Marguerite, "if my books tell the truth, he must have covered himself with glory under Louis XIV."

"That's exactly what I told you. He was, it seems, the favorite, the king's most intimate friend. Near his statue, there's a lake, my dear, a love of a lake, surrounded by weeping willows, whose forms are mirrored in the water. It's very nice to be able to say, 'my lake.'"

"My lake is not mine yet."

"The castle is superb, monumental, I may say," continued Mme. Mirion. "You could make ten castles of it, if you wanted to."

"How about the owner of it? Tell me something about him. In the first place, is he an old bachelor or a widower?"

"Oh! don't think because he's a few years older than you...."

"A few! a good many, it seems to me. I believe he's twice my age."

"What if he is? As long as a man is not fifty, he isn't old. What difference does his age make, if he's young at heart? .... No, my dear, he isn't a widower. A widower! how ridiculous! He has been waiting to find the wife of his dreams. He had sworn that he would never marry unless he found this ideal being; fate caused him to meet her at Geneva."

"Did the hostess of the *White-Horse* tell Joseph all this? You frighten me. I am no such ideal being; I don't feel like one.... But tell me, what did you hear about his character?"

"Oh! he's such a man! How can I describe him! The whole village is full of his goodness and generosity. This very year he gave the people a fountain and a laundry. Some of the stories told about him would bring tears to your eyes. He had a friend, the Marquis De Raoux, who was accidentally killed. He fell from a bridge. How can I tell you about Count D'Ornis .... He couldn't rest until the murderer was caught and punished."

"What murderer? I thought the Marquis fell from a bridge."

"How you confuse me with your interruptions! I meant, until he had destroyed the bridge that caused his friend's death. At any rate, that's what Noirel told us. But that's nothing to what followed. He shut himself up in the house for eighteen months, and wouldn't eat or drink...."

"Eighteen months without eating!" interrupted Marguerite again. "I don't believe that the commander of the Holy-Ghost even...."

"Oh! how you pick me up! I didn't say that he ate nothing at all; but that he ate so little that any one else in his place would have starved. I want to know if a man who loves his friends like that, wouldn't love his wife and make her happy!"

"Perhaps so," answered Marguerite; "only, if he waited for her to fall from a bridge...."

"You must stop this trifling; it's entirely out of place."

"Please don't get angry. I only judge, from what little I know of Count D'Ornis, that he is not as tender-hearted as you think."

"The idea of a young girl like you knowing any thing about such matters! At your age you can't understand how the warmest hearts hide their feelings by an appearance of coldness and indifference. Count D'Ornis takes after his mother. She is a very respectable lady, but it seems that she, too, is very quiet and sedate. What do you suppose she was doing when Noirel saw her? She was preparing a surprise for her son. She had noticed that the hangings of their drawing-room were a little faded, so she had sent for an upholsterer, and was having new ones put up. Nothing was good enough for her dear son. Just imagine this countess, this real countess, doing this ! That's the way the D'Ornis understand domestic life ! There ! I've told you every thing I could think of, both for and against this proposition ; now you must decide."

"What ! right away ?" cried Marguerite, who was becoming frightened.

"Yes, right away. There isn't a minute to lose ; your father must send an answer to-night."

"Please let me talk with Joseph about it first."

"What ! talk with Joseph !" interrupted Mme. Mirion, growing red with indignation. During the last half hour she had taken a spite against Noirel. "Talk with Joseph ! your father's workman ! . . . If I thought that you would presume to ask his advice, or that he would dare to give it to you, he shouldn't stay in this house twenty-four hours."

Marguerite was silent for a moment. She was twisting a jasmine branch in her hands, and the poor flower was suffering sadly. "What would you think, if I should say no ?" she replied at last in a low voice.

Mme. Mirion started to her feet as though pushed up by a spring. "If you should say no," she cried, giving her daughter a terrible look, "you would be guilty of ingratitude toward God. Have you not seen the workings of his hand in what has happened here during the last two weeks ? Have you not seen that Providence, by an astonishing and miraculous dispensation, has wished to make us all happy, to recompense us for all the care we have taken with your education, and for your poor father's forty years of honest toil ? If you should say no, you would no longer be my daughter, and God would no longer keep you under his protecting care."

Like King William, Mme. Mirion had a bad habit of mixing God up with matters that he cared nothing for ; it is true it was her particular God, and not the God of common sense. She also resembled the King of Prussia in being exceedingly obstinate ; she never raised a siege until the place surrendered. At last, Marguerite tired of war, said to her, "Well, you can decide for me ; I'll do whatever you wish."

Then she threw herself upon her daughter's neck, and

pressed her to her heart, calling her her treasure, her angel, her darling child; after which she hurried away to find M. Mirion, whom she also embraced, saying to him, "I've left her free, entirely free, to decide for herself. She says yes, but the poor child is so agitated, that it's best not to speak to her. Don't say a word, but run your letter over in your head. You can't take too much pains with it."

After dinner, the family, whose curiosity as can readily be believed was greatly excited, was informed of what had taken place: this time, however, there was no consultation. Mlle. Grillet and Aunt Amaranth were full of congratulations. "The die is cast, my dear Benjamin," said Mme. Mirion to her brother-in-law, who had not spoken a word. "We are going to give our daughter to this sharper, you unmasked so finely."

"Treat your daughter like the cabbages in your garden, if you want to," he answered. "I've told you what I thought, and now, whatever happens, I wash my hands of it."

CHAPTER XII.

COUNT D'ORNIS IS MADE A HAPPY MAN.

During this time, M. Mirion was engaged in thinking over his letter to M. D'Ornis. This painful incubation made him grave and taciturn. It was nearly midnight before his egg was hatched.

The following was the result:

"MY DEAR COUNT: In answer to the very kind and unexpected request which I had the honor to receive from you, I reply that I have informed our daughter Marguerite of your intentions, and that after taking time for reflection, she has given a favorable answer to the communication. Her mother and myself feel deeply the value of an alliance between our family and the glorious house of Ornis, more than one of whose ancestors died on the field of honor in the reign of Louis XIV. We are nothing more than plain, simple people; but I can assure you that our Marguerite bears a spotless name; morality and honesty being, so to speak, hereditary among the Mirions. It is not without deep feeling, as you can well imagine, that we accede to your gracious request. Our daughter is our joy and pride, and her happiness is the great aim of our lives. We are very confident that you will make her happy; on your side, you may rest assured that if God gives you children, she will set them a good example, teaching them all the virtues which she has seen practiced by her mother, and which have been taught her from her infancy.

"As regards the dowry, permit me to differ from you in regard to the desire which you were kind enough to express to me. It is a principle among the Mirions that the wife should contribute her share toward the family expenses, and as my father often used to say, principles before every thing! This is the foundation of all family happiness. God having prospered my business, I can easily afford to give my daughter a dowry of 300,000 francs, say three hundred thousand, or fifteen thousand francs a year, which will be her contribution toward the general fund. I remember your once saying to me in my office, that a wife ought to belong solely to her husband. This principle, I dare affirm, belongs alike to the D'Ornis and the Mirions. I should be very sorry if you had the least uneasiness in this regard, or if you thought that, because Marguerite brings you something more than her *trousseau*, it can at all lessen the respect she will always have for your desires. I promise you that she will always remember that noble precept of the Gospel, 'Wives, obey your husbands.'

"Please receive my deepest, most respectful, and, if I may be permitted so to say, most affectionate regards, and believe me to be,

"Your humble servant,

"THOMAS MIRION."

Before this letter was sent, it was carefully reviewed by Mme. Mirion; if she was a little confused concerning Louis XIV. and the Crusades, she was perfectly acquainted with her grammar and her *Poitevin*.

Forty-eight hours later, M. D'Ornis, who had climbed up some peak or other and just come down again, arrived in haste at Mon-Plaisir. As he approached, he saw Marguerite on the terrace; without noticing any one else, he went straight up to her, looked her in the eyes a moment, and then took both her hands in his, saying, "Thank you, you have made me very happy." He remained at Geneva only three days, being anxious as he said, to return to Burgundy, in order to attend to important matters there, and to have his castle put in order. During these three days, his actions and manners were every thing that Marguerite could have desired. Although he addressed her neither with compliments nor protestations of affection, he evidently was in love. He gave her speaking glances and treated her with an air of marked courtesy and respect, with which was mingled a kind of fatherly protection.

As regarded the domestic animals that formed what, in his talks with her, he called the Mon-Plaisir menagerie, he bore their questions and officious services with very good grace, and succeeded in concealing his annoyance from them. He was very polite to every body, and his politeness, though it was perhaps a little curt, proved very satisfactory, they all being so well disposed toward him. Mme. Mirion went into ecstasies over her future son-in-law; she almost worshiped him; she watched every motion that he made, and repeated again and again his words, in which she found a depth of wisdom that completely overwhelmed her.

The marriage was fixed for the middle of the following month. Before leaving, M. D'Ornis had a conversation with M. Mirion in which the question of the dowry was definitely settled. Not being able to overcome the obstinate resistance of the good old man, he finally said, "Well, put in your fifteen thousand francs a year. You can give it to your daughter as her own. She can use it for her personal expenses and her charities." The weeks that followed were undoubtedly the happiest of Mme. Mirion's life. She lived in the clouds, and, as Uncle Benjamin said, the Queen of Spain was not good enough to be her cousin. There was not air enough at Mon-Plaisir for her lungs, or light enough for her eyes. Sometimes she was perfectly serene, sometimes her happiness almost took her breath away. She called on all her friends and acquaintances, going from house to house to tell her story. With a satisfied look, and a face lighted *à giorno*, she enjoyed alike the exclamations of some and the ill-concealed jealousy of others. Every one of her sentences began with, Our son-in-law, Count D'Ornis. She no longer called her daughter Marguerite: she spoke of her as the Countess, my daughter, or as our dear Countess. When she unfolded the Geneva *Journal* one morning, and read in the list of legal notices these words, "Contract of marriage between Count Roger D'Ornis of Burgundy, and Marguerite Mirion," she experienced a strong desire to surround the number with a triple band of gold, and to invite the whole editorial staff to supper. It grieved her that she could not climb to the highest tower of St. Peter's cathedral, there to take a speaking trumpet and cry aloud to the whole Republic, "Stupid people, hear me; in two weeks my daughter will be a countess."

In the midst of all this tumult and confusion, Marguerite said but little, except to talk about the *trousseau* with her mother, or to prevent her from doing various absurd things. What she thought may be gathered from the following letter, which she wrote at this time to her *bosom friend*:

"MY DARLING NELLY: I must tell you all about it right away, or it will kill me. Do you want to hear some wonderful news, which I can scarcely believe myself, it seems so strange? Come here and sit down by me, put your arm around my neck and place your hand in mine, just as you used to do when, in the long winter evenings, we read together in the school-room *Gonzalvo di Cordova* and *The Last of the Abencerrages.* Now, are you listening? This is the news: Marguerite Mirion is going to be married. He is about forty-five, is dark and well formed; he has very piercing black eyes and hair a little gray; he fought in Mexico and received two wounds at the taking of Puebla; his name is Roger D'Ornis; he is a count, and owns a castle in Burgundy. This is the way it all happened: he was passing through Geneva on the way to Chamouni; as he is very fond of old furniture, he went into father's store to examine some cabinets, but found nothing there that pleased him. 'The handsomest articles are at my house,' said father to him. 'I'll be glad to show them to you; but I give you notice they are not for sale.' At this point Marguerite Mirion, dressed in pink, appeared suddenly upon the scene, and interrupted this interesting conversation. I don't know how it happened, but Marguerite and the cabinets both made such an impression on him, that he scarcely knew what he was about. He came to Mon-Plaisir, saw the cabinets, and fell in love with them; but father refused to part with his treasures. 'Then give me your daughter instead,' he said, 'otherwise I shall get nothing.' 'Oh! oh! we must have time to think about that.' 'Very well, I'll give you eight days, fifteen hours, and twenty-five minutes to think it over; but I positively must have either your cabinets or your daughter.' With these words he went off like a shot, and for eight days I thought it over. The only reply that came to me, however, a reply which was considered a foolish one, was, 'How can I love him, when I don't know him?' 'What has that to do with it?' was the answer; 'don't you think he has good manners?' 'Certainly.' 'Doesn't he talk well?' 'Yes.' 'Is he deformed in any way?' 'Not at all.' 'There, I knew you loved him!' To all this my only answer was, 'How can I, when I don't know him.' My wise mother replied that people never know each other well until they have been married a year at least, and that, at all events, I could not have any serious objections to a person I did not know. Then she begged and entreated me.... She told me if I refused she would never forgive me. The fact is, if I had no reason for saying yes, I had still less for saying no —and tired of disputing with her, I agreed to do whatever she wished me to. He was at once informed of my decision, and came back immediately; he had not changed his mind, you see. He took both my hands in his, kissed them tenderly, and said, 'You have made me very happy.' Since he believes it, it must be so. I will try my best, at all events, to make him a good wife. I am a good daughter, and good daughters make good wives, you know. But what a strange affair this is, Nelly! It all comes from being so fond of old furniture.... Mother is in raptures, she always speaks of me as her dear Countess. I am.... how can I express it? I am astonished. I'm the most astonished person in the world.

"I inclose his photograph; you must tell me frankly what you think of him. I like his looks very well, only this photograph does not show that, at times, he is absent-minded. He suddenly grows sad, not appearing to hear what is said to him, his thoughts wander away I know not where, his face grows long and solemn, his eyebrows come together, and a deep wrinkle seams his forehead. The other day it frightened me a little to see him so. What was he thinking of? where was he?

In Mexico, perhaps. He came quickly to himself again, however, and took up his sentence where he had left it off.

"I am not only astonished, but also somewhat confused. After reading the *Abencerrage*, we promised each other that we would never marry except for love. We knew a great deal about that article. We agreed that love was something that suddenly came and took possession of you, never leaving you all your life; we called it a divine frenzy. Well, Nelly, my lot is cast, I shall die without knowing what this divine frenzy is! It is not the fault of circumstances; I believe that deep feeling is foreign to my nature. I am too much of a Genevese, as Aunt Amaranth says, too matter of fact, and, moreover, I am the greatest laugher you ever saw. I shall laugh without trouble in my castle in Burgundy, and the castle and its owner must laugh with me. You must take my place, Nelly, and be divinely mad for both of us. Some fine morning you will find yourself face to face with some Ben-Hamet, who will have fallen from the sky or sprung up from the ground; then the frenzy will take possession of you, and remain with you for life. You must tell me all about it, dear, and I will listen as the children do to *Mother Goose*, half believing all you say.

"Now I must leave you, darling, mamma is calling me, oh! so loud. Something must be the matter.... 'Yes, yes, I'm coming in a minute.'... You must answer me at once, and tell me what you think of it all, and whether you believe I have done right or not. Now, Nelly, don't be jealous; I swear to you by Gonzalvo's sword, that you shall always have the first place in my heart. You will answer immediately, will you not? From a future Burgundian, who will love her Nelly forever.

MARGUERITE.

"P. S. Mamma called me to look at my presents, which have just dropped from the clouds. They are exquisite, and in perfect taste; they are a thousand times too good for me. It is very evident he must have gone to Paris to buy them all."

CHAPTER XIII.

A PAINFUL INTERVIEW.

After Joseph's return, Mme. Mirion was careful to keep him away from Mon-Plaisir, until all the arrangements for the wedding had been perfected. She did not wish to have her son-in-law meet a common workman in her house, and eat at the same table with him. She also feared that in spite of her injunctions, Marguerite might try to talk with the secret agent concerning his journey; she was well aware of the effect which is often produced by certain questions and answers on an unsettled mind. As there had recently been two or three burglaries committed in Geneva, which had caused a great deal of excitement there, M. Mirion had pretended to be uneasy about his goods and the money in his safe, and asked Noirel to sleep in the store for a little while. The result was that for more than three weeks he did not visit Mon-Plaisir. This was exactly what he wished; Mon-Plaisir and the preparations that were going on there terrified him. His stay at Geneva was not pleasant; he undertook a task there that was both painful and fatiguing. He persistently endeavored to conquer his passion, and despairing of ever becoming indifferent, he sought to change his love to hate, to persuade himself that Marguerite was repulsive to him. He kept repeating to himself, a hundred times by day, two hundred times by night, that he had been mistaken, that she was like the people about her, that she was mean and narrow-minded, that she was governed by vanity, that although she had pretended to hesitate, she had really taken the bait held out to her from the very first, and that her joy at the idea of becoming a countess had supplied the place of love and happiness. When at last he had, as he thought, convinced himself, his work was in an instant all undone by the thought of two large, brown eyes, that glanced at him with a frank yet saucy look, revealing in their clear depths a happy indifference to all the petty follies that govern the world. Those eyes were like two strangers that gazed, in a curious way, at all the vanities about them, while it was evident that they belonged to a foreign land. M. Mirion's safe was well watched; Joseph did not sleep two hours of the night. Almost as soon as his eyes closed, he would be awakened by an intolerable sense of suffocation; he would sit up in bed, and panting for breath, would rise and walk up and down the floor till morning, tearing with his hands and teeth an inoffensive shaving. If a burglar had appeared, I believe he would have treated him as he did the shaving.

It was five days before the wedding, when Joseph, at the urgent request of M. Mirion, agreed to pass Sunday at Mon-Plaisir. There he saw Marguerite, who appeared more beautiful than ever to him; the near approach of the fatal day rendered her pensive, and the paleness of her cheeks lent a new lustre to her glance. Toward the close of dinner, Joseph was seized with a sudden faintness, and came near crying like a child. As soon as he could, he left the house, and directed his steps toward the most lonely spot in the place. Marguerite, who wished to speak with him, succeeded in escaping her mother's watchful eye. She followed the fugitive at a distance, and saw him enter the woods. She came up to him, just as he had thrown himself down under a willow, his face buried in his hands. He was so absorbed in thought that he did not hear her approach. She had to call him by name before he noticed her; then he sprang suddenly to his feet. There was an angry look upon his face.

"Are you in trouble?" she asked.

There was no reply. She moved back a step. "Do I annoy you? Do you want me to go away?"

"This place is yours," he answered quickly. "I'm the one to go away."

The bitterness of his reply surprised her. "Why! what's

the matter?" she continued. "Are you angry with me? Have I offended you without knowing it?"

He could scarcely contain himself. He leaned back against the willow, crossing his arms upon his breast, as though to still the beating of his heart; his eyes were fastened on the ground. "I can get nothing out of you," she said. "I should like to know what's the matter, though. I've thought for some months that you acted strangely."

"What's that to you?" he answered with increasing bitterness. "Am I a person for you to think of, or be interested in? Am I any body?"

"I believe you are sick," she said in a serious tone.

"I'm sick of life!" he answered in a deep, hollow voice.

She walked close up to Joseph, and said to him:

"You are in trouble. I want you to tell me all about it."

He felt his secret starting from his breast, but forcibly retained it there. "Perhaps I am in trouble," he cried. "If it suits you, you can have it so. I am happy though, very happy. Ask the first workman you meet, and he will tell you I was born lucky. I will sell out my good-fortune, very cheaply. I will exchange it for a crust of mouldy bread. Do you know what constitutes happiness according to my idea? It's to eat and drink, to laugh and cry with your equals; it's to sit with united hearts about a common table. Where are my friends? I'm alone, terribly alone. I have no equals. I am too low for some, too high for others. My comrades shun me and hide from me; they look on me as a fugitive, a deserter. What am I in this house? Nothing but a creature fed, lodged, and cared for by charity. Those with whom I live owe me nothing, while I owe every thing to them. This tree that protects me from the sun knows well that I have no claim on it for shade. It bestows it on me in charity, just as your questions are bestowed. Oh! this feeling of obligation! It's a ball and chain that I've dragged after me for ten years; I might better have thrown myself, ball, chain, and all, into the first stream I met!...."

He had not finished, but his lips trembled, he could say no

more. Marguerite looked with amazement at his face distorted by passion, at the angry curve of his nostrils, at his blood-shot eyes. She remained silent for a moment; then she said, "Obligation, charity: what ugly words!"

Then, after another short silence, she continued, "I can't understand it.... You must be angry with some of us."

"I'm not angry with any one," he replied stamping his foot. "I'm only sorry that I ever was born."

"Please don't!" she said, making a sign to him to stop. "Sometimes we say things when we're angry that we would be only too glad to take back again...."

She went on: "You refuse to tell me your secret, but you will reason with me, will you not? I can reason pretty well, though you may not think so. What do you mean by your debt, by the ball and chain that you carry about with you? You have paid your debt. You have given your services and advice to my father, and have devoted yourself faithfully to his interests. He knows it well enough. If he sometimes says things that displease you, you must not think he intends to hurt your feelings. Do you believe that I approve of every thing he says? He doesn't stop to think, that's all. You mustn't take it so to heart. There's one thing certain, you ought to have some settled arrangement with him. You are very ingenious and intelligent, you are master of your trade. Father is good enough at heart, but he never thinks of such matters. If you'll give me your permission, I'll speak to him to-night."

It was Joseph's turn to be astonished now. Marguerite had never spoken like this to him before. Although he had thought he understood her nature, he had never suspected the depth of this tranquil lake, or dreamt that this lovely girl, whose joyous and contented disposition readily adapted itself to every situation, had reflected so much on the affairs of life. "No; I beg you to say nothing to your father!" he cried. "When the right time comes, I'll speak to him myself."

"You can do better, you can let me know at Ornis, and I will write to him. I never like to trust people who lose their temper easily; they always spoil what they undertake..... In the mean time, if you wish to oblige me, you will drive away those absurd ideas. Workmen, citizens, and counts are all made of the same clay. There's only one true aristocracy; it has its members in the highest and the lowest ranks of society; it is composed of all free and honest souls, who love what is good and beautiful, and dare to despise the rest....Amen! My sermon is ended."

He could scarcely keep from falling at her feet. "You are the only one who thinks and talks like this, and you are going away!" he passionately cried.

She drew her hand across her brow and softly sighed. "It's true," she said, "I'm about to start upon a voyage on an unknown sea. I ask God's blessing on the vessel that's to carry me. I am not like you, however, for I have faith in a happy future. It's so nice to be happy! I'll try all I can to be so .... You'll think of me, sometimes, won't you? And here, to help your memory...."

She drew from her pocket a little box containing a silver ring, in which two diamonds were sparkling. "I was looking for you to give you this," she continued "I had this ring made according to my own idea; these two diamonds were the first that were ever given to me. They were set in a breast-pin that I wore for a long time. You see there's no doubt that they are really mine....I wanted to tell you....You won't get angry, will you? We have lived so long in the same house, and to use your words, have eaten so long at a common table, that I am something like a sister to you, and sisters can say what they please. If you are ever short of money, or want to do it for any other reason, you can sell these diamonds and put false ones in their place. The ring will remind you of me just the same.... I should like better yet to have you give it to your wife when you are married. It shall be her wedding-ring."

"When I am married!" he said with a scornful gesture. "I shall never marry."

"Why! Is that another of your ideas, if I may ask?"

"The ring is too fine for me," he said. Then suddenly changing his mind, he took it without thanking her. He was in great fear that his secret would escape him.

At this moment, Mme. Mirion's voice was heard calling her daughter. Marguerite held out her hand to Joseph, saying, "Remember our understanding: when you're ready to go to court, I'm to be your lawyer. I hope that in return you will pray for my happiness. Come, you know all about Ornis, what good fortune do you wish me?"

He took the hand which she was holding toward him; his own was trembling and his face was pale. He looked steadily upon her as he said in a broken voice, "I have a debt to pay. I wish....yes, I wish that you may be the most unhappy woman in the world, and that you will need a friend ready to die for you."....Then striking his breast, he cried, "I am such a friend."

As soon as he had uttered these words, he fled from her like a thief. She gazed after him, amazed and stupefied. "What a strange boy he is!" she said to herself. "I didn't know him as I thought I did." Then she hurried toward her mother, who was still calling her. She had a letter for her from Count D'Ornis; it informed her that he would be with her the next dav.

CHAPTER XIV.

A NIGHT OF DESPAIR.

This conversation almost turned Joseph's brain. I do not know exactly what he hoped, but he awoke the next morning with the fixed idea of seeing Marguerite again and telling her every thing. The sick toss restlessly about in bed, although they know that one position is as comfortable as another. Joseph was so wretched that he wanted to suffer in some other way, even though he suffered more. This time M. Mirion did not invite Joseph home with him to dinner; Count D'Ornis had arrived that morning. Joseph waited till night and then set out on foot for Mon-Plaisir. His mind was so confused that he could form no plan; he walked straight forward trusting to chance. As he ascended the avenue, he saw two shadows moving to and fro upon the terrace. He approached them and hid himself behind a bush. The two shadows passed by him; they were Marguerite and Count D'Ornis. She was leaning on the Count's arm, listening to an amusing account of his last journey, and there was so much humor in his recital that Marguerite laughed aloud. That laugh was terrible to Joseph, and in a paroxysm of rage, he rent his clothes, lacerating his bosom with his finger-nails. That laugh swept away what little hope was left; it ended all his dreams. He fled back to Geneva, despairing, desperate, with a heart that weighed down in his bosom like a lump of lead.

Two days afterward the contract was signed. The following morning they were married according to the civil form, and in the afternoon the religious ceremony took place in the Protestant church at Carouge, attracting a large number of friends and a great crowd of the idle and the curious. Half an hour before the ceremony, the body and galleries of the church were filled; so crowded were they, a pin could not have fallen to the floor. Outside two lines were formed, stretching for some distance across the square. Count D'Ornis's entrance was a great success; every one admired his distinguished manner, his martial air, his aristocratic appearance, the carriage of his head, and the fire of his glance. Occasionally, however, a cloud seemed resting on his brow; he was not fond of ceremonies, and was impatient for this one to be finished. Ten minutes later Marguerite appeared, pale and trembling. Her father, who was leading her, strove to add to his short stature by walking on his toes; Mme. Mirion followed them, puffed out like a balloon. There was a division of opinion among those present. The mothers thought, "That Mirion girl has been very fortunate." On the other hand, the men all said, "There's a lucky fellow; he's got a bride fit for a king." The ceremony being ended, M. D'Ornis returned at once to his hotel, while Marguerite entered a friend's house near by; they only took time to change their clothes, and then rejoined each other at the railway station. They took the express train for Lyons, where they were to remain two days. Between Bellegarde and Culoz, M. D'Ornis fell into one of those strange abstractions which Marguerite had complained of in her letter to her friend. Alone with her in a compartment of the carriage, he had up to this time given his whole attention to the *lovely flower* which had just passed into his possession. Suddenly his countenance changed, his eyes turned toward the window, and motionless and speechless, he glared into the empty air, as though some horrid phantom stood before him. Marguerite looked on him with amazement; in about ten minutes he seemed to wake, took her hand, put his arm round her waist, and during the remainder of the journey treated her with the most lover-like attention.

What was Joseph doing all this time? At Marguerite's particular request, he had been invited to the ceremony, and a place had been reserved for him in one of the wedding carriages. He did not make his appearance, however. M. Mirion was astonished and twice cried out, "Where's that confounded Noirel?" It did not trouble him long, however; he had too many other things to think of. A Joseph more or less on such a day made very little difference. M. Mirion had given all the workmen a holiday and closed the shop. The invisible Joseph, who had his own key to the work-room, remained there all the morning working furiously. Toward noon, without stopping to take off his blouse, he started for Carouge. He saw Marguerite pass without being perceived by her. By hard pushing he succeeded in forcing an entrance into the church. He remained there looking on and listening until the officiating clergyman said, "Lord God, let thy grace descend upon this wedded pair, who have solemnly promised in thy presence to share each other's fortune, whether good or ill, and always to be one in heart and soul before thee!" At these words, Joseph suddenly turned round, pushed through the crowd, and went out. It seemed to him as he reached the porch, that the world was nothing but a wretched show, that the sun was an old smoky lantern, that the rows of trees which embellished the square had just been taken from a Noah's ark, and that the people passing through the streets were ugly puppets worked by wires to the sound of a hand-organ. There was nothing real; every thing seemed like a miserable farce. He muttered to himself, "What a poor affair it is!" Then he added, "Fortunately life is short."

He walked on without any fixed purpose; chance led him near the house where his helpless mother lived. It seemed as though he were searching for every thing that could increase his pain; he did not hesitate, but entered the house at once. Notwithstanding the sacrifices her son had made to procure an honorable home for her, Mme. Noirel retained all her former habits of negligence and disorder, and squandered in the most foolish manner every cent that was given to her. Joseph found her seated in an arm-chair, dirty as she could be, with her finger-nails in mourning, wearing a ragged dress, and having on her head a torn cap, through the rents in which straggled long locks of tangled hair. She had in her lap a large bag of candies, which on Joseph's entrance, quickly disappeared in one of her capacious pockets. He walked up to her, and stood for a moment gazing on her with folded arms. "This," thought he, "is the mother-in-law I intended for Marguerite Mirion. After leaving the church, I should have led her to this house, and said, 'This is my mother; kiss her rags and ask a blessing from her hands.'"

"Is that you, Joseph?" said Mme. Noirel; "didn't you get to the wedding?"

"No, I refused to go."

"Pshaw! don't be silly! If you quarrel with your master what will become of me?"

He did not answer; his mind was fixed on one idea. He kept repeating to himself, "That's my mother. Where is Marguerite? I want to present her to my mother."

At this moment, the woman who kept the house entered and bowed to Joseph with a deferential air. This young man, who had so much self-respect, and who had for years taken care of a mother totally deficient in that particular, made a powerful impression on this good woman; she looked on him as a superior being. "Your mother grows more childish every day," she said. "I took the money that you gave me and bought some stuff to make a dress for her. While I was away from the house a few minutes, she called in a pedlar and sold it to him. The money is all gone, for she spent it right away for candy." After a moment's pause, she added, "I wanted to tell you of it, Monsieur Joseph; but I thought that to-day, the wedding-day...."

"What wedding?" he cried fiercely, interrupting her. Then bringing his fist down heavily on the table, he continued, "Damnation! leave my mother alone. We were born to live in the mire, and take to it as naturally as a fish does to the water."

"So you've begun to swear, too!" said Mme. Noirel. "I thought it was your father talking.... Any body but you would have increased my allowance long ago; but you care for nothing but your own pleasures, and I'm sure you've taken to drink, just as your father did."

"That's a good idea," he cried. "My father drank, I'll drink too. What's the use of working? What's the use of having a heart? There's nothing in the world so good as getting drunk. I'll make that my business after this."

With these words he left the house, slamming the door behind him. He acted so strangely that the woman was astonished. "I really believe he has been drinking," she said to Mme. Noirel.

He had not been drinking, but he now began to do so. He entered the first tavern that he came to, and emptied three bottles in a trice. His brain was not easily affected, however; he did not succeed in getting drunk. He left the tavern with a clear head, but with his nerves excited to the highest pitch. He wanted to demolish something or somebody. He saw in the distance one of his comrades, named Peter Servan, who was returning from the wedding. He hailed him. The other turned round and bowed, then continued on his way. Joseph ran after him and stood before him in the road. "Come with me," he said in an abrupt tone.

"Where are you going?" asked Servan.

"I tell you to come with me."

"What's the matter with you? Are you joking?"

"I tell you to come with me," repeated Joseph, seizing him by the arm. "I am going to walk; we'll go to some inn, and drink all night. Come on, old fellow! I'll pay the bill."

This last argument was too much for Servan. They started off together.

"I supposed that you were busy about this time in putting down the champagne, Noirel. Didn't they invite you to the dinner?"

"What makes you ask that question?"

"I don't know....you're on good terms with M. Mirion. You're one of the family almost."

"Whoever says that is a liar and a villain!" cried Joseph, clenching his fists. "I one of the family! I hate the whole brood as I do the plague."

Servan could scarcely believe his ears. Joseph was destined to astonish every one that day. "Who are they all?" he continued. "A lot of knaves who keep us working and grow rich by our sweat, who rob us of our labor and our heart's blood. I one of the family! They give me my pittance day by day. Don't they do the same by their watch-dog? We both wear a collar; if we should either of us lose it, we wouldn't belong to the family any more."

Then he began a virulent tirade against the burgher class. His conclusion was that society was in terrible disorder; that it was exceedingly unjust for a workman to work day after day to secure a fortune for his employer and enable him to marry his daughters to counts; that this state of things could not and would not last much longer, that the divine thunderbolts had slept too long, and would soon be launched against the offenders. Servan, becoming more and more astonished, listened with open mouth, reproaching himself for not having understood Joseph better before. He was far from suspecting what was in the heart of this modern tribune; he supposed that M. Mirion had offended him—that he had asked him, perhaps, to wait on the table, instead of inviting him to sit down with the guests. "It's a good thing," he thought. "Noirel will now be one of us."

While thus fulminating his anathemas, Joseph had conducted his companion to a small village named Fossaz. As they were crossing the bridge over the Foron, he caught Servan by the arm, crying, "I wish you could have heard her laugh—such a laugh!"

"Heard who laugh?" asked Servan.

"None of your business," answered Joseph. Then drawing from his pocket the little box that Marguerite had given him, he continued: "Look, here's their wedding gift."

Servan stared at him. "Good heavens!" he cried. "You ought not to complain. Diamonds! and you're not satisfied?"

"You great donkey; don't you see they're false—false as the heart of a tradesman's daughter—false as all she does and says?" and placing the open box on the railing of the bridge, he picked up a large stone, and began to furiously pound the ring. He dented and bent it; his anger kept increasing, he struck harder and harder. The diamonds escaped from their setting, and rolled into the stream, where he threw the ring to keep them company. Servan did not understand this at all; he wanted to take off his shoes and stockings, and wade into the river to pick up the stones, even if they were false. Joseph, however, drew him by main force into the inn, saying, "Now let's drink and forget every thing." He expected to kill his thoughts as he would a dangerous beast. He had learned from M. Mirion, the night before, that the newly-wedded pair would pass the night at Lyons, and he knew by the railway time-table that they would arrive there between ten and eleven o'clock. He had sworn that before that time came, he would drown his thoughts in drink. He worked hard to accomplish this, but did not entirely succeed.

As the village clock struck eleven, the clouds which had obscured his brain seemed to clear away. He thought he saw again the dead oak on the hill at Ornis; it was moving its leafless arms and making mysterious signs to him. This oak was pointing something out, and Joseph endeavored in the darkness to discover what it was. The obscurity was too great, however. He experienced a secret joy at this; he had succeeded in doing what he wished. He pointed toward his glass, saying, "There it is, it can't get out!" He was speaking of his grief. Suddenly a covering seemed to fall from off his eyes, and he saw before him a dimly-lighted room. Marguerite was there; before her stood Count D'Ornis, gazing on her with greedy eyes, like a miser who counts piece by piece the treasure hidden in his chest. It seemed to Joseph as though a red-hot iron had touched his heart; he gave a cry, overturned the table by which he was sitting, sending the bottles and glasses crashing to the floor, and stood erect with pale face and flashing eyes, crying, "Long live the Social Republic!"

Every body was aroused by the noise, and the inn-keeper demanded pay for his broken bottles. At this, Servan, who had been snoring for an hour in a corner of the room, awoke, and in a drunken frenzy, without taking time to ask what was the matter, sprang at the inn-keeper and seized him by the throat. A violent struggle now began ; the blows fell like hail. Joseph was not a man to see his companion badly used ; he tried to rescue him and struck out before him right and left. What followed he never knew ; he was no longer conscious of what he did. The first thing he remembered, he was in the middle of the road, helping Servan along as well as he could ; the latter had left some of his teeth and hair behind him in the inn. He took him to Geneva and saw him safely home ; the remainder of the night he spent in wandering about the fields.

At seven o'clock, he was at work. M. Mirion came to his bench and requested him to walk into his office, where he asked him to explain his strange conduct of the day before. They had hunted for him everywhere without success. What had Monsieur Noirel been doing all day ?

" I thought I wasn't wanted," said Noirel in a dry tone.

M. Mirion indignantly replied, " Oh ! I see where the shoe pinches. You're angry because we kept you in the city the last two weeks. Confound it all, I couldn't help it. What would my son-in-law have thought ?. . . ."

" If I had gone to his wedding, I should probably have done something to disgrace you. That's the reason why I kept away."

At this M. Mirion became very angry, calling his workman an ungrateful fellow. There was a stormy scene between them which almost led to an open rupture. Fortunately, M. Mirion was able to control his temper when he found that it conflicted with his interests ; Joseph was too useful to him to be allowed to go away on so slight a provocation. He therefore ceased abusing him, making up for it by treating him with great coolness for several days afterward. Mme. Mirion's resentment lasted longer ; she often said to her husband, " The idea of his going to walk when our dear Countess was getting married ! It's unpardonable. You were right in saying that the boy hadn't any heart.'

On the other hand, Joseph's fellow-workmen, having been informed by Servan of what had taken place, and of the sentiments which had been expressed by him, treated him with better grace, and made him some advances. He did not reply to them, however. Stern and silent, he kept constantly at work. He did not visit the tavern a second time. That drunken scene, in which he had cast aside his usual dignity and self-respect, had left a painful sting; he felt that he could not repeat it. He formed a new plan, he resolved to emigrate to America. He secretly obtained information on the subject, read accounts of travels in the United States, and gradually collected money enough to pay his passage. Perhaps he regretted a little having thrown away his diamond ring; but he did not demand it back from the Foron.

CHAPTER XV.

MARGUERITE'S LETTER.

Marguerite had been married about three weeks when her dear friend received the following letter :

"Forgive me, Nelly, for not having written to you sooner. Before answering your questions, I wanted a little time to become accustomed to my new position. What story-tellers novels are ! I can tell you that marriage is a dangerous experiment ; you plunge headlong into an unknown future, with your eyes shut. I have had considerable of a fall ; but I have come down on my feet without being hurt. And now you want to know if I am happy. I hope I shall be. That is something, isn't it ?

" In the first place, I live in a charming country, which is the very centre of France. To prove it, there is near here a delightful castle called The Summit. The summit of what ? Of every thing ; you can get no higher. It is agreeable to feel that you are in the centre of something, that you hold France, as it were, in your hand. The fact is our streams are tributary to the Seine, the Loire, and the Saône. My country (it has become mine) is an immense table-land, where the air is excellent, and the spring water is delicious, it's so fresh and sparkling. The ground is very undulating, full of humps and hollows, and is dotted with woods interspersed with meadows, heaths, and immense barren plains. The fields are partly cultivated and partly wild, and the green, mossy valleys are cut through by deep ravines. On every side flow clear, bubbling streams, while the oaks and rushes on their banks look on them as though well satisfied with their own condition, but glad at the same time to see others moving by. They seem to say, 'A pleasant journey to you ! God bless you !' You know I always was passionately fond of water. It is transparent, you can look through it, it is moving all the time; it sparkles, changes color, reflects the clouds, and seems to be talking with the sky. A country without running streams is like a parlor without mirrors. In this particular I am well satisfied. There is a wild spot full of small ponds near here; they call it Little-Scotland. You must tell me what you think of it when you come to see me. What I like better yet, though, are our large meadows used as common pasture grounds. There is nothing more delightful than these immense fields, where you see a great many white horses roving about, and numerous little girls with switches in their hands, driving before them flocks of geese. When I first came here I missed my Swiss mountains; I am beginning now to do very well without them. The other morning, I was seated on a large stone, on the border of a field which rose before me with a gentle slope. This field was being ploughed. On raising my eyes, I could see the crest of this slope, along which the shadow of a cloud was slowly moving. A moment later, the laborers stopped to take breath at the other end of the field, and I saw clearly outlined against the pale, autumn sky, the handles of the plough, the ploughman's staff, and the smoking nostrils of the oxen. A plough standing out against the sky is a thing not often seen at Geneva. After all though, if you look sharp enough, you can find mountains here; they call them the Morvan mountains—they are nothing but little mounds, that I should never notice. On the east, the landscape is bounded by a chain of low hills, on the tops of which are a number of wind-mills. When I have nothing better to do, I watch these wind-mills turn, and my thoughts keep turning with them. Though I am a Genevese, there are some moments when I keep thinking, thinking.

"I promised to tell you every thing. My castle does not please me as well as its surroundings. It is decidedly too large. I had been told of this, but, notwithstanding, the first sight of it was an unpleasant surprise to me. It is a whole world in itself. We live in one wing of the building; the remainder of it is empty and dilapidated. What goes on there? It is unpleasant for me to feel that close beside me are these great empty spaces, these walls which could tell such stories, if they could only talk. I could not help speaking about it, one day, to my lord and master. 'Why!' he answered, 'I thought nothing could frighten you.' I replied that I felt very brave and very timid at the same time; that I thought I could face a known danger well enough, but an unknown one troubled me. ....'Pshaw!' he exclaimed as he pinched my cheek. 'What's the use of troubling yourself about what you don't know?'.... That's the way he reasons. It's all as simple as you please.

"I spoke my mind on other subjects. The first time we went over the grounds, he gave me permission to express my opinions freely. 'Do you like the garden?' he said.

"'There's only one thing I don't like about it.'

"'What's that?'

"'There are no flowers in it.'

"'Why! what do you call this?' he said, pointing with his cane to a miserable little wall-flower, eaten by bugs and dried up by the sun. He really acted as though he were in earnest.

"'A wall-flower doesn't make a garden.' He pinched my cheek again.

"'Next spring,' he said, 'you can arrange it to suit yourself.'

"I then took the liberty of remarking that his park was too dense, that he had allowed the trees to grow in their own way, until they had locked their branches together in such a manner that it was dark under them at mid-day. He looked on me with profound astonishment. 'What, do you like the sun?' he said.

"It evidently seemed strange to him that I should do so. 'I love the sunlight and the water,' I replied.

"'That's good, we've got a lake,' he said.

"I did not dispute with him concerning the lake, which I had heard a great deal about, and which I was simple enough to believe in. It turned out to be an ugly pond, full of croaking frogs. I had been deceived; but I learned long ago the fact that things are not always what they are said to be.

"I have been telling you my little troubles; now I come to more serious matters. When we had finished our walk through the park, we sat down on a bench before the noseless statue of a commander. 'Listen to me,' said Roger, 'I want to give you my ideas of married life....'

"You must also listen, Nelly, and learn the lesson with fear and trembling. What I am going to relate will seem matter-of-fact enough to you. But if we must sooner or later become serious and thoughtful, why not begin at once? Then we can enjoy resting quietly, and looking at others running themselves out of breath, chasing a shadow which they can not catch; then we can say to them, 'Poor creatures, you'll get tired pretty soon, and have to keep still just as we do.' In short, Nelly, I have decided to be very wise, very gay, and very happy all at the same time. That is my programme.

"'You will think me very prosaic, probably,' said M. D'Ornis, twisting the ends of his mustache in his usual manner.

"I replied at once that I had often been accused of having a very practical mind, with much good sense and very little poetry. This declaration entirely reassured him. 'In the first place I must tell you,' he continued, 'that when a child, I was petted and praised until I was completely spoiled. It was not my father's fault; he was a tall man, gloomy and taciturn, who loved nothing on earth except his dogs and horses. He cared little for me; my mother cared too much. She worshiped me, partly because she took pleasure in doing so, and partly because I had an elder brother whom she could not endure. This poor boy had committed the crime of coming into the world with a club foot; his mother never forgave him for it. Every thing was denied him, every thing was given to me. I took advantage of the situation and played all manner of mischievous tricks, for which usually he was made to suffer. He was whipped and locked up. I, on the contrary, was simply told that penitence consisted in confession and forgiveness, contrition and atonement. I confessed and was forgiven; but I was not sorry, nor did I make amends. I always hated sermons, and would rather be whipped than listen to them. To be worshiped and preached to, at the same time, was very distressing to me. It was a happy day for me when I gained my liberty.

They decided to send me to Paris, just as physicians send their patients to the springs, when they don't know what else to do for them. Paris didn't amuse me long, and to get rid of my liberty, I enlisted. I went to Africa as a private, and there won my chevrons. I was made a lieutenant in Cochin China, and a captain in Mexico. Those were the best years of my life. I was treated unjustly, however; I discovered that I could not get ahead, that others more artful and designing kept passing by me, that the captaincy was a difficult place to move beyond, and that being a captain, I was likely to remain one all my life. At last I became disgusted and left the service. When I returned home, my father had been dead about two years; my brother had died a long time before. I found my mother living; she gave up preaching to me, but worshiped me more than ever. I thank her for her kindness and love her very much, though we don't have much to say to each other. In short, I wanted a change....'

"'And one fine morning,' I interrupted, 'you made up your mind to get married.'

"'I had been thinking of it for two years,' he continued. 'The difficulty was to find any one to suit me. I wouldn't give a fig for a doll, or a delicate creature that couldn't walk through the park without a fainting fit. I was born a walker myself. Now I think that marriage ought to be a delightful companionship, and I expect my wife to be my companion in every thing, to share all my pleasures, to walk, ride, hunt, and fish with me, to play billiards with me. ...."

"'Heaven be praised!' I cried. 'I made two caroms in succession to-day, and you told me that you loved me for it.'

"He stroked my hair as he said, 'This head was good for something, I knew well enough.....Do you like my ideas?' he added. 'Will you accept them?'

"'Give me your hand, comrade!' was my reply. He took my hand and pressed it strongly in his own.

"What walks we have taken, Nelly! I walk well as you know. I went with him, bravely marching through the dust on the road, or climbing the rocky foot-paths, jumping from stone to stone. Roger gazed on me with admiration, which made me proud and well satisfied with myself. We have often stopped to rest, at noon, at some tavern on the road, and eaten with good relish an omelette with vegetables, which we washed down with excellent red wine. The other day my foot was lame. He frowned: he could accept no excuse for a lame foot.....Our hunting parties please me less than our walking excursions; they are stained with blood. My best days are those in which we return empty handed. Don't think I have the slightest murder on my conscience. I simply look on; that's more than I want to do. There's one hare that owes me a big candle, Nelly. Diana had lost its trail and was barking furiously in the woods. Suddenly I saw the hare jump from a thicket and run at full speed across a sloping glade, at the upper part of which I was sitting. Just as it disappeared, Roger cried out, 'He must have passed this way. Didn't you see him?' 'No, I haven't seen any thing,' was my reply. You know, you've often said, Nelly, that I couldn't tell a lie.....This is the way the happy pair pass the honey-moon at Castle D'Ornis. You will tell me there are different kinds of honey-moons. I am very well satisfied with mine.

"There is a shadow, however, on the picture. I have a mother-in-law who does not love me. This is in the greatest confidence, Nelly. I must confess that Mme. D'Ornis has not the most prepossessing face in the world. Her features, glance, and voice are all too sharp. I am sorry to say, too, that her piety has soured with age. A sour religion is a terrible thing. Roger had forewarned me that she was exceedingly displeased at his marriage. She worships him; I take him from her, and she is jealous; that's the simple truth. If that was all, I shouldn't care.....She can't forgive me, though, for belonging to the common people, and, what is worse still, for being a Protestant. She refused to come to any understanding with her son, left the castle, and went to live in a little cottage belonging to her, situated at the other end of the village.

"However, there has been no open quarrel. Two days after my arrival, we went to pay our respects to her. I am brave, you know; I put on a bold face. She sent us word that she was dressing. Roger replied that we would wait. She finally appeared, walked across the room, and held out her hand to her son—I said her hand; she gave him only two fingers. He presented me, but she pretended not to notice it, and stood with her back toward me, opening and shutting her fan and telling it (the fan I mean) that she had that morning saved a sparrow which her cat had caught.....The cat and the sparrow, the sparrow and the cat, and the fan opening and shutting all the time—it was very funny, but it wasn't nice. At last, looking at the clock, she said, 'I must leave you now; it's time to go to church.' Then casting a side glance at me, she added, 'That's a duty irreligious women don't attend to.....'

"Irreligious! Am I an irreligious woman? I thought that religion consisted in communion with God, in confessing our weakness before him, in asking him for what we need, in feeling that we are in his presence, and in opening our hearts to him that he may cleanse and purify them....Irreligious! How hateful intolerance is, Nelly! Does not God belong to all the world alike? Does he not understand all tongues, even though they stammer, or are altogether silent, not knowing how to speak?

"Mme. D'Ornis evidently intends not to disregard the ordinary customs of society. She has returned our call. I had gone out. I do not know whether she commenced the story of the sparrow again, but Roger said to her, 'You have decided to follow this course, then? You will not accept the fact that I have a wife, and that it would be proper to ask about her?' She replied, 'I thought I was carrying out your own ideas. You take your wife to taverns, and don't care to present her to your friends, as I suppose.' He became very angry; she begged his pardon and endeavored to appease him. I do not know the result of the conversation. What I have told you, I learned from Fanny, my maid, who had gone into the room to light the fire, but had been quickly sent out again by Roger. She is a good girl ; she came with me from Geneva, and is perfectly devoted to me. If any one should scratch me with a pin, she would scream as though she was being murdered. I do not care to listen to what she tells me though ; I hear enough myself.

"Roger said nothing to me of this interview, but in the evening he remarked, 'I think we ought to give a party.' The very thought of it worried me terribly; but I knew I ought to respect the customs of society. I am glad enough to be through with it though. I understood very well that his mother's remark had troubled him, and that he had determined to show her that he did not wish to hide his wife from the world. I made a few objections, but he had an answer for them all, and night before last, my dear, Castle D'Ornis was illuminated to receive the nobility of the neighborhood. I had arranged every thing myself, and it was all well arranged, I can assure you. I spent two hours at my toilet; I must confess that for the first time in my life, I felt like playing the coquette. Our guests all came : Roger is a man that no one likes to offend, and then people are so curious, you know! My mother-in-law deigned to notice me as she came in, and manifested a surprise which was evidently less agreeable to her than to myself. She recovered herself very quickly, however, and sat down on a sofa, as far from her daughter-in-law as possible. The gentlemen were polite, respectful, and attentive ; the ladies were affected, formal, and patronizing ; their manner seemed very strange to me. They sat in a semi-circle round my mother-in-law, as though they considered her the real mistress of the house. The gentlemen stood about me. I was in high spirits, and the compliments flew fast. Suddenly I heard a sharp voice say, 'You must ask my daughter-in-law ; probably she can tell you.'

"I rose and walked over toward the ladies. 'What can I do for you, madam?' I asked.

"'We were speaking of mortise-chisels, madam. What is a mortise-chisel?'

"'It's a tool used for cutting deep and narrow cavities in wood.'

"'And what is a gouge, madam?'

"'A gouge, madam, is a rounded chisel used for cutting concave surfaces. But why do you ask the question, madam?'...

"'Because the Marchioness Du Rozan has a son who is amusing himself with carpentry, and he has asked her for some gouges and mortise-chisels. She wanted to know what they were.'

"This Marchioness Du Rozan, who sat facing me, was an old crane, whose grandfather had been a rich hardware merchant in Marseilles. The old crane now lifted her neck, and said,

"'It would be very kind in you, Countess, if you would only give my son a little advice. He is very awkward.'

"I am naturally a good-hearted girl, Nelly; I know it is my greatest fault. All these eyes fastened on me, however, made me a little spiteful, and I answered, 'No doubt he needs advice. Carpentry is a very complicated art. It would be easier for him to learn the hardware trade.'

"She blushed to her very temples, and hid her face behind her fan. The women looked angry, my mother-in-law bit her lips, the men were all laughing in their sleeves. As for myself, I was sorry that I had spoken so quickly; but a word can not be taken back. After that, the evening passed very pleasantly. We had a band of strolling musicians with us; the dancing lasted until morning.

"Trouble came from this, though, Nelly. Our unpleasant conversation about chisels and gouges was overheard by Roger. He looked upon it as a premeditated insult, and although I tried my best, I could not prevail on him to pass it by. He went yesterday to call on Mme. D'Ornis, and had a stormy interview with her, which came near ending in an open rupture. I scarcely know what to do, but have formed a plan to call on Mme. D'Ornis myself. Perhaps I may succeed in appeasing her. I talked with Roger about it; he at first refused to listen to me, but finally gave me his permission. I am going right away, and am considerably agitated as you can well believe. Good-by, dear! I must put on my hat and gloves, and go into the lion's den. If the lion eat me, you can compose some verses commemorative of the sacrifice. Do you ever compose verses now? They used to jingle a little, as Professor Bourdon said; as they have grown in years, though, they must have grown in strength.

"P. S. Have I done right or wrong, Nelly? I do not know. I must tell you all about it. I have often noticed that things scarcely ever happen as we think they will. I expected to be received very coolly, or perhaps not to be received at all, which would have greatly simplified the interview. How mistaken I was! A lady came forward to the very door to greet me. 'Good day, my dear,' she said. 'I was very provoking the other evening, but you turned the laugh on me nicely. I'm not surprised at all; you are wise and beautiful as an angel. There's my hand!'

"You can imagine my bewilderment. I took her offered hand and said, 'I am very glad that you feel so, madam, for I called to tell you that I wanted to love you, and to ask you if you wouldn't try to love me a little in return?'

"'Oh!' she answered, 'now you are asking a great deal.'

"'Pshaw!' I replied, 'God is great, as the Turks say. It will all come in good time.' As I spoke of the Turks, she frowned. 'Isn't it proper for an irreligious woman to refer to the Turks?' I asked, laughing.

"'Don't let's talk about such things,' she said dryly; or if we do, let's talk seriously. If I could only hope that some day....'

"'I won't make any promises,' I replied, interrupting her. 'I will try, however, to prove my devotion to you, and I think I can help to make the time pass pleasantly.'

"As I said this I touched my lips to her hand, which I had been holding in my own. It was hard work, Nelly, but I did it. She looked at me, and seemed to be forming some new plan. Remember, during all this time, we had been standing at the door, I outside, and she inside the room. She finally came to a decision, and with a face that was almost smiling, said, 'Come in, my dear, and take a seat.'

"She pushed an arm-chair forward for me, and placed a cushion beneath my feet; then she rang the bell, and ordered some raspberry syrup and orange marmalade, which she makes herself. During this time I could not help admiring the certainty and precision of all her movements; she does every thing in the shortest and quickest way, and I am sure I can not understand why she always carries a crutch with her. I also admired the simple elegance of her dress. She would make a charming picture, if she were not so sharp in every way.

"She began to talk about Switzerland and the Alps, and of a trip she had made in that direction some twenty years ago. She talks well, and seems to have seen much that is interesting and to have remembered it well. She knows more than I do, Nelly; I could learn a great deal from her. But her prejudices! As soon as you touch upon them, she will neither talk nor listen to you. While in her presence, I compared her to a house, the front of which admits the light, while the back is an immense wall without doors or windows, seeing nothing and believing nothing.

"For half an hour we conversed quietly, almost gayly. The lion had not eaten me; it even seemed to have become more tame. As I wanted to leave a good impression, I rose to go; but she made me sit down again, saying, 'You are in too great a hurry, madam.'

"Then turning suddenly toward me, she continued, 'It was very kind of you, my dear, to come to see me. You seem disposed to judge others charitably. Old women have their peculiar ideas, you know. My son is forty-five years old, and I didn't think that he would ever marry. I hadn't taken into account the wonders which a pair of handsome eyes can work. I have yielded my place to you. At my age it's a hard thing to give up a home. I was angry at you, and was foolish enough to let you know it. You forgive me, do you not?....And, now, that you are here, I'll tell you something....My son is very hot-headed. Yesterday, he treated me outrageously. You are very gentle, dear, I can talk easily with you. I will tell you that I should have become reconciled to this marriage much more readily, if I had thought that Roger was a fit person to have a wife. If you can make a good husband of him, you will deserve great credit. He's an old bachelor and is full of whims. You can see how he treats his wife; he takes her with him to the hunt and to the tavern. How can you allow him to so compromise your dignity? He loves you, but he's not respectful. Love is fleeting, while respect lasts forever. My dear, I charge you seriously not to lend yourself to his caprices. You don't know what it may lead to. God knows that I am greatly to blame for his being what he is. I cry *peccavi;* I know that I have spoiled him. He ought to be under some restraint; try to gain an influence over him, and to make him act within the bounds of reason. It wouldn't matter so much if he were simply whimsical. He has, besides, a most violent temper. You'll find it out only too soon. I could tell you some terrible things.... He used to be very intimate with a certain Marquis De Raoux, an honorable man as the world goes, but in my opinion, a vicious, swaggering reveler, who drank immoderately and gambled to excess. I was very sorry that Roger sought the society of this gamester. It seems he had been in the service, and they used to talk of their campaigns and sing their army songs together. Well, one night, just after he had left my son, Raoux was killed by a villain hid near the bridge. It was terrible, I know; but after all, it was nobody but Raoux. My son became a victim of despair, as though the murdered man had been a model of honor and of virtue. I thought at times that he'd go mad. I will give you one fact in evidence of this.... He had a saddle-horse, that he loved as the apple of his eye; he paid eight thousand francs for him. This horse and Raoux were his two idols. The day after the murder, he took a gun, went into the stable, and blew out the brains of this noble animal. How do you like that way of honoring a man's memory? You can see that he is easily excited, and that it's always well to be prepared.... He knows it all; he's afraid of himself. Although he is not sociable, he can not bear to be alone, but must always have some one with him, to stand, as it were, between him and his caprices. While

Raoux lived, he answered the purpose. When he missed Raoux, he thought of getting married. A handsome blonde is a very good exchange for him.... I thought it best to tell you of this, my dear, in order that you might know what to expect. You ought not to be ignorant of what your husband may do in his fits of melancholy. Forewarned, forearmed! You must watch over and control him.'

"This long harangue was uttered in a dry, heartless tone that grated harshly on my ears. I wanted to interrupt her, but could say nothing. What strange creatures we are, Nelly! Before seeking this interview, I had thought about it, and was prepared to hear cruel words and to bear them with good grace; but I was far from expecting this strange outburst of a mother against her son, and was thrown completely off my guard. I experienced a feeling of uneasiness which kept increasing every minute. I remained motionless in my chair, and I am sure that I appeared as awkward and embarrassed as a school-girl; or, what better expresses my idea, I seemed like a helpless bird charmed by a serpent. I wanted to fly, but I stayed and listened, though it seemed as if I were swallowing poison and felt it running through my veins. The curtains of the room were dropped, so that the light entered only by a narrow opening between them. These few rays of sunlight fell upon my face; Mme. D'Ornis could read it easily. Perhaps she experienced a secret joy at witnessing my agitation. When she had finished, I had still strength enough to rise and say, 'If you wanted to frighten me, madam, you have not succeeded.' I said this in an indifferent, almost haughty tone. I was like the boys who whistle when they are afraid.

"She answered coolly, 'Frighten you! you seem to me a very courageous little body, if I can say so without offending you.'

"'Besides,' I continued, 'I don't see any thing so terrible in his shooting the horse.... If any body should ever murder me, I think it would be splendid to have Roger blow up his billiard-table.'

"She accompanied me to the door of the room. 'Well,

well,' she said, 'I'm not sorry that I have made you uneasy. Nothing is more dangerous than a false security. Good-by, my dear. Now you know the way, you must come and talk with me whenever you feel like it.'

"What a weak thing I am, Nelly! I had made up my mind that, if I was defeated, I would at least retire in good order; but, notwithstanding the bold air which I assumed, I felt that I was completely routed; it seemed to me that this rout would end in some terrible catastrophe, and that on leaving the house I should meet with some new misfortune. At last I reached the open air; I looked about and breathed more freely. The sky was blue, the air was full of sunshine, a rose-bush in full bloom stretched one of its fragrant branches toward me. My trouble was dissipated as by enchantment. I saw the sunshine and the roses, and all my former confidence returned; I felt that all these blessings were not at the mercy of an old woman full of jealousy and hate.

"On my return, Roger questioned me. My answers were truthful; but, though I invented nothing, I did not tell all; I omitted the whole of her long harangue. I tell you the whole story. It is so nice to have some one to whom you can tell every thing! Good-by, my darling. Before marrying, learn all you can about your mother-in-law. May your sky be full of sunshine, and your pathway strewn with roses."

CHAPTER XVI.

DAWNING CURIOSITY.

The words we use are ofttimes an active poison. Although we may resolve to believe nothing of what we hear, we generally do believe a little. Marguerite had decided to pay no attention to the warnings which Mme. D'Ornis had been kind enough to give her; she could not keep from thinking of them, however. She had no idea of following her mother-in-law's advice and changing her mode of life, in which she could discover nothing reprehensible. She could not see that her husband was lacking in respect for her, nor that she compromised her own dignity in roaming about the country with him. What harm was there in it? "He has his peculiar ideas about married life," she thought, "and he has a right to his own way of thinking. No one is hurt by it. Let people talk if they want to! They would talk about any thing else just the same." She began to think, however, that she did not understand M. D'Ornis very well, and in order to become better acquainted with him, she began to study him more attentively. Doubt produces curiosity, curiosity creates uneasiness. In searching too deeply, we run the risk of making unpleasant discoveries. Fortunately, Marguerite was not one to borrow trouble; she was determined not to become alarmed without sufficient cause. Her good sense and cheerfulness were a great help to her. I do not know how better to describe her than by saying that she had a happy disposition.

On one of those lovely days in the late autumn which Mme de Sévigné calls crystal days, they started on a long walk which took them farther than they expected. In order to please his wife, Roger had left his gun at home; he simply carried his game-bag, into which he had put a pie, a cold chicken, a bottle of wine, and some ground coffee. They expected to take their meal near some inn, at which they could borrow some plates and forks. At midday they found themselves in an opening in the woods, with no house of any kind in sight. Being hungry, they decided to stop in this lonely place and to eat in the Turkish fashion, with their fingers in other words. They selected a spot near a spring; all about them was an abundant growth of water-cresses, which served admirably as a seasoning to their meal. As they had walked fast and were afraid of catching cold, they started a large fire before proceeding to their repast. Both of them hastily gathered armfuls of dead wood, striving to see which could collect the most. When the fire was lighted, they spread out their provisions on the grass. The pie was speedily demolished. The most difficult thing was to prepare the coffee. By exercising a little ingenuity, they succeeded in boiling some water in a cup, without its tasting at all of smoke.

Their repast being finished, Marguerite, who felt a little tired after the twelve miles she had walked that morning, asked permission to take a half-hour's nap. She lay down, wrapped up in her shawl, with her head resting on a mossy stone. She would have slept two hours, if Roger, becoming impatient, had not awakened her. On opening her eyes, she saw him leaning over her, fanning away the smoke with one hand, and with the other, tickling her lips by means of a long spear of grass. This awakening was delicious; she could scarcely recognize her companion; he seemed to have grown ten years younger. She started up and began to sing; all feelings of uneasiness suddenly passed away; she felt light-hearted as a bird, and when birds are happy, they will sing. "Did the time seem long to you?" she said.

"What do you want to make me say so for? You can judge me by my acts."

"That's not enough. I like to hear people say what they think."

"Very well!" he answered. "I declare on my honor that

the time seemed very long to me." Then he added: "I've read in some comedy that persons should become well acquainted before marrying; otherwise they might find out too late that they did not suit each other.... Yes, this is the line:

'Que tous deux du marché nous nous repentirions.'

We were not well acquainted, and yet I don't see that we're likely to repent our bargain."

An imprudent thing is quickly done. Charmed as well as surprised at the happy frame of mind in which she found her husband, Marguerite thought she would profit by this unusual display of good nature, and try to have an explanation with him.

"I think as you do," she replied, "that we are a well-matched couple, and yet we're not at all alike."

"If you mean in looks, it's very certain that an old graybeard like me doesn't deserve such a handsome wife."

"You must do yourself justice; you don't look to be thirty, this very minute."

"Well, my legs are young enough anyhow, and, thank goodness, yours are also good. So we can take our walks together. You see we agree so far."

"Yes, but there are many respects in which we are very different."

"Suppose you tell me what they are."

"Do you really want me to? Well! in the first place, I am very trusting, too much so perhaps. It's very hard for me to believe that intentions can be wrong, or people wicked, while you...."

"While I am suspicious of every body? Isn't that what you want to say? You are right; I don't believe in perfect characters. Men are governed by the feelings or interests of the moment. You can not tell to-day what they will be to-morrow. It's best not to trust them..... Still, I don't think of any striking proof I've given....."

"Oh!" she answered gayly, "there are plenty of proofs.... The other evening, we were crossing the little wood.... you remember, we were talking about the rain and the fine weather, when we heard a rustling in the dead leaves near us. You caught me suddenly by the arm saying, 'Hush! there's some one here !'.... It turned out to be a dog who was gnawing a bone..... I don't think what he could have repeated of our conversation would have compromised us very much."

He frowned slightly as he replied, "The Italians, who are not fools by any means, have this proverb: 'Be careful of your words; some day or other they may return to you.'"

"Another proof," she continued. "Day before yesterday, you were alone in your room, looking for something in your wardrobe. I took the liberty of entering without knocking. 'Who's that?' you cried in a voice of thunder. Fortunately, you recognized me."

He answered with a forced smile, "If you think there's any thing in my wardrobe that ought not to be there, I'll give you the key any time you want it."

"I won't accept it; I don't want to meddle with your wardrobe."

As she said this, she held out her hand to him.

"Let's be serious," he replied, "since we've entered on this subject. What other difference ?...."

"Well! this for instance. I've always been told that I have not sufficient strength of character; perhaps you have too much."

"What do you mean by that?"

"That you're sometimes....how shall I express it?....a little violent."

"Are you trying to find out all that's bad about me?"

"Not at all. There are some kinds of violence that I admire, and if the story's true...."

"Explain yourself," he cried impatiently, "I hate enigmas."

"I was told that two years—yes, it was two years ago, I think—you shot a horse that you were very fond of."

Nothing is more disagreeable than to step inadvertently on a petard, and have it explode beneath your feet. It was such a surprise that Marguerite experienced on seeing the effect produced by her imprudent words. M. D'Ornis turned pale and bounded to his feet, running his hand rapidly through his hair, as he always did when he was angry. His lips were trembling as he cried, "Who told you that?....who dared to tell you?....I will know....I command you....."

Marguerite was frightened as she looked at him.

"Don't be angry, please," she said. "I had no idea ...."

M. D'Ornis felt that he must visit his anger upon something. He picked up a half-burnt branch, snapped it in two, and threw the pieces far away....."I tell you I must know....What was the story that you heard?"

"I only heard that you used to have a valuable horse which you were very proud of. You used to ride him, accompanied by a friend who was murdered two years ago.....Your friend being dead, you determined to rid yourself of this horse, which recalled to you such sad memories. Another person would have sold him, you killed him instead. If it was madness, I say again, it's a kind of madness I admire."

"And I ask you again, who told you this? Whom have you dared to talk with about me?"

"It ought to be easy enough for you to guess. Whom have I seen since I've been your wife?"

"Ah! my mother.....So you've been questioning her? ....Woman's curiosity....."

He now perceived that tears were standing in her eyes, and feeling somewhat ashamed, at last succeeded in mastering his passion. "After all," he said, "I'm wrong.....There was no great harm in it.....I couldn't help myself; there are some remembrances."....Then he added with an effort, "Never speak to me again about that murdered friend....or that horse....never! never!"....Stopping a moment to take breath, he continued, "What were we talking about? The points of difference between us.....We've displayed a great deal of penetration and subtle wit.....It's not worth the trouble. I'm not a keen-witted person; I never could understand any thing but plain truths. All these differences can be summed up in one word: I'm very dark and you are very light, whence I conclude....."

"Whence you conclude?".... she repeated trying to smile.

"I conclude," he said in an ironical tone, which, in spite of all that he could do, evinced more bitterness than good-nature, "that it's my fate to be ruled by you, for there's no tyrant so oppressive as a blonde."

With these words, he picked up his game-bag and strapped it together. In the feverish haste of his movements, he twice pricked his fingers with the buckle. Then he suddenly cried "Forward!" They walked for twenty minutes almost without exchanging a word. Marguerite, however, soon began to master her agitation and to regain possession of her faculties. Little by little, also, he unbent and resumed his usual manner. Half an hour before reaching Ornis, he took her in his arms to carry her across a brook, and, on putting her down again, said in a cold but pleasant tone, "You're decidedly the handsomest woman I've ever seen." He spoke as though he were praising some piece of furniture. This was sufficient to make Marguerite gay again.

Notwithstanding, this day which had commenced so badly had a bad ending. After dinner, M. D'Ornis asked his wife to sing for him. She sat down at the piano and began a song. Turning her head, she saw that he had fallen asleep in his arm-chair. She closed the piano softly, took up her embroidery, and sat down facing her husband. As she worked, she now and then glanced at him, and as she looked, the mysterious story of the horse came to her mind; it seemed to her that within the heart of this man, who held her fate within his hands, there lurked a secret ready to spring upon her. "Am I growing mad?" she thought. "What's the use of trying to find it out. I don't believe there is a secret."

M. D'Ornis's sleep was troubled. Twice he sighed; then an expression of such agony came upon his face, that Marguerite was terrified. She saw him throw out his arms and beat the air; a moment afterward he muttered in a hoarse voice, "It's yours. Don't be angry. I swear that you shall have it; but, for God's sake, don't tell of it!" The sound of his voice awoke him, and his first glance fell on Marguerite, who hastily dropped her eyes and kept them fixed on her embroidery. "I think I was asleep," he said.

"I think so too," she answered with a forced smile and a slight trembling in her voice.

"It seems to me that I was talking."

"Indeed! I didn't hear you."

He looked at her steadily for a minute or two, and then got up and left the room. Marguerite did not sleep well that night. She kept repeating to herself as she tossed about in bed, "I'll give it to you; but, for God's sake, don't tell of it!" When she opened her eyes in the morning, it seemed as though a change had taken place in her life—as though her happiness was like a precious vase which had been cracked. Thenceforth it could not be touched but with precaution; a single careless movement might shatter it to pieces.

A fortnight passed without any thing of importance happening. M. D'Ornis had resumed his usual manner and appearance. Though a woman may be very reasonable, when once her curiosity is awakened, it is difficult for her to lull it to sleep again. This is not because women are more curious than men, but because they have more time to give to their thoughts, and fewer opportunities to escape from them. The uniform and quiet life which Marguerite led gave little employment to her mind. A walk in the woods is very pleasant; but the woods can not speak, except to the poet's heart, and there are moments when the most unworldly woman would give all the forests in the world, for an opportunity to talk about dress for twenty minutes with another of her sex. What woman could Marguerite talk with? After the party given by M. and Mme. D'Ornis, they had received from their neighbors several invitations to dinner. M. D'Ornis had found excuses for not accepting them, and they had not been repeated. The old Countess went about remarking that her daughter-in-law was a very handsome girl, but that she had good reasons for shunning society; that knowing her own failings, she felt embarrassed in her new position, and had asked her husband neither to receive calls nor make them. "Poor Roger!" she would add with a sigh. Her intimate friend, the Marchioness Du Rozan, shared her feelings of resentment, and confirmed all her petty calumnies. "Your son will come back to you, my dear," she said consoling her. "When a man like him marries such a woman, he always repents of it before long." The women talked in this way; the men reasoned in another manner. Marguerite's beauty had made a deep impression on them, and when they chanced to meet her, they gazed persistently on this forbidden fruit. They found fault with M. D'Ornis for keeping his wife to himself, and depriving society of her presence. Some attributed it to his savage humor, others suspected him of jealousy. A few were persevering enough to call upon them. The coolness of their reception, however, compelled them to cut short their calls.

CHAPTER XVII.

M. BERTRAND APPEARS AGAIN.

If Marguerite did not find much diversion in her neighbors' society, she certainly did not take much comfort in her own. We are often tormented by our imagination, but sometimes it does us a service in return, by helping us forget the realities of life, and we are very thankful when these realities are disagreeable. Marguerite was not one of those winged souls, that fly to the clouds when the earth displeases them. She had never been able to lose herself in the realms of space, nor to fall in love with a shadow or a day-dream. The only passion she had ever experienced was friendship; every thing else was simply a more or less agreeable pastime to her. She liked to read a novel or play a sonata as well as any one, but as soon as she had closed her book or her piano, she found herself again face to face with Marguerite Mirion, now Countess D'Ornis, who recounted all her little affairs to her and asked her advice concerning them. Good-by to music! She had to answer these questions and give her attention to the realities of life. She could not drive away her troubles by dreaming over them; her reason was her only resource. She bravely held her curiosity in check. "Be still," she said to it; "if I should follow your advice, you would render me unhappy."

One evening—I believe it was the 20th of November—a fire broke out in a hamlet near Ornis. Roger, accompanied by his men, was one of the first upon the ground; he always, on such occasions, exhibited great coolness and intrepidity. Marguerite was left at the castle, with no companion but her maid. About ten o'clock, the bell rang violently. At her mistress's bidding, Fanny, who was not the bravest girl in the world, went to the door, much against her will. A few moments later, Marguerite heard her running hurriedly up the stairs. She came in with a terrified look, crying out, "Oh! my lady....it's an ugly man with a great nose and staring eyes....I think he must be a robber."

"What does he want? who did he ask for?" said Marguerite a little frightened.

"The Count. I told him he wasn't in. He said he was always in for him. I asked him to call again to-morrow. Then he began to whirl his stick, telling me not to put on airs, that he wanted to see the Count, that he would see him...."

"Well?"

"Then I pushed the door to in his face; but he kept it from shutting with his stick, and I ran away."

"You're the greatest coward I ever saw," said Marguerite. "Perhaps the man has an important message."

She rose to leave the room. Fanny tried to hold her back, begging her to lock the door and put out the light. "I'm sure that he's a robber," she said.

"There are no robbers about here."

"Oh! yes, my lady, one of them murdered that poor Marquis Raoux...."

"He was guillotined, and I want you never to mention that name, or speak of that murder in this house again," said Marguerite in a reproving tone.

With these words, she took up the lamp, and leaving the room, went to meet the nocturnal visitor. The latter had tried to find M. D'Ornis's room, but had mistaken the way, and had just entered a bath-room, situated at the end of the corridor. The door had closed upon him, and after trying in vain to open it, he was searching in the darkness for another outlet, cursing and swearing all the time.

Marguerite summoned up all her courage and entered the room. She found herself in the presence of a red-faced man, whose eyes gave signs of his having been drinking freely. His tongue, however, moved with ease, and he stood firmly on his feet. On perceiving Marguerite, he remained an instant as though bewildered; he shaded his eyes with his hairy hands, and looked at her from head to foot. "Oh! what a handsome Countess D'Ornis!" he said at last.

"What do you want?" asked Marguerite, not particularly relishing his enthusiasm.

Instead of answering her, he smacked his lips. "Some men are born lucky!" he said as though talking to himself. "Here's an old fellow almost fifty, and black as an ant, and the good Lord sends him a wife handsome enough to make an angel's mouth water.... And then the dowry! may I inquire what the dowry is?"

"What do you want here?" asked Marguerite again in a louder tone. "What are you doing in this bath-room?"

He looked around him. "As sure as I live, you're right," he said with a harsh laugh; "I came near falling into the bath-tub. I know what I'm about though! I've trotted round a good deal to-day, and a little while ago I went into Mme. Guibaud's to refresh myself. I don't know what she puts in her wine, but it makes my head swim a little. It won't last long.... Where's your husband, Countess?"

"You've been told once that's he's not at home. Have you any message to leave for him?"

"A message, did you say? I don't leave any messages for him. I'm in the habit of talking over all my little affairs with him, myself. We're old friends, you see. He wouldn't like it at all, if he knew that I'd come to Burgundy without shaking hands with him. Last summer, I didn't find him. He was in Switzerland, looking for a wife. He's had good luck, I must say, and I ought to congratulate him on it."

Marguerite had never heard of this M. Bertrand, whom Joseph Noirel had had the pleasure of meeting twice at Ornis. His inseparable companion, the large dog, was not far distant; his master had left him in the court-yard, where he was plaintively baying at the moon. Marguerite wondered who this clown, who spoke so familiarly of Count D'Ornis, could be. His dress presented a strange mixture. His coat was of fine cloth with a fur-collar, and in his cuffs he wore two enormous gold sleeve-buttons. On the other hand, his felt hat was well worn and out of shape, and he had on a pair of coarse, heavy shoes, tied with pieces of rough twine. Marguerite finally concluded that he was some horse-jockey, who had formerly accompanied M. D'Ornis in his walks, and who had the bad habit of drinking too much.

"I don't know when M. D'Ornis will return," she said. "Please be kind enough to call again to-morrow, sir."

"Yes, that's very nice," he answered, rolling his eyes about. "You can't get rid of me so easy. To-morrow, the Count will be off hunting, and I'll have to chase after him. Time is money, as the English say. I'm here, and here I'll stay, if I have to wait all night."

In the meantime, Fanny, who from very shame, had rejoined her mistress, bethought herself of an expedient she had heard of, for getting rid of unwelcome nocturnal visitors. Turning toward the door, she began to shout, "Joseph, Jerome, Matthew, John; this man is insulting my lady! Come up and put him out." She would have exhausted the whole calendar, if Marguerite had not placed her hand over her mouth.

The only result of this experiment was to excite M. Bertrand to fury. Striking his hat fiercely with one hand, and brandishing his stick with the other, he cried, "Put me out! me, M. Bertrand! Let your Johns and Matthews all come on! I'd like to see any body in this house that dare touch me!.... Perhaps you don't know that this house belongs to me.".... Then striking the wall with his stick, he continued, "This wall knows me. It knows who I am, and that I've a right to act as master here.... Yes, my dear Countess, if I should take a fancy to add that handsome coral necklace you've got on, to my stock in trade, I'd only have to ask for it, to get it.... And if I choose to insult my lady, as your girl says, who's going to hinder me, I'd like to know?"

With these words he put out his arm, and would have caught Marguerite round the waist, if she had not sprung back. As he started to follow her, his hat fell off, and he stooped to pick it up. Marguerite ran into the corridor, and Fanny quickly shut the door of the room, locking it from the outside. M. Bertrand tried to kick down the door, but without success;

he remained shut up in the dark, swearing, howling, dancing about like a devil in a holy-water basin, pounding the bath-tubs with his stick, and making noise enough to wake the dead. His dog in the court-yard hearing him, answered by a series of unearthly howls, to which all the dogs in the neighborhood hastened to add a chorus.

Marguerite, who was still trembling at the remembrance of M. Bertrand's insolence, was afraid that the door would soon give way, and scarcely knew what to do. Fanny volunteered to go to the village and ask for help. She was about to accept her offer, when M. D'Ornis appeared, followed by his valet.

"What's all this noise?" he asked. Fanny ran up to him, and before Marguerite could say a word, related in a most pathetic tone, how a drunken man, who seemed a very suspicious character, had succeeded in gaining admission to the house, and, on being asked to leave it, had threatened and insulted them, and had even gone so far as to try to put his arm around the Countess's waist.

M. D'Ornis's face grew purple with anger. "Where is the villain?" he cried, and, without waiting for an answer, he ran toward the bath-room. Marguerite followed close behind him, fearful that he would commit some violence. She might have saved her steps. The door had scarcely opened, when his anger left him as if by magic, giving place to a kind of terror, mingled with surprise and anguish. He fell back a step.

"What! it's you, Bertrand?" he stammered, striving to regain his self-possession. "What are you doing?...."

The furious rage to which M. Bertrand had given way had completely sobered him, but he came near having an apoplectic fit. He untied his cravat quickly, as though afraid of suffocating.

"Yes, it's me," he answered in a panting voice. "It's me, Count, and this is the way I'm received here in your house. What do they take me for? Have you ordered them to treat me so? Am I a man to be trifled with? Or are you trying to make me sick of coming here? You might as well save yourself the trouble."

"It's a mistake," muttered M. D'Ornis. "How can you think...."

"Why don't you tell your people who I am then?" answered the other shaking his red head. "You've never told the Countess about me. Explain to her.... "

"That will do," interrupted M. D'Ornis in a haughty tone. He had at last succeeded in mastering his agitation. "I have no reason for presenting you to my wife, and intend to keep you entirely for myself. Cool down now, pick your hat out of the bath-tub, and follow me to my room. We can talk there at our leisure."

M. Bertrand picked up his hat, and turning toward Marguerite with a slight bow, and a side glance that she did not deign to notice, hastened to rejoin M. D'Ornis, who had already started and was turning round to call him.

Marguerite was almost stunned by what she had just seen and heard; it all seemed like a dream. She knew by experience how quick her husband's temper was; she had feared, for an instant, that he would strangle this intruder, who had forced himself into his house and taken liberties with his wife. At the mere sight of him, however, his anger had melted like snow before the fire; he had turned pale, had listened with resignation to the reproaches of this clown, and had finally taken him to his room, to talk over matters with him. Who was this M. Bertrand, who understood so well how to quiet people?

She went up to her room in a deep revery. About eleven o'clock, Fanny, whom she had sent downstairs on an errand, returned saying, "I can't understand it, my lady? That ugly creature has just gone, and the Count went with him to the door. They stood in the vestibule talking a few minutes."

"And you were listening as usual? It's time you put a stop to this. Your ears are growing so large, you'll have to be very careful of them."

"I wasn't listening, my lady; they were talking very loud. M. Bertrand said, 'Very well, we'll meet again a week from now; but I give you warning it's the only thing I'll do.' It was very evident that the Count was angry. 'All right,' he answered, 'only permit me to observe that you're a rascal.' At this the ugly fellow was about to speak; but the Count motioned him to keep quiet, and he went off whistling. I never heard of such a thing, my lady! A drunken fellow tries to put his arm round you, and the Count swallows it like so much honey."

Marguerite ordered her to be quiet. Her own reflections on this subject were sufficient for her; she did not wish to hear her maid's. She took up her embroidery again. Soon she heard her husband's quick, nervous step on the stairs and in the corridor. The door opened and he came in. He had a gloomy expression on his face. As soon as he saw her, he gave her a searching glance; it seemed as though his anger had been long pent up, and was now ready to explode on the slightest provocation.

"Well!" she said, "where was the fire?"

This question took him by surprise; it was not what he expected. "It's scarcely worth speaking of," he said in a dry tone. "It was a shed that caught fire. There was nothing in it but a few pigs, and they were only singed a little."

"Any one would think that you were angry because they saved their bacon?" she answered laughing.

"Not at all! You know I wouldn't harm a living thing."

He began to walk up and down the room with his hands behind him, now and then glancing at Marguerite. Although he was not fond of questions, he preferred them to such silence. In fact, nothing could have been more disagreeable to him than to have his wife say nothing, when he knew she was thinking about him all the time. "It's suffocating here!" he cried. "You've got such a blazing fire. I don't see how you can stand it."

He opened the window as wide as he could. Marguerite approached the fireplace, and pushed aside two logs that had just begun to burn. She could not help making *in petto* the reflection that her fire was a very modest one, and that an angry man always finds something to get provoked about. She then sat down and began to embroider again. Stopping before her, M. D'Ornis said, "What are you doing?"

" Don't you see, I'm embroidering."

" You ought not to work so late ; it will spoil your eyes."

" Oh ! I'm used to it ; it doesn't tire them at all."

" Don't you know that there's nothing so provoking to a man, as to have a woman embroidering all the time."

" Oh !" she answered gayly, " that's an argument that I appreciate." Then putting down her work and leaning back in her chair with her arms folded, she continued, " Well ! what have you to say to me ?"

He slightly shrugged his shoulders, and began to walk round the room. When he came back to Marguerite, seeing that she was determined not to question him, he decided to break the ice himself. " If I may ask the question, where did you pick up that maid of yours ?" he said.

" In Geneva. She comes from my own country. She has been at Paris several years, and is a good clever girl."

" Begging your pardon, she's a goose."

" Why, what has she done ?"

" Oh ! she gets frightened so easily and tells such fearful stories. Didn't she take M. Bertrand for a highway robber ? A little more and she would have roused the whole village. Does he look like a villain ? Did he try to murder her ? You'd better send your girl home again."

" Excuse me. She does get excited very easily, and I have often scolded her for it ; but she was not so much to blame this time. Your M. Bertrand has such a way of presenting himself....I should have been sorry, I must confess, if he had caught your wife in his arms."

" Are you sure that he tried to do so ? He saw that you were frightened, and wanted to have a little fun with you....His joke was in bad taste, perhaps...."

" Yes, I think it was," she interrupted.

" Nothing like that ever happens to women who are not afraid," he answered brutally. " If Countess D'Ornis didn't act like a little girl, no one would ever think of taking liberties with her."

In spite of her gentle nature, this remark provoked her.

"You must excuse your poor Marguerite," she said. "If I had supposed that this man was a friend of yours...."

He started back. "He, my friend! Do you want to insult me?"

"Not at all, only I think you are strangely indulgent toward him."

"Are you sorry I didn't kill him like a dog, because he'd been drinking a little too much?"

"Heaven forbid! I wish, though, that you would show the same indulgence to other people, especially to your humble servant." Then, becoming good-natured again, she added with that childish grace which was so irresistible, "Come, tell me right away who M. Bertrand is, and let's have done with him!"

He experienced some satisfaction at having succeeded in making her ask the question, and became a little gentler in his manner. "I knew you were dying to question me!" he cried. "What curious creatures women are!....M. Bertrand is one of the finest products of this country. After having tried all kinds of business, this child of Ornis is now in a fair way to make a fortune. Beginning as a simple shepherd, and becoming in turn a peddler, a wood-cutter, an insurance broker, and a sampler in a wine-house, he finally grew tired of tasting other people's wines, and swore that thenceforth he would drink none but his own. He doesn't always keep his word, as you have seen. Finally, he became a dealer in *bric-à-brac*, and for some years has had a store in Lyons. Every now and then, he makes a visit to our Burgundian castles, where he always finds something that he wants to buy. My garret is full of old furniture, antiquated things that are good for nothing, and I'm very glad to get rid of them. You see that this man is a useful animal after all, and that your maid is a silly goose."

For the moment, Marguerite was satisfied with this explanation. "Why have you never taken me to visit your garret?" she asked. "You know that I'm very fond of old furniture."

"Pshaw!" he said, "you'd find nothing there but worn-out

things, such as ragged sofas, ricketty tables, chairs without arms, and little trifles which would be of no use to you, but which my man knows what to do with, and is very willing to pay me for."

"Then I'll outbid M. Bertrand. If Marguerite Mirion loves old furniture, Countess D'Ornis has a great regard for family keepsakes."

"Don't be more loyal than the king himself," he answered curtly.

She approached him and held her cheek for him to kiss; he just touched it with his lips. In return she kissed him on the forehead. She did not succeed, however, in dissipating the dark cloud which hung upon his brow.

Marguerite had scarcely placed her head upon her pillow, when, her husband's explanations returning to her mind, she found much in them that troubled her. She knew him well enough to be aware that he had an almost sacred reverence for family relics, and that he would be more likely to burn an old cabinet than to sell it to a peddler. Even supposing he had made some lucrative bargains with M. Bertrand, would that suffice to explain the kind of mysterious power which this clown exerted, or the respect with which M. D'Ornis treated him? Why had he turned pale and fallen back when he first recognized him? She recalled also M. Bertrand's words, "This house belongs to me.... If I wanted that coral necklace, I'd only have to ask for it, to get it." Such expressions seemed strange even in the mouth of a drunken man. Then Fanny had heard M. D'Ornis say, "Permit me to observe that you're a rascal!" Would he be likely to talk in that way to a useful animal, whom he expected to meet again in a week, to talk over the price of a table with him?

After turning many times upon her pillow, Marguerite finally fell asleep. About two o'clock, she woke up with a start. She thought she had seen her husband approach her bed, lean over and gaze fixedly at her for a moment, and then suddenly shake his fists above her, heaving a despairing sigh. She sprang from the bed, crying, "What's the matter? What are you doing?" Her cry brought her to herself. There was no one in the room; around her all was still. On listening attentively, however, she thought she heard some one walking in her husband's room, which was separated from her own by a short flight of steps with a narrow landing at their base. She opened the door softly, and saw that the light was still burning in M. D'Ornis's apartment. Her ears had not deceived her: he was walking up and down the room. A few minutes afterward, he heaved a deep sigh, almost as appalling as the one she had heard in her dream. Fearing that he was ill, she sprang forward to assist him. Her hand was already on the latch, when her courage failed her. She remained motionless a few minutes, holding her breath; finally she said in a low voice, "Roger, are you sick?" Probably he did not hear her, for no answer was returned. Soon afterward, he blew out the light and went to bed. Marguerite lay down again, but could not sleep. Every few minutes she would start up and listen. The darkness frightened her; the night seemed very long. The sun was her great friend; he had always brought her consolation with his beams. She had never had a sorrow which had been able to resist the charms of the early morn—the first bright smiles of a pleasant day.

She rose as soon as it was light, opened her window, and inhaled the cold, fresh air of the November morning; then she lay down again, and slept two or three hours. When she awoke, she sought her terrors, but could no longer find them.

CHAPTER XVIII.

THE OLD COUNTESS PLOTS FRESH MISCHIEF.

That day Marguerite saw little of her husband....He went hunting very early in the morning, without asking her to accom pany him. He did not return till dinner-time. His face was dark, a cloud was on his brow. After dinner, he smoked two or three cigars in the park, then entered the little room where his wife was sitting, and after exchanging a few careless words with her, went off to bed. The next day passed in the same manner. The day following, he stated that urgent business called him to Paris, and without saying what this business was, or how long he would be gone, started for the railway station at Blaisy-Bas.

Marguerite employed her days of solitude as best she could. She took some walks, and passed an hour or two every afternoon with an old woman who was paralyzed, and who interested her very much. The rest of her time, she divided between her embroidery and a new piece of music, which she had every opportunity to learn thoroughly.

She was seated at her piano one morning, when a servant announced the old Countess. She was sorry that her mother-in-law had chosen a time when her husband was away to call upon her. It was better to receive her, though, than to pretend she had a headache ; Mme. D'Ornis had not much faith in her daughter's headaches. Marguerite ordered the servant to show her into the large parlor on the ground floor, whither she hastened to meet her. "What is this they tell me, my dear ?" said Mme. D'Ornis holding out her hand. "You're a widow so soon ? How could you let your shepherd go away ? You must have shed whole floods of tears."

"M. D'Ornis was called to Paris on business," Marguerite quietly replied.

"What an ugly word! When did shepherds ever have business to attend to? I thought that was something unheard of in Arcadia. If I had been in your place, I wouldn't have let him go. When a husband, as much in love with his wife as yours, finds business to call him fifty leagues away from her, it marks a new epoch in married life."

"I'm not worried about it," answered Marguerite; "my shepherd will return to me."

"May I inquire what his business is in Paris?"

"He probably wanted to see his banker."

"Probably? Don't you know for sure? I'm more and more astonished; I thought he told you every thing."

"He does tell me all I care to know."

"That's right, my dear!" answered Mme. D'Ornis. "You are strong in faith. It's not the saving kind, but it's useful, notwithstanding. It keeps you from being jealous. Besides, what good would it do if you were to question Roger? Nothing is more disagreeable than a question. When we lived together, he would often discover, while shaving in the morning, that urgent business required his presence at Lyons, Dijon, or even Paris. I would ask him what his business was. He at first used to make up some story for me; but at last he simply answered, 'I'm tired of home, and want a change.'.... The times are very different now; he don't get tired any more."

"Are you fond of music, madam?" interrupted Marguerite. "I have a new piece upstairs that I'd be glad to play for you."

"I don't like any thing but church music. Keep your demi-semi-quavers for the amateurs, my dear..... By the way," she added, "there's a story in our neighborhood about a scene in a bath-room...."

"You forget, madam," said Marguerite with a laugh, "that there's nothing more disagreeable than a question."

"Unless it is advice," she answered, "and yet I'm going to give you some. One does disagreeable things at my age, and foolish things at yours. I was about to tell you that it would be a foolish thing to draw M. Bertrand here."

"I draw him here! I think I received him...."

"Oh! certainly. I know all about it. Your servants are great gossips, and I've been informed that the gentleman made himself very much at home.....The story has amused every body in the neighborhood. It's not because people are malicious, but they want some occupation, and when they can talk about their neighbors...."

"What advice have you to give me?" interrupted Marguerite again, with something like coolness in her tone. "Are you afraid that I'll encourage M. Bertrand's advances?"

"Let's be serious about it. I have already said, and I now repeat, that it's your duty to watch over your husband and to oppose his caprices whenever you can. I don't know what's come over him; it seems as though, during the last few years, he had determined to sell out his property piece by piece. Why does he find it necessary to turn every thing into money? Last year he sold M. Du Rozan a large field and a strip of woods, answering all my remonstrances by saying, 'Money is worthless trash, but we must have it.' The most absurd of all his whims, though, is his fancy for M. Bertrand. This man has been banished from all respectable society; he's received nowhere excepting at this house. While I was mistress here, he twice visited the castle. I managed so well that he went off without taking any thing with him. Just think what a bad effect it would have, my dear, to see a load of old relics and family portraits leave the castle. And then people would blame you for it. They would say that you were ignorant of the common courtesies of life...."

"They're not to be learned in a carpenter's shop," said Marguerite. "How much the poor carpenters have to answer for."

"I have nothing against them. There's room for every body in this world. It seems to me, though, that this ought to be a matter of honor with you....Among the family portraits that M. Bertrand covets there are some of real merit. That's another strange thing about Roger. Formerly he used to like to have these portraits about him, and had them hung up in his office. Now the wind has changed; in the unsettled state of mind in which Raoux's death left him, he had them all carried to the garret, telling me that he couldn't bear to see them staring at him. I particularly commend to your care a crayon drawing by Latour, about as large as your hand. It's a portrait of a great-aunt of Roger's, a D'Epinac, taken at the age of twenty-five. She is in a ball dress, and has a rose in her hair. Her hair was beautiful, and of a color just like yours, my dear. The poor lady had an eventful life. Her husband, who began by worshiping her, ended by beating her. Such things do happen sometimes. One day she ran away with her lover, and such a lover!—he was a lawyer's clerk. ....May God have mercy on him! When she had had enough of her dear clerk, she entered a convent; she died with an odor of sanctity about her. Her portrait is marvelously beautiful. Picture to yourself a lovely face, with a pink and white complexion, a little pouting mouth, and handsome brown eyes—they were something like yours, too, only they were quite deceitful. You can almost see the lawyer's clerk, if you search them carefully. It would be a sad thing to have such a treasure fall into M. Bertrand's hands. Take good care of it, I beg of you. You ought to talk seriously to Roger...."

"Why don't you speak to him, yourself, madam?"

"It would do no good, I have no influence over him now. You have succeeded to my rights, it's just that you should bear my burdens too....Ah! does your shepherd frighten you? I believe in proverbs, my dear. If you treat the wolf too well, the wolf will eat you."

As she spoke, she drew her cashmere shawl over her shoulders, rose from her seat, and again pressed her daughter-in-law's hand, saying, "You ought to take advantage of your husband's absence to come and dine with me without ceremony; then we can have a good talk together. I can give you an omelette, since you like them, and can season it to suit your taste, I think."

"I'm always suspicious of the seasoning," replied Marguerite with a smile.

"Will you come?"

"I prefer to wait till M. D'Ornis returns."

The old Countess broke into a harsh laugh, which displayed all her pointed teeth. "To tell the truth," she said, "you don't dare to dine with me without asking your tyrant's leave. You certainly are afraid of him."

Marguerite accompanied her to the gate. "Ah!" she said to herself as she saw her moving away, "you are a bad woman, and I shall not try to love you."

She went upstairs again, and opening her new piece of music, played it through. While shutting her piano, she thought of an old woman at Geneva, who was noted for her cross and ugly disposition, and who never called on her acquaintances, without making some spiteful flings at them, or telling them some unpleasant story about themselves, that was circulating through the neighborhood. Uncle Benjamin detested this old vixen, and as soon as he caught sight of her, always cried, "Look out! here comes that hateful animal...." This brought to her mind another phrase of Uncle Benjamin's, an answer that he always gave her, when she was a little girl, and asked him about things that she could not understand. "There, there, Margot," he would say, "when you are grown up, you will find that there are a great many things in a *chosier.*" "What is a *chosier*, Uncle?" she would ask. "It's whatever the Lord uses to put things in. The great *chosier* is the world, and there are a great many little *chosiers*, such as a young girl's head, and it's a harder thing to understand than you have any idea of." Yes, indeed! she thought; it is difficult to understand.

She tried to work on her embroidery, but she was too nervous to fix her attention on it. It seemed as if some venomous insect had stung her. She wanted to bathe in the fresh air. She put on a gray felt hat trimmed with red feathers, threw over her shoulders a cloak of velvet lined with fur, and started for the park. In passing through the parlor, she saw her figure reflected in the glass, and stopped to look at herself a moment. "I don't see but you look well enough," she said. "I don't believe you could find another such handsome head of hair within ten miles of here. The great trouble is, that in your little *chosier* there's a longing for such happiness as can not be found within this house. The ceilings are too high for it."

A moment afterward, she descended the steps, and went into the park, drawing her feet through the dead leaves that covered the walks, and listening to the sad rustling that they made. She soon grew tired of this music, and sat down on a bench at the base of the noseless statue. She gazed for a long time at the castle and its massive architecture. "How immense it is!" she thought, and for the first time she asked herself, if it were not a caprice of fortune that had brought her there..... "The linnet wants a nest, and not an eagle's eyry," she said. "I take up so little room and this castle is so large, I feel quite lost in it. If I had been trained for this kind of life from the time that I was ten years old, I might, perhaps, have grown to like it. The people that I grew up among were no better than any others; they scolded and quarreled and were jealous, just like those that live in castles. They were always frank and open-hearted, though, and they lived too near each other to surround themselves with mystery. When husbands went away, they gave a reason for it, and if their wives were troubled, they always had their household duties, their knitting, or their accounts to occupy them. What have I to do? I'm not permitted to attend to any thing. As soon as the dinner is ordered, I have the whole day before me, and don't know what to do with it. My greatest misfortune," she added, "is that I've always lived with those who loved me dearly, and I've become accustomed to it. There's only one person here that cares for me, and I don't see him very often. Every one else that I meet, is all the time watching to see me say or do some foolish thing. The worst of it is, I can not live without love, for vanity does not help me in the least." She felt herself drawn on by this current of sad thoughts, and her gayety left her for the moment, She rose and, with folded arms, paced slowly round and round the statue. At last, picking up a pine cone from the grass, she murmured, "It's a little pet no larger than this I want. Those little darlings help fill up the time." Then, holding the cone in her hand, she stood looking at the battered statue of James D'Ornis, Field-Marshal and Commander of the Holy Ghost. Notwithstanding the irreparable outrages which time had inflicted on his countenance, his frank and martial face pleased Marguerite. "You look like a good man," she said, "in spite of your missing nose, and it seems as though I could talk with you. You have been in the camp and in the court; you are acquainted with the world and the vicissitudes of life; you have no set ideas and narrow prejudices, like some people that I know. Perhaps if you were to return to life, you would be surprised to find Marguerite Mirion here, talking so familiarly with your statue; perhaps you would be astonished to learn that she had become a member of your family. You must judge things by their fruits, however. If I am ever fortunate enough to present your house an heir, he shall be worthy of you. I will teach him to be noble-minded both in what he loves and what he hates; I will strive to kindle in his breast that courage which enables us to struggle for the right, and even to die bravely for it at Nerwinde,—for that's where you died, old fellow!" she added, leaning forward to read the inscription on the pedestal. At this moment, she noticed that she was still holding the pine cone in her hand. She put it to her lips and, closing her eyes, covered it with kisses, until coming to herself and laughing at her folly, she threw it far away upon the lawn.

CHAPTER XIX.

CURIOSITY AGAIN AT WORK.

Marguerite turned back toward the castle. Her conversation with the field-marshal had rendered her more cheerful; she felt disposed to think better of herself and of those about her. "It's very singular, though," she thought. "I've just promised that old stone hero that I would teach my son to become a brave man, and yet it would be safe to wager ten to one, that I'll not have sufficient courage to even mention the matter of the portraits."

As she thought of the pictures, she became somewhat curious to see them, especially the portrait of that poor young Marchioness D'Epinac, who had been first loved, then beaten by her husband, and who had finally eloped with a clerk. She felt touched by her misfortunes, though she could not excuse her errors; true women are so constituted that they love and pity while they condemn. She hastily returned to the house. Before starting on her search, as she wished to have no one know what she was about, she sent her husband's valet with a letter to the post, and dispatched Fanny with a message to the sick woman whom she was in the habit of visiting. She could not help laughing at her own precautions. "Any one would think it was a crime to visit a garret," she thought. "I'm almost as much frightened as Blue Beard's wife was, when she entered the mysterious room."

As soon as she found herself alone, she went up to the third story, passed through the corridor, ran quickly up a wooden staircase that she found upon her left, and stopped before a great carved oaken door, which had a very uncompromising look, as though it were accustomed to keep away intruders. She opened it, notwithstanding, though not without great difficulty; she had to use both hands to turn the key. The door grated harshly as it swung upon its hinges, seeming to utter a cry of complaint or protestation. It had been taught to dislike curious people.

The garret was lighted by two large dormer windows, and did not appear to be either dark or uncomfortable. It was in good order and not very dusty. The pieces of furniture that filled it were arranged in rows like files of soldiers; it was an easy matter to pass them in review. Marguerite, who was experienced in such matters, saw very quickly that there was nothing among them of much value. She thought she would not try to keep them from M. Bertrand. She passed on to the portraits, which were leaning against the wall; it was easy to recognize the members of her adopted family. All these D'Ornis resembled each other; they were dark and thin, with narrow, compressed lips, hooked noses, gleaming eyes, and dark, stern brows. "What a lot of night-hawks!" thought Marguerite; "those large brows seem full of secrets." She was delighted, at last, at finding the charming portrait of the Marchioness D'Epinac; it was in the bottom of a chest, wrapped up in a piece of canvas. As she saw it, she gave a little cry of pleasure and admiration. The picture was a gem; Mme. D'Ornis had not exaggerated its merits in the least. The expression of the eyes was strange; Marguerite did not discover the lawyer's clerk, but she thought she could perceive within them a gentle sadness, a vague presentiment of evil, a mystery of melancholy and gloomy expectation. She sat down on the chest to gaze leisurely at this portrait which seemed to fascinate her; she could not turn her eyes away from it. "It's true," she said; "it does resemble me a little. The hair, the neck.... Ah! I see, the mouth is too small; it would be impossible to laugh with such a mouth. It may be well enough in a picture, but in real life, I shouldn't like it at all... She must have been a melancholy Marguerite. Her eyes are searching the mysterious future. I would rather have smaller eyes and a larger mouth, I think."

She began to laugh aloud, as though to show the portrait how to do it. As her voice resounded through the garret, it frightened her. It seemed as though it were wrong to be merry there.

"Why shouldn't I laugh?" she said. Then looking at all the D'Ornis staring at her, she added, "That kind of people don't like to see others happy." So saying, she turned their faces back against the wall. As she was about putting Mme. D'Epinac into her chest, she felt that she could not be separated from her. She thought it would be too bad to have this charming Marchioness fall into M. Bertrand's hands, that she would plead her cause when the time came, and, meanwhile, would take care of her, and make a companion of her in her solitary hours.

She carried the portrait to her room, and looked at it often during the day. While she was undressing, it stood upon her toilet table, and when she went to bed, she took it with her, talking to it, and making it tell its story. "So he first loved and afterward beat you," she said. "Why did he do it? You were not a coquette, and he was not jealous. Perhaps you made him angry; perhaps you talked too much with your mother-in-law. You can't be too cautious with such sharp people.... And so, one day, not being able to bear such treatment any longer, you ran off with a clerk. Was he very handsome? Whether he was or not, you soon found out how heartless your lover was.... Then you made your peace with God by entering a convent. There seems to be a charm in a nun's veil; it drives away sad memories. That's a resource I could never have. I should suffer remorse for twenty years. Twenty years of remorse! I think I'd rather kill myself."

She fell asleep still holding the portrait in her hands. In the morning, her first glance fell upon it. Springing from bed, she hastily thrust the Marchioness into a drawer. She had just finished dressing, when she heard a well-known voice and step upon the stairs, and Roger entered the room.

"Has any thing happened while I've been away?" he asked.

"No; nothing ever happens here. How did you find Paris?"

"The same as ever.... Have you received any calls?"

"None at all.... Oh! yes, there was one. Your mother came to see me."

"What did she have to say?"

"She came to ask me to dine with her, but I told her I preferred to wait till you came back."

"You're a good wife, and I believe you mean to do what's right."

He kissed her forehead as he spoke. He was in such good humor that she resolved to speak to him about the portraits. A letter from her father, which was handed her at this moment, however, changed the current of her thoughts. This letter, which had been delayed by some mistake, informed her that Uncle Benjamin had had an apoplectic fit, that the physicians were in doubt as to his recovery, and that knowing how seriously ill he was, he had expressed a strong desire to see his niece. Marguerite showed the letter to her husband, and asked his permission to make a three days' visit to Geneva. "That's very unfortunate," he said, "I wanted you to go with me to the Morvan hills to-morrow."

As she persisted in her request, he finally said with a harshness that deeply pained her, "Yes, you may go, and I'll forgive your uncle, but only on condition that he won't get well again."

The express train from Paris to Geneva passed through Beaune during the night. It was arranged that Marguerite should leave for Beaune immediately after dinner, and the carriage was ordered for eight o'clock. Her husband appeared very much annoyed; she did not wish to speak to him about the portraits: it would be too much to displease him twice in the same day. What should she do with Mme. D'Epinac? The picture was set in a costly frame, ornamented with garnets. Marguerite feared that if M. Bertrand should return during her absence and the portrait could not be found, some servant would be accused of taking it to obtain the garnets. She determined to carry Mme. D'Epinac back to her chest. In the afternoon as she was walking in the park with M. D'Ornis, she was twenty times on the point of telling him of her expedition of the day before, of the prize that she had found, and of the value that she set upon it. She began to speak, but stopped, and although the hero of Neerwinden seemed looking down upon her from his pedestal, and recalling to her mind the brave words she had uttered, her courage failed her. She left M. D'Ornis pretending that she had to finish preparing for her journey, and after stopping in her room to get the picture, stole quietly to the garret to return it to its place.

She found the door wide open, and noticed on entering, that some one had aired and dusted the room that morning. She concluded from this that it was a dangerous place to visit, as M. D'Ornis probably expected his customer there that afternoon. Although she made all possible haste, it took some time to arrange the chest, so that no one would suspect that curious hands had been at work there. As she rose up, she struck her head against a beam; she rested it in her hand a moment, and in doing so, noticed that she had lost a lilac bow, which had been fastened in her hair. She hunted for it a long time without success, and finally persuaded herself that she had dropped it, while passing with her husband through the dense thickets of the park. She prepared to retreat, and had already descended one flight of stairs, when she heard voices on the floor below. She listened attentively; the sounds came nearer. She soon recognized M. D'Ornis's voice, and a moment afterward heard the hollow tones of M. Bertrand. "Now I'm caught," she thought. Yielding to her first impulse, she ran lightly up the steps that she had just descended. At the entrance to the garret, she stopped to think a moment, and reproached herself for her childish fear. "I must be crazy," she thought. "What can be simpler than to explain it to him?.... Yes, but I ought to have told him about it in the park. I left him, pretending that I wanted to get ready for my journey. I've told a white lie already, and he will not forgive me. Besides, he's so suspicious! He will believe that I have the most horrible designs in view; and, moreover, he can't control himself when he is angry. He will speak harshly to me before that man. Every body in the neighborhood will hear of it. It would make Mme. D'Ornis too happy."

The voices had approached still nearer. Marguerite ran quickly across the garret, and hid herself in a dark closet, separated from the main portion of the room by a partition, the boards of which had drawn apart, leaving wide cracks between them. In this closet stood an old arm-chair, half hidden behind an immense chest. Before seating herself in this chair, Marguerite revolved the matter in her mind again. "If they should find me here, it would be a serious thing. Well! I don't care. I'll confess all, and tell them that Mme. D'Epinac is very dear to me, that I don't wish to part with her, that I'm ready to pay a double price, and that she belongs by right to the highest bidder." She thus excused her present fear, in consideration of the brilliant courage she intended to display. So our consciences are formed. As soon as they begin to hesitate, they are sure to find excuses and expedients. The truth is, Marguerite was frightened, and when a frightened person finds an arm-chair hidden behind a chest, it is an easy matter to settle down in it, and take the chances of being discovered there.

CHAPTER XX.

A STARTLING REVELATION.

Marguerite had scarcely reached her hiding place, when M. D'Ornis appeared at the door of the garret, followed by M. Bertrand, who was panting and out of breath. After having closed the door, Roger cast a quick glance about him, as though to make sure that no one was hidden in the room. This glance, however, did not penetrate the thick darkness of the closet. M. Bertrand threw himself down heavily on a sofa in the corner, the worn-out springs of which groaned beneath his weight. "Ugh! Count, I'm all out of breath," he said in a familiar tone. "There was no use in climbing up so far. We should have been much more comfortable in your library.... As regards all this stuff up here, I told you last year what I thought of it. It's none of it worth any thing, except a few frames, and one or two portraits. You look on those as family relics, and you know I always respect such feelings....Still, if you want to make a trade, I'll give you a thousand francs, if you'll allow me to pick out whatever suits me. You could pass the amount over to your credit on our little account."

He rose and walked about the room, as though taking an account of stock, shrugging his shoulders, nodding his head, and puffing out his cheeks with a contemptuous air. He had reached the door of the closet and had already stepped within it, when M. D'Ornis, who had been following him, caught him roughly by the arm and motioned him to take a seat. "Very well! we'll say no more about it," he said, turning his back to the little room. "A count always has a great respect for his ancestors and for all the old things they've left behind them, and is never willing to sell any of them, even when he has a bargain offered him. I understand you very well, though perhaps you don't think I do. Although I'm a low-born fellow, I respect the aristocracy, and think it perfectly right that there should be a class representing refined and noble sentiments. What would become of society without such sentiments, I'd like to know?"

So saying, he sat down again, putting his muddy shoes upon the sofa. M. D'Ornis remained standing in front of him, leaning against a sideboard, and scanning him from head to foot without speaking a single word. "Don't you suppose I know what you're thinking about?" continued M. Bertrand with a malicious grin. "You're figuring up my chances of life. You're saying to yourself, 'There's a stout fellow, with a red face and a short, thick neck; he's certainly apoplectic, and some lucky accident may rid me of him soon'....I'd very much like to oblige you. It won't do to trust too much to appearances though. My father was just my build; he died at eighty-two, and I'm only fifty-three. You see there's considerable margin....By the way, where's the money?"

M. D'Ornis at last made up his mind to speak. "What money?" he asked. "Your demands are ridiculous; I didn't suppose you were in earnest."

"You are mistaken, then. You know well enough that I'm always in earnest."

"May I inquire, M. Bertrand, what you are doing with your money? I'm told that your business is very good...."

"Don't believe it. The times are hard, good bargains are very scarce, and customers are getting more suspicious every day. Suspicion is the great evil of the present time; it's the ruin of such fellows as me. Take pictures for example. The devil himself couldn't sell a picture nowadays. Your customer grins and says, 'What! that miserable little daub! it's nothing but a copy.'....Last year I bought ten Peruginos in one lot, and they were genuine too, upon my honor. I've got them all to-day. No one wants to deal in Peruginos."

"What you mean," said M. D'Ornis with an expression of the deepest scorn, "is that you are living extravagantly, and wasting your money in riot and on women...."

"What if I did spend my money on women!" answered the other with a disdainful air. "Are not women the consolation of life?

It's not often that you'll find such handsome ones as your wife is....You're mistaken, though; I don't give myself up to such follies. My plan is to invest my little savings in real estate. There's a house at Guillotière that I've had my eye on for some time. I want about thirty thousand francs to make up the purchase money, and I come to you to get it. It's all as plain as daylight."

M. D'Ornis violently struck his forehead with his hand. "Have you sworn to ruin me?" he said. "Fifty thousand francs the first time, forty thousand last year, thirty thousand now...."

"Well! that's only a hundred and twenty thousand in all, and you get from your estate six hundred thousand at least. You see you've got plenty left....Then your father-in-law! I've made my little inquiries: they write me from Geneva that he's a millionaire."

"I've shown you my marriage contract. You know as well as I do that my wife brings me no fortune. Her father has given her three hundred thousand francs for her own use, but I have no control whatever over it."

"Is her father such a stingy fellow?" replied M. Bertrand with an appearance of sincere indignation. "Why! he's worse than an old Jew....It seems to me he ought to do more, considering the honor you've conferred upon him....Margoton has become a countess, you see. Those old fellows generally pay well for such things. Don't you think there's some way to make this one settle?"

Marguerite did not lose a single word of this conversation. The latter portion of it grieved her deeply. She remembered how persistently her husband had refused the dowry. What she had looked upon as a refinement of delicacy was really a matter of prudence with him. What was this danger which had rendered him so careful? Who was this insolent borrower, who did not ask for money as a favor, but claimed it as a right? What gave him the power to speak so boldly? He seemed like a gambler holding the winning card. What was this card? Was he not on the point of playing it? Marguerite shuddered as she thought, What am I about to hear? what is this secret? She felt that her future depended on it, that her fate hung, as it were, on the thick, brutish lips of this low fellow, who was now compelling the proudest of men to listen to him, to hear him say, "Margoton has become a countess." The poor girl wanted to fly; but, even if fear had not retained her in the chair, she felt that she was firmly fastened there, by an eager, feverish curiosity.

"You impudent rascal!" cried M. D'Ornis after a moment's silence. "Why did I ever consent, in a moment of weakness and folly, to do this thing. You agreed, for a certain sum, never to trouble me again. You're a robber, Monsieur Bertrand! a robber, do you understand? I'll let you know what I think of you."

"A robber!" replied M. Bertrand without exhibiting the slightest feeling. "Where did you get that idea? It isn't so at all. I'm a man of principle, I'd have you know. I don't believe in doing any thing that isn't right; I understand the laws which govern my trade, and don't intend to break them....There, don't get angry, don't be unreasonable; you'll get your money back again some day. You shouldn't talk of having done a foolish thing. What you did was very sensible, I think. You agreed to pay a ransom for what?....Count D'Ornis's head, that's all. If life without money is worth but little, money without life isn't worth any thing. Come, you mustn't talk so to your preserver, especially when he's so kind to you, and is a man of principle besides. Your ingratitude really pains me. I know very well, that you don't like my face, and don't want to have me calling on you. I've been to see you only three times in the last three years; it seems to me that's considerate enough. This year, too, from a feeling of delicacy, I said to myself, 'Let him enjoy the honey-moon in peace, and since he dislikes the sight of my big nose, God grant he may forget it for three months at least!' I must live, though; I can't put myself out of existence to oblige you. I'm an intermittent bore, that's so much in your favor....Good Lord! if I was in your place, I'd be delighted to see that rascally robber, M. Bertrand, give some signs of life now and then. I come here to ask for money. Damn it, if I hadn't a love for money, Count D'Ornis would be rotting in the ground to-day. Do you want to know what I do with the money that you give me? It's well invested, I can tell you; it quiets my remorse, for every body has a conscience, as you told me once. Every body has some weak point too. I'm no exception to the rule; a door well greased makes no noise, you know.... Perhaps you won't believe me, but on my honor, there are nights when I can't sleep, nights when I see by my bed the white face of the man, who...."

M. D'Ornis did not let him finish; he hurriedly drew out a pocket-book, and threw it violently in the speaker's face.

"Well done!" cried M. Bertrand. "When I have bank bills thrown at me, I'm willing to excuse the way it's done, provided they count up all right."

He opened the pocket-book, and drew out a package of bills which he began to count; then dipping an imaginary pen into an equally imaginary ink-stand, and pretending to write, he said, "Received from Count D'Ornis, one hundred and twenty thousand francs, to be returned upon demand."

So saying, he pocketed the bills.

"Where is my receipt? I want a receipt!" cried M. D'Ornis.

"Go and get one then. What nonsense! Am I in the habit of giving receipts? One merchant ought to trust another merchant's honor. My dear Count, you haven't got a line of my writing, while I have some of yours, I think."

M. D'Ornis here gave way to another fit of passion. He turned toward M. Bertrand with his teeth set and his fists clenched. "Give me that paper!" he cried. "What do you want for it? fifty thousand francs? a hundred thousand?"

"Much obliged!" answered M. Bertrand rising from the sofa. "I might sell it some time perhaps.... A hundred thousand francs is a fair sum. The trouble is, that scrawl of yours hasn't a fixed price. If the old fellow at Geneva should die to-morrow and you should get his pile, that precious little paper would be worth a million."

M. D'Ornis could control himself no longer. He uttered a savage cry, and started forward as though to seize his enemy. The latter, however, caught up his stick, and falling back a step, placed himself on guard. "Don't try that on me," he said; "I know your temper well enough. What's the use of acting so? If you should search me from head to foot, you couldn't find your paper. I don't risk my valuables in such a way."

M. D'Ornis had come to himself again. Showing the door to M. Bertrand, he cried, "Get out, you villain! If you ever dare show yourself here again, I'll have you beaten within an inch of your life."

At these words, M. Bertrand's jovial humor deserted him. Steadying himself on his immense feet, with reddened face and staring eyes, he answered in a voice of thunder, "I'll come here when I please, and if you...."

M. D'Ornis motioned him to stop. He had heard some one coming up the stairs. It was Jerome, his valet, who had come to tell him that the Marquis Du Rozan was below, waiting to speak to him. "So you won't take any less, Count?" said M. Bertrand, changing his tone. "The portraits are not worth so much, upon my honor. Is that the best you'll do?....There's no use in talking then. We'll have to change about; I'll be the seller, and you can be the buyer. You told me you had a great liking for Peruginos, I've got a dozen of them. They're magnificent pictures. I'll send them to you, and I guarantee you'll keep the whole lot. When a man likes such things, you know...."

He began to descend the stairs; M. D'Ornis followed, pushing the door of the garret to behind him. Marguerite left her hiding place, and descended to her room; she did not take the least precaution against discovery, she was so bewildered and confused. Fortunately she was to start that very evening for Geneva. She wanted to begin her journey at once, but before doing so had to take dinner with her husband. The very thought terrified her. How could she control her countenance so that it should not betray her? She trembled like a leaf on her way to the dining-room. M. D'Ornis sent down word that he had a headache and did not care for any dinner. She breathed more freely; still she could not go without bidding him good-by. At eight o'clock precisely, she knocked at his door. "Who's that? what do you want?" he cried in a loud voice.

"It's me.... I'm going."

"Where to?.... O yes, I forgot."

He opened the door half way. Marguerite had been careful to lower her veil. "Good-by," he said in a sad tone. "Come back with your gay spirits as soon as you can, for you are gay and happy as a lark, God bless you!"

"Are you in much pain?" she timidly asked.

"Yes, here and here," he answered, pointing to his head and heart.

During the whole journey, from eight o'clock in the evening to eleven the next morning, Marguerite had but one thought, one occupation; she was reviewing all the details of that interview in the garret, and asking herself the question, "What is the man who calls himself my husband?"

So absorbed was she in these gloomy thoughts, that on hearing the cry, "Geneva! all out here!" she shuddered and said to herself, "Geneva! am I in Geneva? What did I come here for? Oh! I remember, my uncle is sick, perhaps dead. What difference does it make to me? It will not lessen my gay spirits, for I am bright, and gay, and proud besides, as the wife of Count D'Ornis ought to be."

CHAPTER XXI.

MARGUERITE AT HOME.

Uncle Benjamin was not dead. Favorable symptoms had set in, and, to use the mythological language of which he was so fond, had brought him swiftly back from the dark shores of Acheron. They had sent the news to Marguerite two days before, but the letter had not arrived in time to prevent her journey.

If there ever was a joyful home, it was Mon-Plaisir on this long-to-be-remembered day. A little boy, watching his cows in a neighboring field, was the first to see Countess D'Ornis. He gave the alarm at once. The news spread like wildfire; cows, dogs, horses, and chickens, all caught the infection, and from kitchen to parlor, from poultry yard to stable, every heart danced with joy. Scarcely had Marguerite's foot touched the ground, when she was surrounded, questioned, petted, and pushed about from every side. In this storm of words and kisses, it seemed to her as though Mon-Plaisir had a hundred doors, from each of which came forth a father, mother, aunt, and cousin. She scarcely knew what to do or say.

When she had answered, as she could, their questions, and returned their greetings, her mother, who was impatient to have her to herself, threw her arms about her waist and drew, or more correctly speaking, carried her to her room, on entering which she locked the door. Then she took off her hat, made her sit down in an arm-chair, knelt on a cushion at her feet, took both her hands within her own, and fixed her eyes upon her face. "Well! my darling, are you happy?" she cried in joyous tones. "Very happy, mamma," replied Marguerite, as soon as she could catch her breath.

Thereupon Mme. Mirion talked to her for two hours in a steady stream. "Dear me! how lovely you look!" she said. "I believe you've grown handsomer than ever. You're a little pale and your eyes look heavy, but it all comes from your journey, and will soon pass away. You are happy, are you not? He worships you, doesn't he? You owe it all to me. You always had so many ifs and buts, whenever we talked about the marriage. You must confess that you didn't like it, and that I almost forced you into it. How sorry I am that he didn't come with you! They all laugh at me, and pretend that I'm in love with him. That stupid Benjamin with his prophecies of evil.....To hear him, you'd think we had driven you to the slaughter. Dear me! I'm glad he's getting better, but I never did feel worried about him; disagreeable people always do come round all right. Every thing here must seem small enough to you; the ceilings are very low. We can't help it, dear; we haven't a castle, you know. Then your lake! tell me all about it. What! it's only an ugly pond? Pshaw! ask your husband to make you another then. A man who worships you, couldn't refuse you a lake. Your letters, you see, are very good, only they have no news in them. You write, 'The weather is fine; I am well and love you dearly.' We have to guess all the rest. One thing, I've guessed, is that your mother-in-law pets you a great deal, and that you have a party nearly every day. I gave Mme. Patet a dose, the last time I saw her. You know those people feel very grand because their Emily married a rich merchant. When they heard of our marriage, it made them pretty sick, and I heard that they went about saying, 'Those Mirions are trying to reach too high; they'll get enough of it before they're through.' Day before yesterday, I met the old fright with her three freckled-faced daughters, and took occasion to tell her that you were the happiest of wives, that your husband worshiped you, and that every single day, you had a baron to breakfast and two or three duchesses to dinner. She almost died with envy. But that isn't all. There's one question I'm dying to ask you.....What! isn't it so? I remember how it was with me; the first I knew I wanted oranges, oh! so much. Haven't you felt so at all? I want you to make haste, for I must have four little D'Ornis, at least. We'll fix it so that your doctor will order Swiss air for them, and every year I'll dance all four of them together on my knees."

M. Mirion was as much pleased as his wife, but he did not talk so much. He was satisfied to look at Marguerite, and to cry as he tossed his suuff-box in the air, "There's our dear girl home again !" Cousin Grillet gazed humbly and silently upon her, as a beadle contemplates a bishop. Mlle. Baillet questioned her concerning the manners and customs of Burgundy, and concluded from her answers that there were only two things wanting to complete the happiness of the people there, an equestrian order and a grand duchess dowager. As regarded Uncle Benjamin, who had not yet left his easy-chair, when he saw her entering his room, he cried, "Margot, your uncle has seen Charon's boat very near, but the grim ferryman would not receive him ; he begged me to return to earth again, and I am glad now it's so, since I see you so happy and contented. Does every thing go well with you ? Do those D'Ornis treat you with respect ? Is your husband kind to you ? Well, well, this affair has turned out better than that mother of yours deserves. She talks of nothing but her son-in-law, and regales us with him the whole day long, making the most horrible rollings with her eyes and tongue. To hear her, you'd think that D'Ornis was spelt with three *r*s and four *s*s. The devil take such nonsense ; I've had enough of it."

Mme. Mirion made all manner of plans to exhibit her daughter and her delight. She was not one of those misers who keep their treasures to themselves, and are careful never to display them in public ; she wanted the whole universe to share her happiness. Two different ideas came to her. One, which she kept to herself, was to hire a show window in the most public street of Geneva, and to have Countess D'Ornis stand in it for an entire day. The other was to give a grand dinner party, followed by music, an illumination, and Bengal lights—this was the way her parties always ended. Marguerite had hard work to dissuade her from this scheme ; she told her that she had only three days to spend at Mon-Plaisir, that such an affair could not be gotten up without preparation, that the musicians were so engaged that they could not come, that she had brought no party dresses with her, and that she preferred her dear old room, with its empty flower-stands and withered rose-bushes, to all the Patets in the world. She could not, however, refuse to go occasionally with her mother to the city, where Mme. Mirion invented all kinds of pretexts to make her walk the streets for hours, while her flashing eyes seemed to say, " Sound the trumpets ! She is here !"

Although she was spared the party, Marguerite found no rest during the first two days she spent at Mon-Plaisir. To have one fixed idea preying on the mind and be compelled to conceal it from every eye, to so command the face and voice that no suspicion be aroused, to hold back the starting tears and keep a forced smile upon the lips, is a cruelly fatiguing task. Mme. Mirion said to her daughter, "Now tell us all about your parlor, and how it's furnished." All the time that she was giving the description of the parlor, Marguerite saw before her a garret and two men disputing there. Uncle Benjamin, who loved to talk, inquired of her what the history of Ornis was. While answering that Ornis was a model canton, where all the virtues flourished, where the husbands were all faithful, and the wives above reproach, she kept saying to herself, " What is this mystery ? what is this horrible debt that a hundred and twenty thousand francs will not suffice to pay ?" When they asked her if her husband was not thinking of taking her to Paris or to Italy, she answered that Ornis was such a charming place, they could not bear to leave it, and at the same time she thought, " I'll tell him that I was there, that I heard every thing, that I can not sleep and can not live, unless he tells me the whole truth, unless I know who it is that I now call my husband !"

The day before her departure, Marguerite received a call from the Protestant minister of the parish, the one who had prepared her for her first communion, and afterward had married her. Although this worthy clergyman had no confessional in his church, he took great pleasure in confessing his flock whenever he had an opportunity, a taste which he possessed in common with a number of his brethren. He questioned Marguerite at length, asking her whether marriage had proved to be all that she expected, whether she had found her husband to be the ideal of her dreams, and whether, thus far, she had met with any unpleasant experiences or painful deceptions ; last of all, he offered her his sympathy and his advice—he had come prepared at every point. She met his curiosity with a calm, impenetrable face, eluded his questions, and declined his proffered services with a polite dignity which somewhat mortified him. Men of the church, whether Catholics or Protestants, love to see others seeking their holy ointments.

As he was about to leave her, he said in an affected tone, "Persons of your character think they are above temptation. It's a dangerous illusion."

"What is my character?" she inquired with a smile.

"Certain souls," he answered, "conceal strong passions beneath a cold and calm exterior."

"Passions! I don't know what they are. I have but little imagination and little force of character; it would be impossible for me to be very angry, to violently hate, or passionately love any human creature."

"You mustn't trust too much to appearances. When you were my pupil, I looked upon you as a tranquil lake, and I have often noticed that these quiet lakes are the most terrible in storms. It's always well to keep a watch upon yourself."

"And to confess to your minister," mentally added Marguerite, as she accompanied him to the door. "My tongue is tied," she thought, "and I know of no one in the world, who can help me bear the burden that is weighing on my heart."

CHAPTER XXII.

AN OLD FLAME REKINDLED.

Marguerite passed the night that followed battling with her thoughts. Not able to sleep and yet not quite awake, she would lose her senses for a moment and then regain them with a sudden start, only to pass from frightful visions to still more terrible realities. In these waking dreams were mingled her remembrances, presentiments, and terrors; they brought before her a confusion of large noses, red beards, English horses, little mouths that never smiled, pale faces seeking something, she knew not what, and dead eyes which opened in the night to terrify the living. She finally had a dream much more distinct than these confused and painful visions. The scene of it was in a garret. She saw herself seated in an arm-chair which she thought concealed her; little by little the back of this chair became transparent, and a voice at which she shuddered cried, "She has my secret, I will have her life!"

She sat erect in bed and tried to gather up her courage; she could not find it, it had all been spent during the last two days in smiles and falsehoods. In a few hours she was to return to Ornis. What should she do? Would she be bold enough to speak, or strong enough to keep silence and dissimulate? Every thing appeared frightful or impossible to her. She had no counselor; she was alone in the world, alone with her secret. She was filled with terror; Ornis seemed like a gloomy cavern to her, her future was shadowed by dark clouds.

Scarcely were the first faint streaks of dawn visible on the horizon, when Marguerite arose. After dressing hastily and throwing an old shawl over her head, she went out, hoping that the fresh morning air would comfort her. This time, however, the dawn brought no consolation with it. Neither earth, nor sky, nor dew, nor the gray eyes of morn, to use the poet's words, had any thing to say to her. She crossed the garden, and walked straight forward, seeing nothing but the dark pictures of her dreams, hearing nothing but her troubled thoughts. On reaching the clump of willows, her strength deserted her; she dropped wearily upon a bench, and placing her face within her hands, burst into tears. She little suspected that a man had followed her and was looking at her, and that this man was Joseph Noirel.

Joseph had remained faithful to his design. Since Marguerite's departure, he had been slowly amassing a sufficient sum to carry him to America, to place the sea between himself and his sad thoughts. He sighed for the day when, newly landed on the wharf at New-York, he should be able to shake off the dust of the old world, and the ashes of his dead folly. He kept steadily at work; no fault could be found with him in that regard. He was often busy at his bench until late at night. He had obtained M. Mirion's permission to take his meals at the eating-house and to sleep in the shop. Sometimes a week would pass without his appearing at Mon-Plaisir. M. Mirion dared not complain; he knew that at the first remonstrance, Joseph would desert him.

On the evening of her arrival, Marguerite was surprised not to see Joseph at the table, and asked what had become of him. "Don't speak to me about the boy!" Mme. Mirion had replied. "He's completely spoiled. Blood will always tell, he will end up like his father. We don't see him any more—the society of honest people doesn't seem to please him. I'd be willing to bet that he has taken to drink, and is going to ruin. He's got a stone where his heart ought to be. Would you believe that since you've been away, he has never asked after you but once, and that, one day when I was reading a letter of yours out loud, he went out of the room laughing."

"You're too hard on the boy, Marianne," M. Mirion replied. "He never takes any amusement and is nearly killing himself with work. I admit that he's cross and sulky, that he reads bad books, that he's growing to be a socialist and an incendiary, and that it's almost impossible to talk with him. If we're only patient, though, it will pass off like the chicken-pox."

"Couldn't he be informed that I should be sorry to go away without seeing him?" asked Marguerite.

"He'd only keep away the more," her mother answered.

On learning from M. Mirion of Marguerite's unexpected arrival, Joseph was seized by a feeling of intense bitterness against fate, which, by compelling him to look again on the enemy of his repose, seemed to take delight in reopening his wound and preventing it from healing. He determined to keep away from her, and for two days adhered to his resolve. On the evening of the third he felt his determination growing weaker; his desires were more powerful than his reason. His eyes longed to look once more upon those wavy tresses, to gaze entranced upon that smile; his ears were waiting to catch the accents of that well-remembered voice. He went to Mon-Plaisir by night, and slipped quietly into his room. He passed the hours of darkness, as he had often done before, stretched out upon the floor, his head whirling, his heart on fire. At times, it seemed as though the floor again became transparent, and his closed eyes gazed into other eyes which smiled upon him, upon loosened tresses which he caressed, upon fair shoulders which he covered with warm kisses; deceived by his dream of passion, his sad heart became a habitation of delight.

At daybreak he heard Marguerite move about her room, then open her door and descend the stairs. He looked out of the window and saw her cross the garden. He immediately left the house and followed her; she did not hear his footsteps, so deeply was she absorbed in her sad thoughts. Having assured himself that she was going toward the willows, he took a shorter route, and reaching the spot before her, hid himself within the trunk of an immense hollow tree. It was the same place where, three months before, she had surprised him in a tumult of despair; at that time she smiled. He saw her stop, seat herself, place her face within her hands, and, could he believe it? he saw her weep. Yes, indeed, she wept; not only did her tears fall, but convulsive sobs shook her frame. A delirium of joy took possession of him, while his eyes shot fire and his breast was filled with a maddening hope. His wish then had been fulfilled! It was misfortune she had found at Ornis. Misfortune removes all barriers and places every one on the same level; misfortune despises no one, it grasps eagerly the first hand stretched out to it, it clothes itself with patience and condescension, it listens to advice, is docile and obedient, and receives with gratitude the sympathy and devotion of the poor and weak. Joseph felt reconciled, for a moment, with the government of the world; it seemed to him that all was changed in heaven; that blind fortune had been dethroned by an omniscient justice, which had decreed that henceforth each one in turn should have his desires fulfilled, and that bright and happy days should dawn on the oppressed. Thus we transfer to heaven the feelings of our hearts, and thus our desires, denied or satisfied, frame our philosophy. The heart of man is the cradle where all the gods are born.

CHAPTER XXIII.

MARGUERITE FINDS A CONFIDANT.

Joseph did not hesitate a second. He left his hiding-place, and softly moved toward the bench. A moment later, Marguerite raised her head, and saw him standing there before her. At first she was confused and troubled; the soul has its nudities which a glance profanes. Besides, would not this man demand the secret of her tears? She could not tell this secret; it belonged to another. She looked on Joseph with troubled, almost angry eyes, striving to frame some answer to the question she expected, asking herself what invention would be most likely to satisfy his curiosity. Suddenly something which she had forgotten came distinctly to her mind. She remembered that in that very spot, Joseph had said to her, "I hope that some day you will need one ready to die for you." No, she was not dreaming, those were the very words he had used. She looked about her as though to ask the grass, the trees, the walks, if it were not so. Yes, they all had heard, they all remembered. Then she raised her head again, and fixed on Joseph a piercing look, which he could scarcely bear; it seemed to read the very secrets of his heart. Marguerite thought, "They speak ill of him, yet on his brow is the mark of a noble nature. This young man is neither dissipated nor ungrateful; he's simply proud, and, not being understood, is constantly wounded by unintentional slights and provocations."

After gazing a long time upon him, she came to the conclusion that this workman, this son of a poor beggar, was the only true soul she had met within the last three days, and an impetuous, irresistible desire took possession of her, a desire to share her secret with this soul, as one divides a bit of bread with a companion on the road saying, "Let's eat together." It seemed to her that it would be a great comfort to do this, that half the weight she bore would be taken from her, that thenceforth she would be able to move calmly on, making her way as best she could over the sharp stones and through the thorns of life.

She could not, however, quite make up her mind to break the silence. He spoke first, saying, "Do you remember, here, three months ago...."

"You wished misfortune to come upon me," she interrupted in a sweet, sad voice. "Your desire has been granted; I hope you're satisfied."

"I shall only be so," he answered quickly, "when you permit me to devote myself to your service. I told you, if you ever needed help, to call on me. I have not much to give; but what I have is yours."

She fixed her calm, clear eyes upon him: "What have I done to inspire you with this devoted friendship that you offer me?"

He changed color; his lips trembled. "Must I repeat what I have already told you? I owe every thing to your family. My debt weighs heavily upon me, I wish to pay it off. How can I do otherwise? I am proud, I can't feel that I am free until it's paid. It's in your hands, though, I wish to make my payment. You seem nearer to me than any one else. Did you not say, yourself, that I was almost a brother to you?"

"How is it then that, though I've been here three days, I see you now for the first time?"

"I was afraid you had forgotten me.... It's so easy to forget! I'd rather not see those I love, than to find them changed."

Then he added, "What can I do for you?"

She hesitated no longer. "Listen to me.... I'm going to reveal a secret to you...."

Then stopping a moment, she continued, "But first you must promise the strictest secrecy. You must swear that you will never repeat a word of what I tell you...."

A thrill of joy ran through his frame. Henceforth there

would be a secret between them, which would belong to them alone, and from which all the rest of the world would be excluded. This secret would unite and wed their souls. "I promise," he answered in a steady voice.

"That will not do," she continued. "You must take a solemn oath. Swear by what you love best in the world.... Swear by that pride which with you is honor."

"I swear by my pride," he answered, "and I swear by the horror and scorn I should feel for myself, if I should break my word."

She held out her hand to him. "And I swear," he added, "by this hand which I hold in mine, and which I should not dare to touch, with the crime of perjury upon my soul."

"That will do," she answered. "Now sit down by me, I will tell you....."

As soon as he was seated, she recounted the scene that had taken place in the garret; she toned down the coloring of the picture, however, and said nothing of the frightful conjectures which she had made. Strange to relate, as she told the story, she looked at the matter herself in a different light, her fears were dissipated, the pouring out her secret into a sympathetic heart acted like healing balm upon her own, and opened again to her the consolations of hope.

"Now you know what makes me so unhappy," she said in conclusion. "I have found that M. D'Ornis is in a condition of humiliating dependence upon a man to whom he has given his signature, for some reason, I know not what. His freedom, his fortune, and his honor all seem compromised by this fatal paper, and his misfortune is also mine. How can this have happened? What service has this insolent fellow rendered him, to be able thus to abuse his power? I suspect that he was a soldier or sutler in Mexico, that he met the Count there, and that in the vicissitudes of the campaign, he at some time saved his life. M. D'Ornis is a man who acts on the impulse of the moment. In his first transports of gratitude, he probably agreed to every thing, and signed whatever was presented to him. I ought to ask him for an explanation, but I am not brave enough. He is proud and quick to take offence. He can not bear to speak of the past; he wishes to share with me only the present and the future. What a future it will be, alas ! if I do not succeed in delivering him from this usurer, his evil genius and my own ! Whoever will discover the answer to this enigma, find out who this Bertrand is, and help me to rescue M. D'Ornis from his hands, whoever will do this, will restore to me my peace and dignity, and acquire an eternal claim upon my gratitude.... But do I not expect too much ? Am I not asking an impossibility ? Am I not wrong in telling you?...Why have I disclosed these secrets to you ? You saw my tears, your eyes were questioning me. I was so unhappy, I could not tell you an untruth ; but I trust your promise and your oath. You swore to me that you would keep my secret."

Joseph's heart bounded with joy. He now knew that Marguerite's feelings toward her husband were those of friendship, not of love. Love is bold and not afraid to question ; love is jealous of its secrets, and never permits another person to come between the loved one and itself. "I swore to you," he cried, "that you could do with me as you wished, that I had chosen you from among my benefactors, as the one whom it pleased my pride to acknowledge as a creditor. Yes, I owe you a debt, and I promise you I will pay it.... Within a fortnight, this man at Lyons shall become my employer, and I will learn how to make him reveal his secrets.... But to know them is not all; I must disarm him by destroying this dangerous paper which gives him so much power over others. Even if I risk my life...."

"Risk your life !" she said in a trembling voice. "You must not think of it. You must promise that you'll do nothing without consulting me.'

"Do not fear, there are no dangers except for those who are afraid," he answered proudly. Then he added, while his face was lighted with an expression of strange joy and triumph, "Since you have confidence in my oaths, I'll take one more. I swear to you by the horrible den where I was born, by all the doors where I asked for alms and received but insults, by all the evil thoughts which came to me, by all the evil acts I meditated, by the hospital where I saw my father die, I swear that I will bear this paper to you, saying, 'Now my debt is paid!'"

"May God hear you, bless you, and reward you!" she said warmly pressing both his hands.

He fixed upon her a strange look. "Why should God reward me?" he replied. "I shall have done nothing but my duty. If you are satisfied, that's all I ask."

But as she turned toward him with a questioning glance, he felt that his eyes revealed too much. He succeeded in mastering his passion. He rose, saying, "It shall not cost you a farthing. All I ask in return for what I shall have done, will be that you will listen to me, while I tell you what I have upon my mind....An hour of patience, that is all! If I am full of pride, I'm also crazy with ambition. For some months, I've been thinking of going to America. I'm tired of this old world. Certain peculiar ideas have come to me, you see; I should not dare confess them to a soul....They've told you, perhaps, that I've taken to drinking. It is not true—I never drank but once. My thoughts are what intoxicate me. I want to tell you what they are some day; perhaps you can give me some good advice. You will hear me, will you not? On the day I give you up that paper, I can tell you all, and after you have heard me, however great my folly may appear, you will answer me without anger and without scorn?"

"Tell me now," she said; "I'm ready to hear you."

"I shouldn't dare to do so yet," he answered. "I want first to prove to you that I'm good for something more than putting a smooth face on a board."

It is very rare for two such interviews to take place without at least one of them being disturbed. Some weeks before, Mme. Mirion had almost broken in upon a meeting between Joseph and her daughter. This time, she interrupted the conversation with a cry of astonishment and indignation. She had gone up to Marguerite's room, and not having found her there, had started out to look for her. She was shocked to see her seated on a bench, talking familiarly with the ungrateful workman. Countess D'Ornis was not maintaining her dignity, she thought.

"What are you doing there, dear Countess?" she cried as she approached them. "Breakfast is waiting for you."

Marguerite hastened to join her mother without stopping to say good-by to Joseph. If she had turned her head a moment afterward, she would have surprised him in an attitude and occupation that would have given her cause for serious reflection. After moving away a little, he had hastily retraced his steps, and had fallen on his knees upon the ground, at the spot where Marguerite, in talking with him, had left the imprint of her foot in the damp earth. He gathered up a handful of this earth, pressed his mouth upon it, smeared it on his lips, and, I verily believe, he ate it. After this repast, he ran at full speed to the workroom, where, during the whole day, he astonished his companions by the fire of his glance, by his feverish and loquacious humor, by his whistling and his singing. For some months before, he had not been heard to sing a note.

Meanwhile Mme. Mirion had said to her daughter in a reproachful tone, "What are you thinking of, my dear? What would your husband say, if he were to see you so familiar with a workman of your father's, especially one who doesn't stand well in my books?"

"You don't do him justice," replied Marguerite with unusual vivacity; "he's better than you think he is."

"If he hasn't all the vices I suspect," answered Mme. Mirion, "he's an ungrateful fellow at the best."

"I'm afraid you don't understand how to manage him; you worry him by constantly telling what you've done for him."

Mme. Mirion made a sharp reply and scolded her daughter for at least five minutes. That was the extent of her ill-nature though. Love spats do not last long.

Marguerite was a prey to two opposing feelings. Now she was astonished at what she had done, at the boldness of speech which had suddenly come to her, and at the temerity of her confidence. "My secret has escaped; I can not take it back," she thought. Again she experienced a kind of magical relief at the thought that she had made known her misfortune to another—that a friendly heart had taken her sufferings upon itself, had bound itself to hers by a solemn vow, and had promised to aid and comfort her. She saw again in imagination Joseph's face, with its irregular but expressive features; his hands which were well shaped, though hardened and browned by toil; his pale and hollow cheeks; his gray eyes full of mystery and unrest; and his thick dark hair, which fell upon his forehead with a kind of savage grace. "He's homely rather than handsome," she thought; "but his face is full of character, and his eyes full of intelligence. They express resolution, boldness, pride, and obstinacy; they reveal a thoughtful yet savage nature, at war with all the world and determined to struggle to the bitter end. At times, he seems like a madman, full of fantasies and stormy passions—then his expression softens suddenly, his eyes grow tender and sympathetic, and you recognize within him a heart capable of devotion and of love. He freely acknowledges his faults. He speaks boldly of his pride, of his ambition, of the debt that weighs upon him, of the old world which wearies him, and of his castles in America; he is sincere, at all events. No, I have not misplaced my confidence."

She was so absent-minded during the morning, that her father noticed it and chided her. "You're no longer here, Margot," he said; "you're back again at Ornis. A plague on wives who are too devoted to their husbands!"

In the afternoon at three o'clock, the whole family accompanied her to the railway station. They all kissed and embraced her again and again. As the train started, she looked from the window and saw a workman in a gray blouse, who was standing by the track and waving his cap to her. She waved her hand in return; then sitting back in a corner of the carriage, she closed her eyes and slept soundly for five or six hours. She had great need of sleep after three nights of wakefulness and unrest.

CHAPTER XXIV.

AN ANGRY HUSBAND.

How quickly our thoughts change! Because she had seen a hat waving in the air near the depot at Geneva, Marguerite Mirion, Countess D'Ornis, had slept soundly and peacefully for several hours. Scarcely had she awakened, however, when her mind experienced a sudden revolution. She felt that she had committed an irreparable fault; she foresaw its consequences and was terrified by them. "There's nothing surer in this world than courage," she thought, "and the wisest part to take is always that which costs the most. It was my duty to confess my involuntary fault to Roger as soon as it was committed. I didn't dare to do it. Now I am condemned to silence. If I should tell him to-day that chance had made me a witness of that horrible scene in the garret, his first words would be, 'You've just spent three days at Geneva; swear to me that you've not told a soul what you have seen and heard.' How could I answer him? My only resource would be to tell him an untruth.....She wondered whether she were capable of doing this. It seemed to her like trying to raise a mountain, only to have it fall back again and crush her. Marguerite Mirion had little force of character, and if later she showed some strength of will, it was the result of circumstances, such as sometimes constrain our natures, making them unrecognizable even to ourselves. Though she was weak, however, she was honest and sincere; the truth was in a certain sense her native air, she could breathe no other freely.

She arrived at the castle just after her husband had started on a hunting trip. "The Count will not be gone long, for he was very impatient to see my lady," Fanny remarked as she was dressing her mistress's hair. "He can't keep still a moment. He was afraid that you'd remain some time at Geneva, I think; when he received your dispatch yesterday, he was just strapping his valise to go after you."

"Has any one called to see him since I've been gone?"

"The old Countess took dinner with him day before yesterday. They've made up again; and if my lady will let me tell her...."

"No, I don't care to hear," said Marguerite; "your stories are too long."

It's very certain, she thought, that Mme. D'Ornis makes it a point never to come here, unless one of us is absent.

How great was her astonishment, when she saw the portrait of Marchioness D'Epinac hanging in the most conspicuous place in her sitting-room! How had the portrait come there? This question, and the answer which came most naturally to her mind, greatly troubled her. M. D'Ornis did not make his appearance until evening. He bowed politely to his wife, and inquired concerning her health and her uncle's; but all the time he wore a singular air, as though he had something to say, and was only awaiting a suitable time to say it. He conversed very little at the table. After dinner, he smoked a cigar in the park, and then rejoined Marguerite in the sitting-room.

"You haven't thanked me for the little surprise I planned for you," he said showing her the portrait. "That's a charming picture."

"Very charming," she replied, concealing her emotion as best she could.

"I want to tell you about that handsome, light-haired girl, who, it seems to me, looks a little like you."

By the glance he gave her, she knew that he was putting her to the test. "I've heard the story," she said; "your mother told it to me."

"Did she tell you how the unhappy woman lost her husband's love? How she could not distinguish between what was his, and what her own? My mother seemed to think that the portrait would please you. Take a better look at it."

" I've seen it before," courageously answered Marguerite, making a faint attempt to smile.

" Indeed?" he said in a sarcastic tone. " Hereafter when you're hunting about the garret, don't drop your ribbons there."

So saying, he drew from his pocket and placed on the table the lilac bow which Marguerite supposed had been lost in the park. He walked two or three times up and down the room ; he was afraid, himself, of what he was going to say. Finally, throwing himself into an arm-chair, he asked, " Will you please inform me what day and what hour you...."

She felt her head whirl a moment ; then it seemed as though some other person took her place and answered, " It was all chance. I was there and heard every thing."

Then the consciousness of what she had done returning to her, she threw herself at his feet and, in a choking voice and with streaming eyes, told him how it happened. When she raised her head again, the expression of M. D'Ornis's face terrified her. She felt that a change had come over him, that he did not and could not love her longer; that his heart, which had opened for a moment, had closed again, and that this heart was now a tomb on which was written this inscription, " Here lies a friendship that survived three months."

He rudely pushed her back, crying, " Chance ! do men of my age believe in chance, ...and women's stories ?....I'll tell you what you've done—you've been spying out my secrets !"

Marguerite shuddered, her heart throbbed. " Do you think," she asked with a piteous smile, " that I look like a spy ?"

He seized her by the wrists and, raising her to her feet, dragged her before the portrait. " You look enough like her to be her sister," he cried. "She's worthy to become your patron saint."

He pressed her wrists so strongly that a groan escaped her lips. Releasing her from his grasp, he fell back in his chair, where he remained for some time motionless and frowning. Suddenly he laughed aloud. It was the first time she had ever heard him laugh. "After all, what does it amount to?" he said. "It was scarcely worth your while to climb into a garret, and to hide there in the dark, holding your breath and keeping as quiet as a spider on the watch.... On the watch for what, I'd like to know? Have I got any secrets? You didn't make any thing by your spying.... I use the same word yet, madam. What did you find so wonderful in the garret? Two men talking angrily with each other.... I'm sure I had good reason to be angry. I'm never angry except for cause. That Bertrand ... that Bertrand is a rascal.... That Bertrand".... He stopped. His trembling lips could not find the word they sought. "That Bertrand," he continued after a moment's silence, "that Bertrand is a wretched usurer. Cursed be the day in which I fell into his hands! What else could you expect? I was dissipated, I gambled, I had all the fashionable vices. My childhood was so dull! I was trying to amuse myself. Bertrand serves to amuse me now. I wanted money, he lent it to me at twenty per cent. It must be paid.... You see what it is, madam, to marry a libertine."

She sat down at his knees, her cheeks bathed with tears. "You are not a libertine," she said, "any more than I'm a spy. I deserve your confidence, your entire confidence, and will try to prove it to you. I have a heart and I love you, although you seem to doubt it. You see me at your knees; I beg you to hide nothing from me. Do you want money, a great deal of money to free yourself from this man? You shall have every thing I own. Tell me all! I'm sure I know how it happened; I'm sure this Bertrand saved your life and took advantage of your generosity, making you sign promises you can not keep. It was in Mexico, wasn't it? What is this pride which keeps you from telling me the truth.... Ah! tell me all, how at the fatal moment he appeared, turning aside the blow and killing the assassin...."

M. D'Ornis's face was terrible to look upon. "What assassin?" he cried in shrieking tones. His cheeks were pale, he gazed at her with haggard eyes. She thought he was going mad. He quickly came to himself, however, twisted the ends of his mustache, and bit his lips until they bled; it was a punishment he was inflicting on them. Then he rose and, crossing the room, pulled the bell cord so violently, that he tore it from its place. Fanny appeared. "Mme. D'Ornis is faint," he said, "Quick! bring the salts!" Fanny returned a moment afterward with the bottle; she offered her services to Marguerite, who refused them and sent her out again.

M. D'Ornis took plenty of time to recover his composure. It was with a firm voice, cutting and sharp as steel that he continued: "Smell the salts, madam; you need them, you seem to be out of your head. Are you subject to these attacks? I am very uneasy about you. It seems that my usurer has the sad privilege of disturbing your brain. Now you take him for a robber, and lock him up in a bath-room. Now you make a melodramatic hero of him, and imagine all manner of queer things. He saved my life, he killed a Mexican who held me by the throat....There's no truth in any of it, except that there's a bill I've got to pay, no matter what it costs; but out of my money, my own money, for I'm not like you, I make a distinction between mine and yours....I'm a proud fool though. See how madly I deceived myself! When I met you by chance at Geneva—this time it was really chance—I thought I had found the woman to make me a good wife. I said to myself, 'She's a Genevese, and Geneva is the classic land of common sense; she belongs to the middle classes, and is probably as well bred as a marchioness; it is Marguerite Mirion, who on becoming Countess D'Ornis, will thank me for the change, and show her gratitude by conforming herself to my humors and my tastes; last of all, she's a Protestant, and whoever marries a Protestant has the inestimable advantage of having a wife who does not confess to a black-robed priest every thing about herself, her conscience, her sins, her husband, and her household. It has turned out that this Genevese is a flighty person, that this well-bred girl is more indiscreet than Marchioness D'Epinac herself, that Marguerite Mirion does not care to fulfill her obligations, and that this Protestant....Ah! I hope that I'm not mistaken in this respect.

Thank God! you've no confessor, madam! Tell me, you've no confessor, have you?"

He glanced at her. He saw that she blushed and looked confused. He cried, "What! you've not been able to hold your tongue? There's some one at Geneva to whom you've told your visions?"

She did not answer. He walked toward her with clenched fists; she thought she saw again her horrible dream. She laid her head upon her knees, hiding her face within her hands. "What! you've been base enough!"....he continued. "Who is your confessor. I want to know him, to talk with him. I know how to talk to such people."

She had lifted up her head. He waited a moment for an answer which did not come to him. He again seized her hands, and pressed them with all his force, as though to crush them in his grasp. She still continued silent. "Do you hear me?" he continued; "I want to know the name of this receiver of stolen secrets."

She raised her large eyes wet with tears; soft and supplicating as was their glance, those eyes announced a firm determination not to yield to his demand.

"It's very foolish for me to ask the name of your confessor. You may have ten or twenty for all I know. I'll guarantee that you had scarcely arrived at Mon-Plaisir, before the great family council was gathered in the parlor, and you served me up alive to the hungry crowd."

At last she made up her mind to answer him. "I've spoken to no one," she sadly said, "except a discreet and devoted friend, and not a single word has escaped my lips, that did not bear witness to the esteem and affection which I have for you, and which you have just put so rudely to the test. He saw me weep and questioned me. I confessed to him that I was sad, because I feared you had some great sorrow....I will try to make amends for my fault, which I know will cause no future trouble....I promise you that after this....Have I not already proved that I know how to hold my peace?"

M. D'Ornis's anger was rekindled. "Once more, I ask, who

is this man ?" he repeated, stamping his foot. "Is he a Protestant Jesuit ? is he some low-born lover, who has been made a sacrifice to your parent's vanity, and whom you are now repaying with your confidence ?"

Standing before her with folded arms, he fastened upon her a fierce and steady glance, crying angriiy, "I'm waiting ; I want to know who this man is." When her continued silence at length convinced him that he would obtain no answer, he abded, "At your own pleasure, madam ! I'll think it over." With these words he left the room.

CHAPTER XXV.

MARGUERITE A PRISONER.

Scarcely had her husband shut the door, when Marguerite burst into tears. When she had somewhat recovered her composure, her conscience spoke to her; they had a long conversation with each other. "You are very unhappy," this honest conscience said; "but is it not your own fault, O weak and cowardly soul? You are now overthrown because you have met with a difficult situation and an intractable nature!" "I should be thankful if that were all," she answered. "Can my eyes forget what they have seen, or my ears forget what they have heard? Oh! that he had been artful enough to really deceive me!" "What is the use of these vain imaginings and conjectures?" replied her conscience. "Some day all will be explained, and you will blush for your foolish thoughts and idle fears. In the meantime, you must make amends for your fault and repair your errors." "I am ready to do all I can," answered Marguerite. "Will you not promise me that by patience and submission I shall succeed in touching this hard heart, compelling it to see me as I am, and at last to return to me." Her conscience promised all she asked. It was a youthful conscience just awakened and perfectly sincere, which, not having yet become acquainted with the world, took pleasure in believing that, in this life, virtue always meets with its reward.

The first thing Marguerite did, was to write the following letter:

"MY DEAR JOSEPH:

"Your friend is a foolish creature, who gets frightened at nothing, who weeps without cause, and talks without reason. Her only excuse is that she is not yet twenty-one. I have received an explanation of the famous mystery. M. D'Ornis has told me all about it, and I am as ashamed as a linnet that has been frightened by a scarecrow. The whole affair is finally reduced to an ugly creditor, who has the bad habit of drinking too much, and of saying foolish things when he is intoxicated. A little patience and we shall pay him, and be freed forever from his importunities. I beg you to forget my foolish fancies, and to give up the journey you were proposing to make on my account, as it would be perfectly useless now. I have made up my mind to become a sensible person, and not again to be frightened by my shadow. I feel that I am changed already; what will never change, however, is my friendship for you, and my deep gratitude for the devotion you have shown me. When I again visit Geneva, we will talk over your plans, your ambitions, your pride, which pleases and pains me at the same time, and your castles in America, which I should like to help you build. Farewell! Forget my unreasonable fears, but do not forget the unreasonable person who signs herself,

"Yours affectionately,

"MARGUERITE."

She was interrupted more than once while writing; at the slightest sound, she laid down her pen and hid her paper. For the sake of greater safety, she inclosed her letter in a second envelope, and addressed the latter to the woman with whom Joseph's mother lived. The next morning, she watched behind her curtain, and as the porter's daughter passed beneath the window, she threw her out the missive, asking her to carry it immediately to the post.

A few hours afterward, she met with her first surprise, which was soon followed by many others. She had passed the morning in her sitting-room, embroidering a little and reflecting a great deal, with no other company than Marchioness D'Epinac, who was gazing on her from the wall. Marguerite looked at her small, sad mouth, the mouth that never smiled, that told the story of her sorrows, her deceptions, her quarrels, her sufferings, and her long repentance in the convent; then she said to herself, "What can I do to obtain my pardon?" She thought for a long time, but could find no answer to her question. Time and patience, a long infinitude of time and patience, this was the only remedy her reason could suggest. But could she not divert her thoughts and forget the past? She gave a side glance at her piano, which had not been opened since her return. There was a silence in her soul which could not bear the sound of music. It seemed to her that her gayety was inclosed within this mute piano; she thought she heard it humming among the wires, like a fly imprisoned in a box. "I'll not open you," she said, "until he pardons me. Heaven grant that on that day I may not find you ruined!"

The clock had just struck twelve. She prepared to descend to the dining-room, and her heart beat quickly at the thought of again seeing her husband. Her maid entered, glancing at her with a singular expression. "Is it true, my lady?" she inquired.

"Is what true?

"That you are sick, and will take your meals up here?"

"Who told you so?"

"The Count."

"In that case, it must be true," she said with a forced smile. Then she added, "In fact, I don't feel very well, and think I'd better keep my room."

She passed the afternoon entirely alone. She said to herself, "He has thought of this as an expedient to avoid me for a few days. It's better for him, as well as for me. Thank Heaven, though, I am well; I'm not an invalid, except in the imaginations of other people."

At seven o'clock, Fanny brought up her dinner. She had a constrained air, walked on tip-toe, and spoke in a low tone. She was somewhat reassured when she saw that Marguerite had not lost her appetite. A youthful digestion does not yield to the first assaults of trouble.

An hour later, Marguerite had another surprise which powerfully affected her. She saw M. D'Ornis entering her room. She rose to meet him; he bowed to her without speaking, and motioned her to take her seat again. He sat down himself, drew from his pocket a number of the *Union*, unfolded it and read it through from the first line to the last. She asked two or three questions ; he acted as though he did not hear her. When he had finished his paper, he folded it up, put it in his pocket, and left the room.

The second day passed like the first, the third day like the second. On the fourth day, as she looked in the mirror, Marguerite was struck by the paleness of her face and by her sunken cheeks. To say nothing of the uneasiness and sadness that had been preying, night and day, upon her mind, this silent cloister life to which she had been condemned, was painful to her bright and happy nature ; she could not bear it long without becoming pale. Her appetite deserted her ; she experienced a nervous trembling from time to time. The evening before, while M. D'Ornis, mute and impassible, had been studying his paper, she had been compelled to stop embroidering, her tears fell so fast upon her work. After his departure, she had remained an hour as though stupefied, listening to the ticking of the clock, and comparing it with her thoughts, which shot to and fro like a shuttle through her brain.

Toward the close of the morning, she threw a cloak upon her shoulders, drawing the hood over her head, and went out into the park, following the path that led to the pond. She was astonished, on turning her head, to see Jerome, her husband's valet, following her. He stopped when she stopped, and moved forward when she moved forward, regulating his pace by hers. It was a cold and gloomy December morning. A thick mist was rising from the pond, and the willows that surrounded it were covered with a thin coat of ice. Marguerite stepped upon the bank. Her twenty years, which only asked to be amused, took some pleasure in looking at these white willows ; gnarled and twisted, they leaned over the surface of the water and seemed endeavoring to see their image in this dim mirror, which vaguely reflected their wrinkled forms. She approached one of them and, leaning forward, shook from it the ice, which fell like sleet upon her hood and in the water. Suddenly she felt some one pulling at her dress. She turned round quickly, and found herself in the presence of Jerome, who was looking at her with a startled air. "Ah ! my lady, how you frightened me," he said in a reproachful tone, drawing her down with a firm but respectful grasp.

"What are you afraid of? Let go my dress, you'll tear it."

He did not loose his hold until he had drawn her from the bank. "Yes, you frightened me well, my lady!" he repeated heaving a sigh of relief, as though he had just saved her life.

"Were you afraid my foot would slip?"

"No; but it seems my lady is not very well, and if it were not for the respect I owe her...."

"Ah! you thought I wanted to drown myself?" she asked with a nervous laugh. "Don't trouble yourself, I love my life too much for that."

She started to walk on again, and Jerome, faithful to orders, began to follow her, after she had moved a few steps in advance of him. She stopped as she was passing the Commander's statue. She looked at him with a troubled gaze which seemed to say, "Since you wish me well, give me your advice." The Commander, who had formerly been an active man in warlike matters, appeared unable to find an answer to this appeal; he could not understand this new case presented to him, and knew not what to say to a young wife borne down by her domestic sorrows.

Marguerite was not yet through with her surprises. On the morrow, she received a call from the physician of Ornis, M. Crotet, a little old man in spectacles, rude in speech, awkward in manner, talking through his nose, who concealed his ignorance beneath a multitude of apothegms, and whose empty head had never invented any thing better than quack remedies. This worthy man had gained a footing in the place through the patronage of Countess D'Ornis; he was perfectly devoted to her, seeing only through her eyes, and trusting only in her name. "So! so! madam, we're a little out of sorts?" he said in a familiar tone. "Well, well, we mustn't get discouraged. It's our business to mend the machine when it's out of order. I've an idea you don't want to see me. You must be careful, Countess; it's a bad sign to hate the doctor. Let me see your tongue and feel your pulse!....A little too quick and not quite regular. It isn't enough to kill a man, though, or a woman either for that matter. Young women are very easily affected; but they recover very fast. Then, besides, we're an only daughter, they say; we have been spoiled, badly spoiled. The first time we're crossed, our imagination boils up like so much porridge. We must keep it from boiling over, if we can."

"I don't know what you're talking about," answered Marguerite, assuming a gentleness of manner she did not feel.

"Without taking into account," he continued, "that sudden changes of fortune predispose us to melancholy; all surprises, whether good or bad, disturb the machine. It's very true that since '89 the trades stand higher than before; but it's no less true that there are some adventures that astonish one. To go to sleep at night in a carpenter's shop and wake up in the morning in a castle...."

"Don't you see the shavings in my hair?" said Marguerite running her fingers through her tresses with an angry gesture.

"You must keep quiet, madam," he cried moving uneasily on his chair. "Where did you get that idea from? Look in the glass; you'll see a very handsome head of hair there, but no more shavings than I've got in my eye. When such ideas come to you, you must shut them out at once. If you yield to them, you are lost. But, pshaw! you'll get over it; youth recovers very quickly."

Thereupon he asked her a great many questions, all of which might have been summed up in her mother's inquiry about the oranges. Marguerite answered him with angelic sweetness. He obstinately insisted on his point; the worthy man clung to his ideas: such is generally the case with people who have but few of them. He had, however, to give it up. He afterward asked her other questions, to which she gave him no reply.

Suddenly his face lighted up, as though a ray of divine wisdom had just passed through his mind, and was now darting from his eyes and through his spectacles. "I have the solution of the question," he said, tossing his snuff-box in the air. "You have had a great fright on one of those days when young women ought particularly to avoid all emotion.... First, there was the fire; then that ugly Bertrand arrived and you took him for a robber. A week later you met him unexpectedly again. That was enough to induce lypemania. Consult the masters of the art, and they will tell you that all lypemaniacs are very sensitive and irritable, that a little matter makes a strong impression on them, and that the most ordinary events appear like new and strange phenomena, invented expressly to annoy them.... Tell me now, what you thought you saw and heard in the garret."

A shudder ran over her from head to foot.

"Never mention that garret to me again," she cried in anger.

He nodded his head with a satisfied air.

"Didn't I tell you I had solved the difficulty?" he said; "I have my way of getting at a thing. Rest easy, Countess! we'll say nothing more about the garret. There! there! don't think you're worse than you really are. It's only an hallucination, a false perception. You thought you heard and thought you saw strange things; but, Heaven be praised! you'll soon get over it. The best way is to say to yourself, I really didn't hear or see a thing. Then when those gloomy thoughts come over you, you ought never to walk near the pond."

"There's no great harm done," she interrupted; "they pulled me out and I'm all safe now."

"It's no joking matter. Lypemaniacs always ought to avoid the water. But it is nothing serious, Countess. In a couple of months, I trust our little trouble will be over. We'll have to be a little careful in our living. Rest, solitude, and silence.... Those are the sovereign remedies for troubled minds.... Now and then a short walk to refresh the ideas, and then good, nourishing food besides. No highly seasoned or farinaceous dishes. A little veal or chicken, and some nice ripe fruit, that's what you want!.... My dear patient, I'll call on you again in a few days, and I hope to find you with a smile on your lips and roses in your cheeks."

He rose and held out his hand. She bowed to him with folded arms. A week afterward he returned. This time, she received him coldly and refused to talk with him at all ; he could make no impression on her, and retired shaking his head mournfully and repeating to himself, "Yes, yes, it's a bad sign to hate the doctor."

CHAPTER XXVI.

THE OLD COUNTESS'S TRIUMPH.

A few hours later, Mme. D'Ornis called on Marguerite. Although the old Countess could perfectly control her countenance, the sparkling of her eye betrayed her; she could not conceal her happiness. A moment before she had said to Marquis Du Rozan, who had inquired concerning her daughter-in-law, "Ah! my dear Marquis, is there any thing so sad as to see a young girl of twenty lose her reason?"

"Poor dear!" she said to Marguerite as she embraced her; "what is the matter with you? You know, my darling, I don't love you very much, and yet I'm very sorry.... I really hope with all my heart, that you will soon get well. I can't bear to see young people suffer. How did it happen, dear? After such a bright beginning!....Every thing smiled on you, the wind was fair, you had a husband who adored you, who was always at your feet, who gave you the first place in his thoughts. What has caused this dreadful melancholy?....Don't be offended at my question; I only ask it because I am so much interested in you. Are such affections common in your family?"

Marguerite exerted all her self-control and answered gayly, "Don't be uneasy, madam, the Mirions' heads are well set on their shoulders."....Then moving her own about, she added, "You can see, mine's well fastened on at all events." "Dear me!" she continued after a moment's pause, "M. D'Ornis thinks too much of me and is altogether too much troubled about my health."

"I wish I could believe you. M. Crotet tells me, though...."

"M. Crotet is a stupid fool," interrupted Marguerite. "He called me a lypemaniac, an ugly name I don't understand, but which I don't like at all. He can't tell when you're making sport of him. I dare say he told you...."

"About the shavings! O yes, he told me that."

"He commenced the talk himself. I'm not a person to despise shavings. They bring back happy memories to me, and if I should find any in my hair, I'd be very proud of them."

Marguerite pronounced these words with a little excitement in her tone; as she did so, she saw a smile of malignant satisfaction pass over the thin lips of her mother-in-law. She immediately resumed her former coolness of manner, and Mme. D'Ornis could easily see that there was nothing serious about her malady. The conversation lasted for an hour. Though Marguerite received no pleasure, she gathered some instruction from it. She had wondered several times whether Mme. D'Ornis possessed her son's secret. She now knew that she did not. Mme. D'Ornis thought that, acting on her advice, Marguerite had made certain suggestions to her husband, that he had become angry, that they had had a quarrel, that her daughter-in-law had made up some excuse to pass three days at Geneva, that on her return there had been more quarreling, that Marguerite had not been able to bear up under so much trouble, that like a spoiled child she had pretended to be sick, and that she was now in a fair way to become so in reality. She flattered herself that a reconciliation would, every day, become more difficult. She was too well acquainted with her son not to know that he was both proud and selfish, that properly speaking he loved no one but himself, and only evinced an attachment for another, on account of the gratification he expected in return; if he found he was mistaken, he never forgave those who disappointed him. The most he could do was to forget them; but he could not forget his wife, it was much more likely he would hate her.

Marguerite's beauty was the only thing that troubled Mme. D'Ornis. She wanted to persuade the invalid to go away for a time, to try the effect of her native air. She made a few insinuations of this kind, telling her that Roger, who was always well, could not bear to have a sick person about him; that change of air and scenery was the best cure for melancholy, and that there probably were in Geneva much better physicians than M. Crotet. Marguerite turned a deaf ear to her, and the old Countess had to beat a retreat, reserving her attack for a more favorable occasion. "I thank you, madam, for the affectionate interest you have shown in me," said Marguerite as she accompanied her to the stairs. "If M. Crotet will leave me alone, Roger will have his companion back again before three weeks have passed."

Meanwhile M. D'Ornis hunted by himself from dawn till dark, and when he had any thing to say, he said it to his dog. The woods heard; but they are silent and discreet. In the morning, before starting out, he inquired concerning his wife's health; on his return, he again asked about her; then he took his dinner, walked about the park, went to Marguerite's room, and unfolded his paper, silent and frowning as on that first dreadful evening, never lifting his eyes except to give a quick, circling glance about him. There was a fierce rapidity in this glance that caused Marguerite to shudder. One evening, feeling that her strength and patience were about exhausted, she resolved to make an effort to put an end to this intolerable situation. Resting her work upon her knees, she said, "Roger, we can't live this way any longer. It seems to me like a painful dream.... I prefer your anger to your silence. Say what you please; only speak to me."

He settled back further in his chair and kept on reading. She approached him. "Tell me what you intend to do," she said. "Are you putting me to the test? I'm sure I bear it well. What is your opinion?"

He fastened his eyes upon his paper and buried his face within its folds. "I hardly dare tell you what is on my mind," she continued in a trembling voice. "It seems to me that here, three weeks ago, you had a horrible thought. You said to yourself, 'She has discovered half my secret, and she will not rest until she has learned the rest. She will learn it, too, some day, for she's a regular domestic spy.... As she has no heart and can't control her eyes or tongue, she won't be able to keep from talking, and so becoming a witness against me. I'll spoil her testimony by making her pass as a crazy woman

....If she ever appear against me, I'll say to the fools who are tempted to believe her, "Ask Dr. Crotet, ask my mother, my servants, my porter; they'll all tell you she is mad."'.... Roger, if that's your thought...."

He gave a start and his paper trembled in his hands, but he did not stop his reading.

"Look at me," she continued; "look me in the eyes. Don't you know me any more?"

She tried to wrest the paper from his hands, but did not succeed in her attempt.

"You think I have a confessor at Geneva," she continued. "That friend who saw me weep, Roger, do you want me to repeat word for word all I told him, and also the letter I wrote to him the other day? If that letter is not enough, you can dictate another to me."

He raised his eyes and fixed a stern look upon her; then he began to read again.

"Will you never learn to know me?" she cried, wringing her hands in anguish. "If you should confess to me this very minute ....Yes, if by any strange chance there has been a crime connected with your life, and you should make it known to me, I would not let my conscience speak; I would think only of the confession, and forget the fault....I will say more. It seems to me that I should love you better. Your confidence would inspire me with a deep affection, a mingling of sorrow, joy, and fear. You and your crime would belong to me alone. You would have given me your whole heart, and my heart would respond to you, and be ready to break before parting with your secret."

She burst into tears. He let his paper fall and gazed on her a moment; that hard heart seemed about to soften, but suspicion and pride soon got the better of this momentary tenderness. She sprang forward to throw her arms about his neck. He rose suddenly, and pushed her back with so much violence that he threw her from her feet. In her fall, her head struck the corner of the mantel; the blood streamed from the wound. Her eyes were closed; she opened them with difficulty. She thought she saw him leaning over her, and looking at her bleeding face with a terrified and pitying glance. She smiled at him; her whole heart was in that smile. Her eyelids grew heavy as lead, but her thoughts were active still. She said to herself as though talking in a dream, "This is the vital moment on which depends my future; if he take me in his arms and reveal his secret to me, I shall be his forever." She succeeded in opening her eyes again and, raising her head, she tried to smile. In this smile she again offered him her heart, a heart willing to be sacrificed, and yearning to devote itself to him. This offering did not satisfy him. Pointing to the half-opened mouth which was reaching toward him, he muttered, "Forever false!" He gazed fixedly upon her. His glance was like a thunder-cloud, and in this cloud she thought she saw a flash of pitiless hate. Then she knew that all was over; she gave a feeble cry and lost all consciousness.

When she came to herself again, it was two o'clock in the morning. She looked for a long time at the bed-curtains, which were covered with flowers sprinkled on a white ground. Her eyes collected these flowers together and formed bouquets of them. While she was thus engaged, she strove to recall her memory which had fled. She rose up in bed and cast her eyes about her. M. Crotet was seated at her side. "Doctor," she said, "ask him about it; I know I smiled." Then her reason entirely returned. They questioned her; she answered them with pious lies.

"So you fainted suddenly?" they said.

"Yes. I was crossing the room, when suddenly my limbs failed me, and I fell. We can't look out for every thing, doctor. We keep away from ponds and meet a mantel-piece. I suppose you think I tried to kill myself."

Suddenly her eyes fell on M. D'Ornis, who was seated on a sofa across the room, his hands resting on his knees. She gave a cry and, turning her head, hid it beneath the clothes like a frightened child.

From that moment until evening she was without consciousness. She had a burning fever accompanied by delirium. At intervals she kept repeating, "O the poor girl! they don't believe her!" Then she cried, "Take away his paper; tear it up!"

At sunset she regained her senses, and for a few moments retained the use of them. She heard her maid say to Mme. D'Ornis, "The Count has come back." A moment afterward she saw him enter in his hunting-dress. The doctor, who accompanied him, was saying, "She hated the doctor, and you see what's come of it." The four then formed a group in the centre of the room, and talked together in a low tone for a long time. Marguerite heard the words brain fever; and soon she understood that they were discussing the important question as to whether it would be necessary to shave her head. Fanny was making supplicating gestures. M. Crotet said, "It would be a shame to do it!" Roger seemed to be of the same opinion; but Mme. D'Ornis was insisting that the sacrifice should be made. Marguerite thought, "She is right; a bald Marguerite would no longer be a dangerous rival." She raised herself in bed and cried, "Take them; they're of no more use to me." She then fell back upon her pillow, and her reason again deserted her. They did not, however, rob her of her tresses. She was mistaken, they were yet to be of use to her.

CHAPTER XXVII.

M. MIRION LOSES JOSEPH.

A few days after his conversation with Marguerite, Joseph Noirel, having put his affairs in order, went to M. Mirion, and in a firm tone, which announced an irrevocable determination, told him of his decision to go away and seek his fortune. As he listened, M. Mirion began to rub his eyes as though to make sure of being awake; then in a sarcastic tone he begged Joseph to repeat the story of his life, asked him if he was sure his reason had not deserted him, and finally, being convinced that Joseph meant what he said, tried to argue with him. When he at last made up his mind that Joseph was a prey to vain ambition, he grew angry and heaped all manner of reproaches on his head. He had noticed for a long time, he said, that Joseph had been ruining himself by reading bad books and adopting evil doctrines, that he had lost all principle and all respect for those above him, that he had been nursing in his heart a hatred of all social institutions and a scorn of those wise distinctions which assured the happiness of the State, and without which there can be no morality, no religion, no God, no devil, nothing at all in fact. M. Mirion was not absolutely wrong, but he had a most unhappy way of being right, and in this world the form is more important than the matter. Joseph happening to smile, he became furious, declaring that he would have nothing more to do with him; that Joseph Noirel would appear in the annals of humanity, and particularly in those of the cabinet-maker's trade, as an example of the blackest ingratitude; that ungrateful adventurers always came to a bad end; and that he felt it his duty to remind him of his father's fate: after all which he went into a long enumeration of the benefits he had bestowed upon him. Nothing was omitted, from the dozen fine linen shirts they had given him the day of his first communion, to the culinary delicacies with which they regularly welcomed Saint Joseph's day; at the head of these figured Mme. Mirion's celebrated cream-fritters. Joseph ate those fritters for the last time that day, and they gave him an indigestion for the remainder of his life.

He listened to this chant, the words and air of which he knew so well, with an impassible and, at times, sardonic face. He quietly answered that he remembered it all, but that, on his side, he had given all his time and skill to his employer. He added that he intended to remain in the shop until M. Mirion found some one to take his place. M. Mirion was not only sorry to lose a clever workman, who had become his factotum, but his vanity suffered also at the thought that he was not discharging Joseph, but that Joseph was leaving him. He was delighted at this opportunity to save his dignity by changing rôles. "Get out," he cried, "and never let me see your face again! I want you to understand that I'm discharging you."

Joseph did not wait to hear these words repeated. A few hours later, he went to Mon-Plaisir to get his clothes. He tried to see Mme. Mirion, in order to say good-by to her and thank her. She refused to let him in. Aunt Amaranth and Mlle. Grillet joined with the husband and wife in expressing their indignation. At dinner and during the entire evening, nothing was spoken of but the monstrous perversity of Joseph's heart. Uncle Benjamin alone, who with his health had recovered his belligerent humor, pleaded various extenuating circumstances.

When Joseph went to say farewell to his mother, the evening before starting for Lyons, the housekeeper handed him Marguerite's letter, which at first filled him with dismay. On reading it a second time, however, he was entirely reassured. It seemed to him that this retraction had no real meaning, that Marguerite had a remorseful feeling, that she was sorry she had been so indiscreet, and that, perhaps, she did not trust her confidant. "She fears," he thought, "that I may be tempted to abuse her confidence." He pondered a moment over this reflection which made his heart beat quickly. If he was feared by any one, it was because he was somebody. Whatever he might be, he was determined to do what he had promised, to solve this profound mystery. He started on his journey without answering Marguerite.

From Geneva to Lyons, he conversed only with his thoughts; they gave him sufficient occupation. He had read some ancient tales of chivalry; he pictured to himself a knight-errant, searching for adventures in order to gain his lady's love and win the right to wear her colors. For the first time, something had happened to him, his life was big with an event, he found himself excited by the novelty of an adventure. He looked at his hands, those obscure and indefatigable workers, which all his care had not been able to keep from becoming hard and brown. "You have a new work before you," he said to them; "you must unravel the mysteries of a dark intrigue." Up to the present time these hands had wrought on oak and pine, now they were to work on human souls; in their days of glory, they had carved out ovolos and leaves, now they were to create tragedies and passions, joys and sorrows, smiles and tears; they found themselves engaged in executing the decrees of fate, and Joseph in his simple pride felt that fate was somewhat under his control. He snapped his fingers and shook them in the air; he thought he saw puppets dangling from them, which danced and laughed and wept at his command.

His heart was a prey to contradictory feelings. When his pride was silent, he only saw Marguerite in tears; he suddenly became again her confidant and friend and, examining his heart, found himself capable of the noble devotion and heroic silence characteristic of great sacrifices. A moment later, he gave himself up anew to the fever of desire and hope: his future, taking shape before him, brought to his view such visions of delight, that his form trembled and his temples throbbed. His pride, which was never quiet long, added to these visions other delusive dreams of satisfied revenge. If he should succeed in his attempt, what scandal, what piercing sorrow his triumph would create among those vain and sanctimonious people whom he detested. They would look upon it as a sign of the times, and all the Mirions in the world would lift their hands in horror. They would have good reason to do so, he thought, for this triumph would be an example—a public event which would mark the date of the revenge of the employed on the employers, of the scorned upon the scorners, a deep blow struck into the crumbling strata of the old and worn-out social order, and the signal for the universal overturning. If, by any possibility, Marguerite Mirion, Countess D'Ornis, should some day give herself to Joseph Noirel, such an event would dawn upon the world with the light of the new era. Such were the shadows and desires which pressed upon this soul, possessed at the same time by Marguerite and the spirit of the Gracchi, and filled with dark clouds of passion, tinged with the rosy hues of love. It was not a vulgar soul, it belonged to a noble family; great deeds and sublime devotion had their attractions for it; but there were bitter dregs within, by which its virtue was corrupted. It had its griefs against fortune and against mankind; it believed it had been the victim of injustice and of scorn; it had sworn to make others expiate the misfortune of its birth and the defeats of its ambition; its rankling bitterness mingled something of gloom and horror with its most noble feelings; its tenderness resembled wrath, its dreams of happiness resembled vengeance.

If Marguerite could have read her preserver's thoughts, she would have been seized with terror. She had placed her secret and her life at the disposal of a man for whose soul God and Satan were disputing. Which was to gain the victory? Capable of generous emotions, but incapable of scruples, this workman's heart had the fierce desires, the bold flight, and the savage cry of a bird of prey.

CHAPTER XXVIII.

JOSEPH FINDS A NEW EMPLOYER.

M. Bertrand was in his store one day, between four and five o'clock in the afternoon, when a young workman appeared at the door, dressed in a short blouse, with a knapsack on his back and a stout stick in his hand. The dealer in *bric-à-brac* did not deign to notice this new comer. He was talking with a customer, whom he was attempting to deceive without success, which fact provoked him very much. M. Bertrand flattered himself that he was an adept in the art of *making a customer bite*, as he expressed it. His plan was to exhibit first all the daubs, the refuse of his stock. After having tortured his customer by keeping him for a long time contemplating these horrors, he would pass on to other paintings of some merit, and show him some apocryphal canvas, scratched and re-touched in twenty places, which he would characterize as a masterpiece and call by the most pompous names. He thought that after having lived some time with negroes, it would be natural to mistake mulattos for whites. If the amateur was a hard customer, and his judgment was able to withstand this double assault, M. Bertrand would have recourse to his great expedient, to what he called his boxed-up picture. "Is that all?" the customer would ask; "haven't you any thing else?" "That's all," the shrewd merchant would reply, "and it seems to me it is enough. I see you are tired of looking at so many. As regards my Perugino and my Rembrandt, I never exhibit them except on great occasions." The purchaser, who thought his visit entitled to be called a great occasion, would insist on seeing them. M. Bertrand would hesitate awhile, and at last would lead his man, with a condescending air, into a small room, entered by a door of solid oak, carefully locked and bolted. This sanctuary, in which a mysterious twilight reigned, contained a couple of cases, before approaching which,

M. Bertrand always made a profound and reverent bow. His experience had taught him that a customer is less likely to bite at a Rembrandt than at a closed case which might contain a Rembrandt. His own inclosed only copies. Solemn as an officiating priest, taking out the masterpiece with an infinity of precautions and with a pious hand, he would begin to sing its praises, and to grow pathetic, his voice would tremble, and sometimes tears stood in his eyes. Then, mingling the serious with the sweet, he would recount the birthplace and the history of the masterpiece, its varied fortunes, its peregrinations, the galleries of which it had been the finest ornament, the principal sales in which it had figured, the ruses which he had employed to gain possession of it, how, for instance, having discovered it in a garret at Rome, he had had the greatest trouble in getting it across the frontier, the holy father having determined to claim the treasure for the Vatican, and not to allow it to be taken from his States.

The day that Joseph made his first appearance in M. Bertrand's store, the customer had not taken the bait. It is proper to add that this customer was a Belgian, and according to Bertrand, the Belgian was a cool and reasoning animal. The child of the Scheldt had not bitten at either the daubs or the paintings of merit, at either the locked door or the pine case. Silent and observant, he had looked and listened almost without opening his mouth; he had not, however, been able to keep from smiling once or twice, and in order to conceal this smile had put to his lips the gold head of a cane, which M. Bertrand would willingly have broken across his back. After returning to the shop again, he began to examine a wooden chest, carved in Gothic style.

"You won't find its equal in the *hôtel de Cluny*," cried M. Bertrand. "It is splendidly preserved. It hasn't been retouched at all. It's just as it left the maker's hands." The Belgian made no reply; he simply placed his finger on two of the carved figures; one was antique, the other modern, and the contrast between them was easily to be seen. Thereupon he bowed and left the store.

The *bric-à-brac* merchant was very indignant, and wished all the Belgians at the bottom of the sea. He felt aggrieved that his customer had not allowed himself to be deceived, to say nothing of the fact that large robberies did not disgust him at all with smaller ones. The day after he had caught a trout worth thirty thousand francs in the pond at Ornis, he could not bear to miss a carp or gudgeon. He acted on the precept of Socrates, who advised his disciples to despise nothing.

His bad humor sought for some object on which to vent itself; it was on Joseph that the storm fell. Suddenly perceiving him, he cried, "What are you doing standing there like an idiot? Did you come to beg? You've got hold of the wrong man! You can look for the right one in the street."

Joseph was not disconcerted by this reception. "My good sir," he answered, "I called to see if you wanted a good cabinet-maker, who is willing to work, and understands his trade."

"Go to the devil with your cabinet work!" cried the other. "What do I want of a lazy fellow like you? You'd better leave as quick as possible."

"Excuse me," replied Joseph; "I've been running about Lyons all day without finding any work, and I can go no further."

With these words, he laid his knapsack on the floor, and, without any ceremony, sat down in an easy chair, which held out its arms invitingly toward him. "That's cool!" said M. Bertrand. "Upon my word, the little scamp takes it easy." Then running toward him, he cried, "Quick! out of this!" As he was about taking him by the shoulders, he recognized him as some one he had seen before. "Your impudent face is familiar to me," he said. "Where have I had the pleasure of meeting you?" Then he began to ransack his rich memory, which was one of those dark places that can not be searched long without making unpleasant discoveries. He began to pass his numerous acquaintances in review, when Joseph came to his assistance, saying, "We met in the court-yard of Castle D'Ornis....You remember, I came near being eaten by your dog."

"He wouldn't have digested you. He's used to better food. What were you doing at the castle?"

"I was in Burgundy buying wood for my employer; while traveling about, I was looking at the country."

"You amused yourself so much that your master kicked you out. If you don't hurry up, you'll have the same luck here."

So saying, he opened the door into the street; he did not, however, try to put Joseph out. He remembered that at Castle D'Ornis, the little scamp had treated him in such a cool and resolute way, that he had been compelled to lower his tone. Though M. Bertrand was familiar with every body, and rude to his inferiors, he never raised his hand except to the inoffensive and the weak. He avoided quarreling with others.

Joseph rose, picked up his knapsack, and placed it with a sigh upon his back. Instead of going out, however, he stood with folded arms before the chest which the Belgian had just examined, and looked at it a moment. "Your customer was right," he said. "There was mighty little skill in the restoring of that chest. It must have been a fool that patched up those twisted columns. Then look at those two monks singing matins....See, that's the original, and that's the copy, and one's as much like the other as a turnip's like an orange."

Self-confident people always made an impression on M. Bertrand. He was not wanting in confidence himself; but he had acquired it by study, and used it as a cover for his ignorance. When he found it in a natural state in other people, he at once conceived a high opinion of them. This coward, who pretended to be bold, had no respect for any thing but insolence. Joseph's speech attracted his attention. "What's that you say?" he cried. "Are you acquainted with those little machines? It's easy to talk, but I'd like to see you do the work."

"I'll be hanged," proudly answered Joseph, "if it will take me more than an hour to turn you out a monk's head singing matins....You'll be ready to swear that he never did any thing else all his life, and that the brute of a joiner who spoiled that piece of furniture for you is only a bungling workman."

It was now the turn of the great fisherman to bite. "Enough

said!" he answered. "There's a piece of wood and there's the tools. I'll take you at your word. If you make your monk, I'll give you your supper; but if you're only talking, you'll be kind enough to clear out at once, and take your knapsack and your boasting with you."

In two hours' time, Joseph had nearly finished his monk's head, which was an exact copy of the model. He had reproduced the face and all the details, the distended veins of the neck, the puffed-out cheeks, the dimples in the chin, the slight frown, in fact every thing to indicate a singer who was exerting himself to the utmost. M. Bertrand stared and, leaning toward him, said, "That isn't bad; you shall have your supper."

He led him into his room, where the table was already spread, and gave him a seat opposite his own. There was nothing remarkable about the meal; M. Bertrand did not spend much on his table; he made his investments in other quarters. They washed down their simple fare with a pale wine, which, in spite of its innocent look, went very quickly to the head. Joseph drank a great deal of it; when an idea had possession of him, he could swallow any quantity of wine, without being at all affected. M. Bertrand tried to draw him out; the young man told him all he wanted to know.

Toward the close of the meal, the worthy merchant said, "You're a good sort of fellow, and I see we can make something out of you. Now tell me honestly what your former master paid you."

"My former master was a stingy fellow," answered Joseph. "He never paid me much of any thing. I've left him in order to do better."

Thereupon he demanded such exorbitant wages, that M. Bertrand could scarcely believe his ears. They disputed the question for a long time; Joseph would not yield at all, but evinced a desire for gain, that was very revolting to M. Bertrand's stern morality. They finally, however, came to an understanding. The *bric-à-brac* merchant owned the miserable house, the ground floor of which was occupied by his store. He rented out the second story and lived in the third himself; above the latter were two small lofts. It was agreed that he should give Joseph his board and lodging, and in consideration of this, the latter was to be satisfied with reasonable wages.

This bargain being concluded, Joseph, well satisfied with his day's work and with having installed himself in the heart of the enemy's works, went up to take possession of his loft. It was not a pleasant spot; the cold was intense, and there was scarcely room to turn around. It seemed a delightful place to him, however, and he did not regret at all his comfortable attic-room at Mon-Plaisir. "Prudence and wise delay," he said to himself as he tried to warm his fingers: "those are the things that gain success." The last thing he thought of before going to sleep was the little bridge where he had met M. Bertrand for the first time, when leaning on the rail and gazing into the water, he had muttered, "Keep still, old fellow; what is done can't be helped!" "Yes, what is done can't be helped," thought Joseph, "but sometimes it can be looked after." Then placing his fingers on his lips, he threw into the darkness of the night a kiss, which knew well where to take its way.

It required only a short time for the shrewd boy to gain his new master's good will and confidence. M. Bertrand was delighted by the way he worked. In order to save all he could, he had employed none but low-priced workmen; he had now in his service, without any more expense, the king of Josons—this was a friendly nickname he had given him. Joseph repaired, with patient and ingenious industry, the old furniture which filled his employer's store-rooms, and which had cost him little more than the expense of transportation, so well did he understand the art of bargaining. Joseph dressed the wounds of these dilapidated articles with a light and delicate hand; he not only brought his fingers to the task, but he possessed, besides, taste, style, and a genius for the work. Up to that time, M. Bertrand had given all such work to a master cabinet-maker, with whom he had made an agreement, and who according to his story overcharged him heavily. He confided the most delicate work to Joseph, and the first cabinet he finished was sold the same day, bringing twice as much as he expected. It was during the enthusiasm caused by this first sale, that M. Bertrand called him the king of Josons.

His workman appeared to be a pleasant fellow. He was discreet, easy to get along with, and simple in his manners; he kept his place, took in good part his employer's familiarities, listened to his stories, and laughed at his jokes. When M. Bertrand had been unsuccessful in his projects and was in a bad humor, Joseph knew how to smooth him down again. He spoke to him something like a character in a certain comedy: "I say, Gotte, I have read in some book or other that, in order to make your fortune in this world, you must have neither honor nor humor." There was only one objection M. Bertrand made to him: he thought he stood up too firmly for his rights. One day when, under some pretext or other, he had endeavored to keep back a portion of his wages, Joseph had threatened at once to leave him. At another time, on a single word of remonstrance concerning a tool he had mislaid, he had mounted hurriedly to his loft, had thrust his clothes into his knapsack, and started off without saying a word. He had already reached the street, when M. Bertrand running after him, caught him by the blouse and coaxed him to return. A statesman said recently to a young prince, who was leaving to take possession of a vacant throne, "Don't pay too much attention to the Spaniards; they will care for you, if you don't care for them." Joseph understood diplomacy without having studied it, and Spain now held him by the blouse.

At first he took his meals in the shop, but little by little, M. Bertrand got into the habit of inviting him to his table, and generally they passed the evening together after dinner. During the dessert, the pale wine helping him, our worthy merchant became communicative. He told his workman about certain customs of the trade, or informed him of his commercial and financial speculations, which consisted in buying up old houses at a low price, repairing or rebuilding them in an economical way he well understood, and then selling them at a great advance. He also made known to Joseph his dreams of the future, which he was impatient to realize. His idea was to cross the sea, to settle in a slave country, and become a planter there. The paradise of his dreams consisted of some hundreds of blacks, men, women, and children, who were all to belong to him. He already saw himself governing this woolly tribe, with a whip in one hand and a handkerchief in the other. He was anxious to take possession as soon as possible ; and in order to hasten the happy moment, he lived very economically, denying himself present pleasures, but enjoying in imagination all the delights of his future Nabob life.

CHAPTER XXIX.

THE TRAP IS SET.

If M. Bertrand was satisfied with his workman, Joseph was no less satisfied with his employer. He studied him curiously and quietly, and soon began to understand his character. He found out at once that he did not belong to the class of heroic knaves. His clown's face was not deceptive; there was not in him the stuff of which great criminals are made; the most that could be said of him was, that he was the king of rogues. He had no scruples, yet he was very cautious. His strange and noisy impudence served to conceal the weakness of a will that was never sure of itself, and was always afraid of accidents; this iron bar had flaws in it, which rendered it liable to be broken suddenly. If any one were weak enough to yield to his effrontery, it carried every thing before it; if opposition were made to it, it gave way at once. One day, in Joseph's presence, he had a lively altercation with a builder who had come to collect some money on account. He tried to put him off at first by a number of miserable excuses. The other becoming urgent in his demand, he refused him boldly and endeavored to intimidate him; he was dealing, however, with a determined man, who turned on him at once, threatening to sue him. As soon as this occurred, M. Bertrand gave him what was due. From this and various other incidents, Joseph inferred that his employer was formidable only to those who had good cause to fear him. If Count D'Ornis submitted himself to this humiliating tyranny, he evidently had some great crime upon his conscience.

Joseph made another observation. Although it may seem strange to compare M. Bertrand to a flower, this coarse man did, in one particular, resemble those beautiful blue and white morning-glories, the corollas of which, opening at the rising of the sun, close again as soon as he has sunk below the horizon. Like the morning-glories, M. Bertrand's gayety was fresh and sparkling in the morning, and unless something unpleasant happened in his business, he abounded in coarse jokes throughout the day. On the approach of evening, a sudden change took place, a cloud hung upon his brow, he became uneasy and nervous, if it is proper to speak of a clown's nerves. He then had recourse to the bottle to animate his drooping spirits, and society became very necessary to him. Before Joseph's arrival, he had been accustomed to spend his evenings at the coffee-house or in some little theatre; but since good fortune had brought the king of Josons beneath his roof, he no longer found it necessary to go away from home to seek for company and amusement. After dinner, they lit their pipes, and played interminable games of dominos together. On the other hand, he always tried to isolate himself during the hours of sleep. At eleven o'clock he sent Joseph to his loft; the cook retired to her room; a shop-boy made his bed on the first floor; he then shut himself up in his own apartments, which consisted of four rooms, the doors of which were fastened by double bolts. He slept there alone, watched over by a lamp that burned all night, and by his dog who lay at his feet upon the floor.

Joseph's loft was situated immediately above M. Bertrand's sleeping room, and the partition between them was quite thin. Joseph, who for some months past had slept with one eye open, thought he heard strange noises in his employer's room. He listened, he even pressed his ear against the floor; as we know this was no new thing for him. He heard nothing but a low groaning or grumbling sound, the creaking of loose boards beneath a heavy tread, and sometimes the howling of the dog, who perhaps was suffering from bad dreams and telling them to the moon. It seemed to him that his new employer's sleep was broken and troubled. "It's not indigestion that makes him so uneasy," he thought. "Can it be that he, too, has something on his conscience? I've discovered already that he has nerves; if he has a conscience besides, he's a very complete clown."

One evening, M. Bertrand notified his workman that early the next morning he had an important business engagement at the other end of Lyons: fearing that he should oversleep himself, he gave Joseph a pass-key, asking him to wake him at exactly four o'clock. It was half-past four when Joseph awoke. He dressed himself hastily and went down to his employer's room. As he was crossing the hall, a groaning sound fell upon his ear. He looked through the key-hole, and by the light of the lamp, saw M. Bertrand, who had slid from the bed to the floor, and who, with his eyes shut, was throwing his arms about, as though struggling with some hideous dream. Soon he uttered, in a mysterious tone, the same words that Joseph had heard him use before, "Be still, old fellow, be still!" Joseph kept quiet, thinking he might hear more; but that was all. M. Bertrand was again silent; at intervals he moved his lips, but no sound came from them. Finally Joseph rapped upon the door. The dog barked, and his master, rising suddenly, sprang into the bed, which groaned beneath his heavy weight.

"Who's that? what do you want?" he cried in an angry voice.

Joseph entered, saying, "I came to wake you up, as you asked me to last night."

"Oh! it's you, is it?" answered M. Bertrand in a milder tone. "Excuse me for speaking so; you just awoke me from a most delightful dream.... I thought I was stretched out in the shade of a palm-tree, with two lovely black girls near me; one was fanning me with a peacock's tail, while the other was delicately tickling the bottoms of my feet."

"I'm sorry I frightened your black girls away," said Joseph. "I had an idea that your dream was a bad one, for you spoke and said...."

"What did I say?" asked M. Bertrand, suddenly changing countenance.

"You said, 'Be still, old fellow?'"

"Did I, really?.......O! yes, I remember. An old negro had come to complain that he had been whipped for something he hadn't done, and I was sending him away.......What did he want to complain of that for? A little whipping wouldn't hurt the fellow. It's silly enough to talk in your sleep. Do you ever do it?"

"No," he answered; "I can't afford to dream, nor to keep black girls either."

With these words he went away. From that day, M. Bertrand never asked him to wake him in the morning.

Joseph Noirel knew how to act. He remained two months with M. Bertrand without asking him a single question, or manifesting the least curiosity concerning his affairs. He seemed to think only of his work and of making money. At the end of the two months, he asked for an increase ot wages. The *bric-à-brac* merchant protested, and tried to pay him in fine words and promises. Joseph threatened to leave if his demands were not complied with; his employer finally gave him what he wanted, and this discussion only increased his confidence in Noirel.

Joseph at times, however, was sad and silent; this surprised M. Bertrand, who said to him one evening, "What's the matter, my boy? You seem very dull to-day." To which Joseph answered with a start, "It's nothing." Then he affected a noisy gayety, which did not seem natural to him. Another time he allowed himself to be surprised with his head buried in his hands, and plunged in a deep and endless revery. "You are troubled about something," M. Bertrand said; "tell me about it." "We all have our troubles," Joseph answered. "Mine are not worth speaking of." M. Bertrand was not satisfied, and continued to question him on the subject. He liked to become acquainted with other people's affairs; some profit can be gained from every thing. Joseph did not enlighten him at all; he gave him nothing but evasive answers.

One Sunday, as M. Bertrand was dilating for the hundredth time on the joys which he anticipated in Brazil, Joseph interrupted him saying, "That may be well enough for you; I couldn't be happy in Brazil."

"What would make you happy then?" asked M. Bertrand.

"Revenge, if you must know!" he answered in a sullen tone.

"Revenge! whom do you want to be revenged on?"

Noirel bit his lips, as though he were sorry he had said so much. "On nobody," he said. "Is it likely I'd hate any one? I was talking nonsense, that is all."

M. Bertrand's curiosity was now thoroughly excited; on several occasions, he endeavored to discover Joseph's secret. The following Sunday, he persuaded him to drink more than usual, and when two bottles had been emptied, made a direct assault upon him. "What are you so mysterious about?" he said. "Don't you like to talk over matters with your friends? Tell me what troubles you, old fellow! If you've got an enemy you want to be revenged on, you may get some advice, and some help, too, perhaps."

Joseph did not yield for a long time. At last he began a story, in which fact and fiction were strangely mingled. He said that he had been apprenticed in his youth to a master-joiner at Geneva; that his benefactor had certainly been very kind to him, but had always treated him in a haughty way; that under these circumstances, he had been unfortunate enough to fall in love with the daughter of the house; that finding she was receiving attentions from a man of rank, he had been so foolish as to declare his love, which had been scornfully refused; and that finally, he had been spurned from the house as though he were a dog.

"What's your former master's name?" asked M. Bertrand.

"Haven't you seen it on my certificate upstairs?"

"I don't remember; I think there's an ink spot over it."

"His name is M. Mirion."

M. Bertrand started. "Mirion!.... I've heard of him before.... Your sweetheart is Countess D'Ornis now?"

"Countess of any thing you please," answered Joseph with a sullen air. "When you met me at Ornis, I wasn't there by chance, as I told you the other day. Those idiots had sent me there to gather information; they wanted to make sure that he was a real count.... A real count, you understand! If he'd been white with leprosy, they would have given him Margot all the same."

"Yes, I see....what did Margot think of it?"

"Oh! she's a kind of saint....She's always willing to do every thing you want her to. She was delighted, though, I know; her eyes betrayed her happiness." Bringing his fist down heavily on the table, he continued, "Ah! if I could get those upstarts in my power! How scornfully they treated me! They trod me under foot as though I were a worm."

Then, letting his imagination have free play, he gave M. Bertrand a long account of the miseries and insults he had endured. "The trouble was, you looked too high," replied the latter. "I saw your Margoton, one day, at one of the castle windows. She's handsome as an angel.....Then the money! how about the money? I've heard that those people were millionaires."

"That's no name for it," said Joseph. "I'll take my oath, though, I didn't care a straw for their money. I was dead in love. It was Margot I wanted, and if she brought me nothing but her night-cap and her slippers...."

"Her expectations were not to be despised," interrupted M. Bertrand. "You're a sly rogue, ain't you?"

Joseph assumed an offended look. "I was a great fool to tell you that," he answered in an angry tone. "You're a bourgeois, too, M. Bertrand, and the bourgeois all understand each other, like so many thieves....they're all leagued against us, and treat us as though we were the offscourings of the earth. Well, what is said can't be helped; but I'll be hung if I ever....A shut mouth catches no flies."

"Keep cool," said M. Bertrand, slapping him on the back, "I'm a good fellow. To prove it, I'll sign an agreement to give you my daughter with a dowry of a hundred thousand crowns. Only you'll be kind enough to wait till the young lady's born."

He laughed long at his joke and at Joseph's angry look, and then proposed a game of dominos. He played badly that evening, however; he was so preoccupied that Joseph could not help noticing it.

CHAPTER XXX.

M. BERTRAND TAKES THE BAIT.

For several days M. Bertrand appeared absorbed in thought. Noirel pretended not to notice it, and did not speak again of Marguerite. It was Bertrand, himself, who brought the subject up the second time. One evening, after walking a long time up and down the dining-room, whistling a lively air, he stopped before his workman, and placing his hand upon his shoulder, said, "You've only got to say the word, to be revenged on those Mirions."

"Leave me alone," Joseph answered in a sulky tone. "You joked enough about it the other night, I think."

"I say again that if you want to be revenged on your benefactors, you've only got to say the word. I can furnish you the means."

As Joseph looked at him in astonishment, he continued, "Answer a few questions for me first. Those people are rich and vain. Which influences them most, their money or their vanity?"

"Their vanity, most decidedly."

"Yet you told me they were mean enough not to give their daughter any dowry."

"You don't understand. They were willing to give her every thing, they had this marriage so much at heart; it seems, however, that M. D'Ornis was a man of peculiar delicacy. He refused to receive a dowry in order to show that he was not marrying for money."

M. Bertrand shook with rage. "What! *he* refused! Then in an accent of honest indignation, he added, "The miserable rascal!"

"What's that?" asked Joseph.

"I'm asking questions now," returned the other in a haughty tone. He took a large glass of wine to calm his ruffled temper, and then continued, "On what terms are they with their son-in-law?"

"They glory in him, and address him on their bended knees as they would the Eternal Father."

"If he should ask them to-morrow for half a million, would they give it to him?"

"Ah! now you're going too fast. The day before the wedding, they would have given him their last cent; to-day, in my opinion, they'd refuse him."

"Suppose Margot should join with him in asking for the hundred thousand crowns?"

"That's a very different affair. They would give her the entire million. With her soft ways, she leads them all, and, if she wanted to, could make them go through the eye of a needle. She's the real shepherd of the flock."

M. Bertrand's face lighted up. He sat down in a rocking chair, and began to drum with his fingers on his forehead; then rising again, he said, "How is it with you and Margot, have you had any quarrel?"

"O no! I don't think she has the least idea that I was ever rash enough.... I talked with her mother, and she said nothing to her.... What would be the use of that? It's easier to kick a poor fellow into the street, and say nothing to Margot about it.... There, I'm getting angry again. Let's play dominos, Monsieur Bertrand."

He shook the dominos from their box. M. Bertrand caught him by the arm saying, "If you should go to Ornis, would they receive you there?"

"I don't know whether they would or not; but if I was the only one to travel in that direction, the grass would soon grow in the road. If any one offered me ten thousand francs...."

"There, that will do, you rogue!" interrupted M. Bertrand. "If any one gave you ten thousand francs, you'd not only go to Ornis, but into the devil's den itself!".... As Joseph rose with an angry gesture, he added, "Lord! how quick you are! Pray sit down and listen to me. Suppose," he continued in a mysterious tone, "some one should go to Margot, and whisper in her ear, Madam, your noble husband, of whom you are so proud, has a crime upon his conscience, which no one knows about, thank Heaven, but which, if it was known, would make it very unpleasant for him...."

Joseph bounded from his seat. "What has he done?" he cried. "Has he committed forgery, or broken into some banker's safe?"

"That's none of your business," answered M. Bertrand; "that is my secret. Answer the question I put to you. What would she say to such a person?"

"Don't deceive yourself, the Mirions are no fools, and she has a sound head that reasons and will believe nothing except on abundant proof."

"Suppose," continued M. Bertrand, "this person had his proofs with him."

"She would require conclusive and unanswerable ones, such as could be seen and felt...."

M. Bertrand leaned toward him and, seizing him by his ears, which he pulled vigorously, said, "Proofs that can be seen and felt!....What would you say, if I had such proofs?"

Joseph remained for a moment dumb with astonishment. At last, coming to himself, he cried, "In that case, I'd say it was a splendid thing, and I'd like to take a hand in it."

M. Bertrand began to laugh. "Look at the innocent fellow, who never loved any thing but his sweetheart. Don't speak to him of money; it will break his heart....I say, my boy, if we avenge you, you've nothing else to ask for. Let's play dominos, Monsieur Joson!"

"One moment," answered Joseph, seizing his arm in turn. "I don't care for the money; but the vengeance that you offer me—the devil! it's one of those dishes I can eat without being hungry."....Then snapping his fingers as though they were castanets, he added, "So you want to bleed those Mirions, eh? I'm your man; only I don't know how to play my part...."

"Oh! you'll do well enough; and you shall have your share

too. Whoever puts his hand in the pie will have something stick to his fingers. You shall have your share, large or small, according to the size of the pie."

Then resting his elbows on the table, he continued, " Listen to me. You must start for Ornis early to-morrow morning; you must present yourself before your sweetheart, saying that you've come to ask her to plead your cause with your old employer. You've been driven away, but you are homesick; you want to return to the old place. If she receives you kindly, you can show your gratitude by warning her of danger; if she will not hear you, you can get angry and threaten her with revenge. In either case, you must reveal to her that your new master, Monsieur Bertrand, dealer in *bric-à-brac* and other articles, is the owner of a paper which threatens the safety of Count D'Ornis; that the said Bertrand is a dangerous man, and that this little paper is probably for sale, the only thing being to fix the price. You can make up any story you please to explain to her how you know all this; above all, you must give her to understand that she is lost, if her husband ever suspects her....The devil! he'd just as leave kill her as not. You must therefore advise her to observe the strictest secrecy....In short, you are a stupid rascal, if you don't bring me back word that the lady will meet me at such a day and hour and place, to question me and make a bargain for my little scrawl."

In proportion as M. Bertrand developed his plan of operations, Joseph, who had been very eager at first, pretended to become more doubtful and hesitating. He was full of difficulties and objections, representing to his employer that their common enterprise seemed very hazardous to him, that he feared he was not a fit person to attend to it, that, as nearly as he could judge, he would neither be received nor believed at Ornis, and that, at his first words, before he could gain time to explain himself, he would be turned into the road. M. Bertrand grew excited and told him he was a coward. "What do you want to send me for?" Joseph asked. "Why don't you write instead?"

"I never write," he answered. "The only writing I care for is that of other people."

The next day, Joseph acted in the same manner. The cooler he became, the more excited M. Bertrand grew. "Don't be angry," Joseph said at last; "since you're so determined, I will try it; but I'll not answer for my success. You'll find that you're engaged in a desperate game."

The day afterward, he was on the road to Ornis.

CHAPTER XXXI.

CONVALESCENCE.

We sometimes say, "Strong as a Turk;" we might better say, "Strong as a young girl struggling with sickness and misfortune." She is considered lost; her physicians have given her up; her friends, if she have any, are already mourning for her. She does not cease to hope; she defends herself with calm persistency against the assaults of the pitiless enemy who has caught her in his iron grasp; more pliant than the willow or the vine, she meets his furious attacks with a gentle and patient resistance. Her days have been so few! She looks forward to the future with such longing and desire! "Wait for me, happy days!" she cries. At last, moved by pity and repentance, Death softly steals away.

Marguerite was for several days at the point of death. M. Crotet had already pronounced the fatal sentence, when suddenly she began to improve as though by miracle; her most alarming symptoms disappeared, her eyes, for a moment paralyzed, regained their natural lustre, her fever passed away. At the end of three weeks, she became convalescent; her appetite and strength returned, and a few days afterward she was walking about her room. She was not, however, the Marguerite of former days. She seemed to have lost forever her bright color, her quick and graceful movements, the elasticity of her step, the quick flash of her glance, and that charming smile which always lurked in the clear depths of her eyes. The greatest change was in her voice, which had been so fresh and sweet that it reminded one of the linnet in the woods, when, in the bright spring days, it carols forth its happy song. That voice now was soft and faint; having nothing but sad things to say, it had no use for its former ringing notes. Her form, too, like her voice, bore the impress of a languid grace; her beauty, however, still remained. It was not a destruction, it was only a metamorphosis. Grief had touched with his sceptre that youthful and smiling brow, over which the hours had heretofore so lightly flown ; it had left upon it a settled gloom, the imprint of a sad memory. This, however, did not prevent M. Crotet from admiring the astonishing rapidity of his fair patient's recovery—it was indeed wonderful, from the fact that she had had to contend not only with her malady, but also with her doctor, who had treated her in a barbarous way, administering remedies fit only for a horse. " My dear Countess," he said, " I've never seen such a recovery from meningitis before." He had taken a liking to her on account of all the leeches he had applied. Such are the considerations that determine the friendships of physicians.

Marguerite, while convalescing, had regained the use of her mind and memory. She clearly recalled the past; but she saw it in the distance, as it were. It seemed to her that her sickness had lasted a long time, that entire years had rolled away since the day when, carrying a picture to the garret, she had overheard a conversation that had frozen the blood within her veins. Her memory was very clear; but her impressions being deadened, she asked herself if her imagination had not had something to do with her fright and her despair.

She said to herself, " I'll think no more about it, till I've regained my strength." When one is recovering from brain fever, it is necessary to start anew in life. She bravely went to work to learn again to use her hands and feet and head; she applied herself to this like a faithful scholar to his tasks. She had plenty of time: all her hours belonged to her. Every three days, she saw her husband for three minutes, when he spoke three words. This seemed more than enough to her, so much did she dread any excitement or emotion. She sometimes saw her mother-in-law, and had no reason to complain of her. Mme. D'Ornis treated her as though she were a sick child, not responsible for the foolish things she might say or do. She seemed to think it very strange that she was able to put two words or ideas together, or that she had any common sense at all. Her maid was of the same opinion. Marguerite soon discovered that this girl had changed during her sickness, that she was now playing the spy upon her, and was in communication with the enemy. Another thing happened which made her sad. One morning, as she was walking in the park, she heard the porter's son call to his sister, who was playing in the snow, "What are you stopping for, you big fool?" His mother placed her hand quickly over his mouth, while she cast a glance at Marguerite; she remembered that it is not proper to speak of a rope in the house of a man who has been hung.

Marguerite's courage alternately rose and fell. Sometimes she thought she could discover in herself an inexhaustible fund of patience and resignation; she felt strong enough to tire out her grief. At other times, life weighed so heavily upon her, that her mind seemed to fall to pieces. Marguerite, however, would not yield; she went to work to repair the ruin.

Her only amusement was carriage riding. For some years, M. D'Ornis had owned no horses; he hired them whenever they were needed. She expressed a wish to buy a pair with her own money; he gave his consent at once. The Marquis Du Rozan sold her two good trotters, whose lively ways had given the Marchioness much uneasiness. She selected for her coachman an old man who had formerly been a diligence postilion. M. D'Ornis only required that Jerome, his valet, should always accompany her in her rides; his orders were never to lose her from his sight.

It happened, however, that one day toward the middle of February, Jerome was called away for a short time. Marguerite did not wait for him; she ordered her old postilion to start on, and made him drive her a long distance on the road to Arnay-le-Duc, to the foot of a rocky hill that commanded an extensive view. Descending from the carriage, she climbed by a foot-path to the summit of this hill. When a stone wall at last concealed her from her coachman's sight, she folded her arms upon her breast, and looked upon the landscape spread out before her. The snow had fallen heavily during the few preceding days, and had covered the whole plain with a thick white shroud, through which the undulations of the ground were visible. Clearly defined against this background, were long rows of poplars, tufts of yellow osiers, old and stunted oaks covered with dry leaves, clumps of elms and beeches whose dark forms and naked arms had fixed themselves in tragic attitudes, patches of thorny brushwood, still agitated by long struggles with the wind and revealing their anger by their savage gestures, and here and there a few lonely pines, bending beneath the weight of years and looking sadly down upon the snow. The hills which bounded the horizon were half concealed by a thick gray mist. The air was still; nothing was moving on the ground or in the branches of the trees. The plain and all that it contained was frozen into immobility and silence. Over this landscape hung a dull, leaden sky, which seemed tired of gazing on the gloomy scene below.

Marguerite was in low spirits, and this view was not calculated to console her. Her sadness whispered low to the sad things about her, to the frozen, lifeless fields, to the bare and gloomy woods, to the earth and sky, both prisoners of the winter and believing no more in the coming of the spring. Her heart was frozen like the plain, her future appeared as dull and dark as the gray horizon. Suddenly the clouds opened, and the pale sunlight struggled through them for a moment. The valley seemed astonished, it did not recognize the stranger; he, himself, felt that he was out of place and disappeared. So a traveler sets out to find a friend, and stops at the wrong door; unfamiliar faces meet his gaze, he finds out his mistake, and quickly moves away.

"How the sun is changed!" thought Marguerite; "I never saw him with so sad and wan a face. He has been sick like me; he has lost his color, too. Formerly, we loved to look upon each other; I don't know which was the gayer of the two. Ah! what has become of our old friendship?....And yet," she continued, "when I saw that death had spared me, I was thankful for it. What a fierce desire to live! Is life of any value without happiness? Could I believe in happiness again? I did believe in it; I can not do so now. How simple I was then! every thing seemed easy to me! I used to be so young! How old am I to-day?"

She sat down on a stone, first brushing the snow off with her handkerchief. She leaned forward and closed her eyes. It seemed to her that within her was a springtime surprised and ravaged by the frost; her heart was strewn with unfulfilled desires and disappointed expectations, with withered branches and dead flowers. "If I had a child," she said as she raised her head, "I'd teach him to believe that life was but a snare."

CHAPTER XXXII.

THE MEETING IN THE SNOW.

As Marguerite was about to descend the hill and rejoin her coachman, whose horses she thought might have become uneasy, she threw a last look over the valley. From the place where she stood, she could see upon her left the prolongation of the road which, after bending toward her, descended in zig-zags to a stream, beyond which she could trace it running for a long distance in a straight line. Marguerite noticed in the road a black point clearly defined against the snow. This point was moving, it was approaching her. She regarded it with interest; it was the only living being this solitude contained.

Suddenly an unaccountable emotion seized her. She had an idea that this traveler was not a stranger, that she knew his name and that he knew hers, that this very moment he was thinking of her, was looking for her, and was bringing something to her. He disappeared at one of the angles of the road; she did not wish to go without seeing him again. Wrapped in her thick furs, she did not feel the cold. Her feet alone were growing numb; she stamped upon the ground to warm them. Suddenly the man appeared. She gave a cry, as did the Israelites of old when they saw the manna falling in the desert. She was not mistaken—this traveler was acquainted with her life and history; he knew her name and loved to have it linger on his lips. He had been a witness of her youth, he had seen this flower grow, he had heard this bright bird sing. he could certify that Marguerite Mirion had once been loved and happy; and this traveler, who had known her so long, did not pass by; he had come purposely to see her, he had, indeed, brought her something, for under his gray blouse, beneath his woolen vest, there was a heart devoted to her, a soul that belonged to her, that had sworn obedience to her will. In her first transport of joy, she cast about her a glance of triumph, as though to say to the trees, the rocks, the snow, the mist, "I am richer than I thought; if you have never seen a true and honest soul, here is one, a soul that belongs to me." ....Then she waved her handkerchief, with as much excitement as a ship in distress would display on seeing help approaching. Joseph saw her, raised his cap, hastened his steps, and soon, leaving the road to climb directly toward her, she saw him leap from stone to stone, jump over bushes, force his way through the brushwood, and run swiftly over the snow. He was not more than twenty paces from her, when he stopped, all out of breath and ready to sink down with emotion. Again he started toward her. She held out both her hands, which he seized and pressed within his own, fastening a look on her, in which she thought she saw nothing but the respectful inquiries of a tender and devoted friendship; perhaps, at that moment, his eyes revealed no more than this. She drank in his glance, as a shipwrecked mariner, who still feels the salt waves washing against his lips and threatening him with death, drinks the first glass of wine that a merciful hand presents to him.

This transport of joy was of short duration. Her memory, which had been weakened by her sickness, now came back in all its power. In seeing again this man whom she had made her confidant, she had also seen the past, and shaking off its torpor, her mind suddenly awoke. Since she had returned from death to life, she had tried to persuade herself that the only cause of her unhappiness was that she was no longer loved. Before Joseph had spoken a word, she knew that he had brought all her former terrors back to her.

She looked at him uneasily; he gazed on her with astonishment. He found her changed, and no longer recognized the bright young girl whom he had carried across a ploughed field two years before. Her paleness, the dull fire of her glance, her emaciated features, her face on which disease had left its traces, and the bright color of which had given way to a touching languor and penetrating charm, all served to bewilder him. What had become of Marguerite Mirion? After looking at her for a short time, he felt that he did not love her less, but that he loved her in a different way. He experienced a feeling of sad tenderness, he could have sat down at her feet and cried; he was capable at that moment of risking his life for her without asking any thing in return. "What has happened?" he asked. "Have you been sick?"

"Alas! my poor Joseph, I've been very, very sick," she answered with a faint attempt to smile. "I have escaped as though by miracle, and you see me surprised at being still alive, and not knowing whether to rejoice or weep. Life has some good in it, however, since sooner or later we see our friends again."

With these words, she held out her hand to him the second time. "But what chance has brought you here?" she said.... "I wrote you two months ago; didn't you receive my letter?"

"Forgive me," he answered. "I disobeyed you, and it is well I did, for that scrap of paper of which you spoke to me exists; it has been most carefully preserved.... It has fallen into terribly bad hands. Fortunately they are hands that open when they see gold within their reach."

She nervously twisted the ribbons of her hat. "Tell me quickly all about it," she replied in a trembling voice.

He briefly told his story, while she listened to him, gazing into his face with haggard eyes. She kept interrupting him, exclaiming, "Is it so?....do you believe it?....can it be true?"

He concluded with the following advice: "After having thought it over, I believe it will be well for you to see this man. He is not fit to approach you, or to speak to you,....but it can not well be helped. You mustn't be afraid of him; he is a coward. Then I won't be far away, for I wouldn't consent for any thing in the world....You had better write me a few lines that I can show him, which will give me an excuse to accompany him here. He is very suspicious. Your letter must be carefully worded....You must pretend that you will believe nothing unless you see the proofs with your own eyes. He must come here and bring his paper with him, so that you may know what it is.... Perhaps, in spite of what he says, it don't amount to any thing. In that case, you can send him off again."

While Joseph was speaking, Marguerite was a prey to the most cruel uncertainty. Her first impulse was to push away the cup thus offered to her. How did she know but a deadly poison lurked within it? At the same time she thought, "My present situation is so painful that I can not bear it longer. An opportunity is now offered to escape from it. If I can become the possessor of this paper and restore to M. D'Ornis his dignity and lost repose, I shall compel him to give up his horrible suspicions, and to do me justice. He has told me that my words are false; he must believe my deeds. I'll not ask him to love me, for that he can not do; but the greatness of this service will oblige him to put faith in me, and thus make life endurable again."

She made her decision, and as Joseph finished speaking, said, "You're right. I will write to you.... Then I will ask for proofs; you can see for yourself that it is so.... I must have proofs!...."

Suddenly a voice behind her cried, "Proofs of what, I'd like to know?"

She turned round quickly, and saw M. D'Ornis, who, with his hands in his pockets, was looking at her in a threatening way.

While his wife was riding, he had started for a walk, first having slung his gun across his back. As he was crossing a meadow, he saw at a distance the carriage standing in the road, and curious to know what this halt meant, had turned aside from his intended route. The coachman told him that Mme. D'Ornis had left the carriage, and that he had become uneasy about her, but had not dared to leave the horses, as there was no one else to stay with them. Thereupon, M. D'Ornis had climbed the hill in haste, and had arrived in time to hear the words, "I must have proofs!"

"Proofs of what?" he asked again, looking from Marguerite to Joseph, and then from Joseph back to Marguerite.

She immediately regained her presence of mind, and for the

first time in her life she boldly lied. She knew that he loved her no longer, and she felt that she could not love him.

"This is a good workman," she said in the calmest tone, "who has lived twelve years with us." (She strongly emphasized the *us*.) "They have discharged him for a supposed offense, which he tells me he has not committed. He is intelligent and honest, and his only fault is that he can not always control his tongue. He has come to ask me to intercede for him. I have promised that I will write to my father, and ask him what proofs he has that this young man has deserved to be discharged. I must have proofs. Don't you think, Roger, that it's the best thing I can do?"

Judging from his past experience, M. D'Ornis considered her incapable of telling an untruth. He almost believed her now, which fact, however, did not prevent him from looking at Joseph with an arrogant and angry glance. "What is your name?" he suddenly inquired.

"Joseph Noirel," replied the workman, after hesitating a moment whether to answer him or not.

"Well, M. Joseph, if you have come to Ornis on purpose to have a consultation with my wife, you will make nothing by it, and it may be it will cost you something."

The sudden appearance of M. D'Ornis had thrown Joseph into a tumult of excitement. He was no longer the same man; his passions were rekindled, his heart was full of violent desires, which cried aloud to him as the young eagles cry when they ask for food. His first idea, which was not a very unreasonable one, was to seize Marguerite in his arms and carry her away, crying, "Who will dare to take her from me?" Fortunately, she looked at him, and this glance brought him to himself. He answered M. D'Ornis, "I hope that the Countess." ....He could say no more; it was impossible for him to hold any communication with this man.

"You have no business to hope," answered M. D'Ornis as he approached him, "nor to keep your cap on in the presence of a superior." So saying, he struck his cap and sent it flying through the air.

Joseph's face grew white as the snow on which he stood; he was on the point of rushing headlong on M. D'Ornis, and it was with great difficulty that he finally controlled his passion. His lips trembled, he nervously rubbed his hands together; he said to his pride, "Be still, your hour has not yet come." Marguerite had run after his cap; she picked it up, brushed it off, and presenting it to Joseph, said, "The man who controls his temper is always the superior. You may depend upon me. I will write to-morrow to my father."

She had just lied to her husband; now, for the first time, she braved him. She was astonished at her own audacity, at the change which her destiny was already working in her character. M. D'Ornis also seemed surprised. Two minutes afterward, Marguerite stepped into the carriage; before closing the door, she invited her husband to take the seat beside her.

"I prefer to walk," he answered. Then turning to the coachman, he dryly said, "Hereafter, when Jerome is not at liberty, you need not go."

He waited till the carriage was out of sight, and then climbed the hill again to make sure that Joseph had departed. The man with the cap had already reached the road; he was walking at a rapid pace, and singing a battle-song in a loud voice. This song was interrupted now and then by hoarse, sharp cries, like those of a wounded hawk. The song and cries breathed forth a savage joy, a frantic hope, a fierce and passionate hate, the tumult and confusion of a soul that could no longer recognize itself.

CHAPTER XXXIII.

M. BERTRAND OUTWITTED.

Joseph Noirel presented himself to his employer with a long face and downcast look, like a man who brings bad news. He told him that he had with great difficulty succeeded in obtaining an interview with the Countess Marguerite, but had scarcely mentioned the subject of his errand, when she became indignant and drove him from the house. "You're a fool," said M. Bertrand; "you didn't know how to manage it. Never mind, we won't give up so soon. Young women are quick-tempered; they get mad and won't listen at first, but afterward they think it over and are mighty glad to talk. I'm only afraid that she will tell her husband, in which case, I'll lay it all on you, and send you off as a traitor and a spy!"

"I knew very well," replied his workman, "that was all I had to expect."

A week passed, during which nothing more was said. The eighth day, at supper-time, Joseph's employer handed him a letter. He opened it hastily, and as he read his face betrayed some emotion. M. Bertrand unceremoniously snatched the paper from his hands; fortunately, it was an easy letter to understand. It read as follows:

"I have written to request your pardon. They answer me that your conduct was unjustifiable, without giving me any further explanation. You have exiled yourself forever from a home which you ought surely to regret; you received there many favors, for which you have made a poor return. I am sorry for it. Gratitude is a noble trait, and my father is right in saying that ungrateful people always come to a bad end. If you need money, let me know. I shall be very glad to help you. It seems to me, however, that so good a workman as you are ought easily to find a way out of this difficulty, without having recourse to any unworthy or deceptive tricks. Can I speak in any other way of the commission you undertook? What does your new master take me for, that he thinks he can so easily disturb me? He evidently thinks that all young women are credulous and jealous. You might have told him that the members of my family always take things coolly, and never believe any thing unless they see the proofs. I should have blushed to have thought for a quarter of an hour of the few words he sent you to whisper to me, and I shall be glad to tell him so, if he ever come to Ornis. Perhaps he would prefer to write; in that case, I should advise him to disguise his writing, as it probably is well known here."

"Good Lord!" cried M. Bertrand as he folded up the letter, "what a strange mixture of cunning and stupidity women are! Here is one who takes plenty of precautions. In the first place, she has mailed her letter at Arnay-le-Duc, as the post-mark proves; then she hasn't signed it, and probably she's disguised her hand besides, which last fact pleases me, for I conclude from it that she's afraid of her husband and has said nothing to him on the subject. On the other hand, this very cautious woman is simple enough to think that I'm going to write to her. What does she take me for? You can set it down as a general rule that those who write are fools. Add to this that my lady is incredulous and is never disturbed; that she would blush to have thought for a quarter of an hour of those few words, and yet that she does think of them a week afterward. Your Margot is an innocent creature; we were so afraid we couldn't interest her, and here she is excited by a single word. I'd only want to have a few customers like her.... The great trouble is, she has left it for me to appoint the time and place of meeting. What shall I do? I'm looked upon at Ornis as a white wolf would be."

"All I ask is that you won't send me there again!" answered Joseph with a scared expression. "They treated me like a dog, and I'm a little proud, you know."

"What will you sell out for?" his employer asked with a sly

glance. "You mean well enough, my boy; but you want a little training."

Another week passed by. M. Bertrand hoped for a second letter from Marguerite. As nothing came, he finally became impatient and tried to persuade Joseph to write to her; he refused, however, repeating his employer's aphorism: "Those who write are fools."

"How can it hurt you?" asked M. Bertrand.

"There are certain things that the law looks out for," he answered. "You want me to pull the chestnuts out of the fire. You'll take the chestnuts and leave me to the police."

"Don't be such a fool as to talk of the police. Say rather that you're afraid of being laughed at."

"I'm not afraid of any thing," answered Joseph; "but I don't intend to be imposed upon."

M. Bertrand treated him coolly all the evening, but Joseph pretended not to notice it. Only one thought troubled him: what influence could he bring to bear to make his employer take him to Ornis with him? M. Bertrand kept thinking the matter over without coming to any decision. He was willing to trust no one but himself. As Joseph was preparing to retire to his loft, he asked him to call at his room the next morning at five o'clock. "We may have something to talk about," he said.

It was still dark when Joseph, who had slept but little through the night, heard M. Bertrand moving about his room. After a while he went out, but soon returned again. At half-past four, Joseph went down stairs, and suddenly entering his employer's bedroom, surprised him preparing for a journey. A large iron safe, set in the wall and furnished with a patent Fichet lock, stood open; on the table lay a large leather pocket-book, fastening with a key. M. Bertrand quickly slipped the pocket-book into his coat, buttoning it tightly over his breast. "Is that the way to come into a room?" he asked in a surly tone. "What are you doing here? It isn't five o'clock."

"Excuse me for disturbing you," said Joseph. "If I can help you in any way in getting ready for your journey...."

"What journey?"

"Why you seem to be going away; I can't help noticing it. ....There! frankly, M. Bertrand, you had better not attempt it."

"Not attempt what, you fool?"

"I shouldn't say any thing about it, if it were not to keep my conscience clear, for you know well enough it makes no difference to me. Your life is your own, and you can dispose of it as you please. I would guard against surprises, though, if I were in your place. I don't know what you've got in that big pocket-book you just put in your coat, and I don't care to know: it's none of my business, anyway. The Countess Marguerite is very cunning, though, and to-night I began to suspect....What would you say if she had let her husband into the secret, and if he had dictated the letter she wrote the other day? We must look out for every thing. Are you sure that you're not being drawn into a trap? You will arrive there and be assigned a rendezvous, when suddenly three big fellows will spring on you and rob you....The fox expected to eat the hen, but it's the hen that catches the fox at last....Believe me, Monsieur Bertrand, you'd better not attempt it!"

M. Bertrand grew thoughtful; he sat down astride a chair, with his elbows resting on the back. "There's nothing in my pocket-book," he answered after a moment's pause, "except some receipted bills and two or three bank notes."

The tune of his song did not agree with the words, and Joseph learned all he wished to know. "Oh!" he answered carelessly, "if that's all you've got, what's the use of going to Ornis?.... Margot is a Mirion, and the Mirions never yet bought a thing without knowing what it was."

M. Bertrand looked at his finger-nails for some time without speaking. The vision of the three men evoked by Joseph made him thoughtful. The more he reflected, however, the more improbable did his workman's suggestion seem. Marguerite's letter excluded the idea of any plot; he had put it in his desk, he now took it out and read it again. "You are all wrong this time," he said to Joseph. "When people set a trap, they generally bait it. Read that letter. Don't you see that Margot wants to see me and at the same time is afraid to do so? She would like better to have me write. You're a coward, but you've made a mistake in trying to frighten me."

Joseph argued the question with him for a long time. "This is my conclusion," said M. Bertrand, rising as he spoke: "who risks nothing gains nothing; only for the sake of greater safety, I'll take you with me, and you can act as courier and scout."

"Thank you!" said Joseph starting for the door. "Ornis is not a place I like, and I prefer to stay at home."

M. Bertrand caught hold of him and forced him back into the room. "Upon my word, you're a queer fellow," he said. "If there's any thing to be made, you're always ready; I never saw such an appetite for gain. We mustn't ask you to take any trouble, though. If we do, your pride is afraid of a rebuff, your conscience is afraid of the police, and your long ears are afraid of being cut off. You're fond of sinecures, and want the money to come in while you're asleep.... Listen, my boy, I'll buy your pride, your conscience, and your ears, all in a lump. What do you want for them?"

Joseph looked him in the eyes as though to assure himself that he meant what he said. "Two thousand francs," he answered in a trembling voice, "and I'm your man."

M. Bertrand made a gesture of dismay. "Two thousand francs!" he said; "are you crazy? Where shall I get them from?"

"You expect to get five hundred thousand out of this affair," answered Joseph.

"Five hundred thousand francs....wouldn't I be happy if I had them. You don't understand the times, my boy; a man's signature sells as cheap as his honor now; you can't get more than the market price. Besides you exaggerate the importance of my little paper. I overestimated it the other day. No doubt Margot will be glad to get it, but if I ask her a cent too much, she'll send me to the moon to get my pay. And then, too, this may happen. She will, perhaps, begin to cry, and I have a tender heart. I know just how it is: when I see a woman cry, it's too much for me, I always melt into tears.... You'll see that I'll give her my little paper for a thank-you."

M. Bertrand's tears! If a sea monster had told Joseph of its excessive susceptibility, he could have believed it much more readily. He insisted on his price. The discussion became animated; his employer finally had to yield, and although he did not like to write, consented to sign a note as follows: "M. Bertrand hereby agrees to pay the sum of two thousand francs to his workman, Joseph Noirel, when the latter shall have faithfully performed the work committed to him." Joseph pretended to find nothing objectionable in the words or form of this note, which his employer gave him, saying, "Now, are you satisfied? You complain of getting too small slices. This one may give you an indigestion."

CHAPTER XXXIV.

THE CONSPIRATORS AT ORNIS.

M. Bertrand took time to leave a few instructions with his clerks, and then set out with Joseph for the station at Vaise. At half past six the train started, and at ten o'clock our travelers arrived at Beaune. There they took a closed carriage, which carried them at a rapid pace to Rousset, a hamlet near Ornis. M. Bertrand stopped at an inn, where he ordered dinner. "Be off!" he said to Joseph. "It's a principle of mine to attend to business at once."

Joseph quickly left him and soon reached the outskirts of Ornis, which place he carefully avoided. He turned one side and gained the little wood, where three years before the Marquis De Raoux had been murdered. He wandered about there for some time, in the hope that Marguerite would appear in the park, and that he could approach her without being seen. He waited in vain. Evening came on; it had snowed heavily the previous day, and the sky now being clear, the cold was intense; the paths in the park had not yet been cleared, and it was very improbable that Marguerite would care to walk there. Joseph retraced his steps; there was nothing for him to do but to enter the castle, and to enter it, moreover, by the door.

Unfortunately this door was guarded, and at the very moment that Joseph arrived before the gate, the porter stepped out in front of his lodge. Seeing Jerome sweeping the snow off the steps in the court, he asked, "Is it true that the Count will not be back to dinner?"

"He's going to dine with Marquis Du Rozan," replied the other; "he won't be back before eleven or twelve o'clock."

This news pleased Joseph very much, and his face lighted up at once. "You don't say so!" continued the old porter as he took a pinch of snuff. "The Count is on good terms with the Marquis then?"

"He has sold him his mill. They sign the papers to-night."

"His mill! Next year he'll sell his park. What on earth has come over him?"

The worthy man remained thoughtful for a moment, with downcast eyes, and as gloomy a look as Hamlet's when he cried, "The time is out of joint." As he regained his lodge, he met Joseph, who had just passed through the gate. "Where are you going? what do you want?" he said.

"Is Count D'Ornis at home?" asked Joseph.

"No! If you want to see him, call again to-morrow."

"To-morrow!.... But I must see him to-day. Is the Countess in?"

"The Countess don't receive strangers."

"I'm not a stranger; she knows me very well. She promised that if I ever was in trouble....."

"We don't allow any beggars here. Come, leave!"

"You are very harsh," said Joseph. "The Countess is better than you. Before sending me away, please tell her that I wish to see her."

So saying, he advanced step by step to the centre of the court, in spite of the resistance which the porter made.

"What is your name?" the porter asked.

"Joseph Noirel."

"That's good. The Count told me a week ago, if Joseph Noirel came here, to shut the door in his face. Come, my boy, clear out!"

"Wait a minute, I know that fellow," said Jerome as he came nearer, broom in hand. "Yes, it's the same one. He was prowling about the park one day, and in crossing the court, he met M. Bertrand, whose dog tried to bite him. Dogs don't fancy him, it seems. Let's loose Diana, and we'll see some sport."

"You miserable rascals!" cried Joseph in a loud voice, hoping that the sound would bring Marguerite to her window; "I defy you, brooms, dogs, and all."

His manner was so determined, that Jerome and the porter hesitated to begin the attack. Each gave the other an encouraging look, but left his companion the honor of commencing the assault. Suddenly the cracking of a whip was heard under the vaulted passage before the gate; the porter hastened to open it.

A moment afterward, a carriage rolled into the court; in it sat the old Countess, who had borrowed her daughter's horses to make a call in the neighborhood. Something had startled them; instead of stopping before the steps, they passed by them, and the coachman had great trouble in reining them back; they reared and pawed the ground. Mme. D'Ornis, who was easily frightened, gave a scream, and thrust her head out of the carriage window.

At this instant, Marguerite, who had heard the noise of the quarrel, appeared at the top of the steps. She saw Joseph at once, and blushed deeply with emotion and surprise. Mme. D'Ornis noticed her agitation and, motioning Jerome to approach, asked him who that man was. She had scarcely finished her question, when Joseph, running up the steps and taking off his hat, said in a loud voice to Marguerite, "I hope the Countess has not forgotten the promise she was good enough to make me." Then he added in a low tone, without any perceptible motion of his lips, "The man is here; where and when will you see him?"

Marguerite shuddered. She turned away her eyes and looked for a moment at the winter sun, which was about to sink below the horizon, and which resembled an immense wafer, red as blood; then turning toward Joseph, she whispered, "To night, at nine, in the orangery."

"If you want me," said Joseph in the same tone, "clap your hands.... Now, get angry and send me off."

At the same instant, Mme. D'Ornis, who had just alighted, looked straight at her daughter-in-law and cried, "What is it, my dear?" She had heard nothing, and could not understand what was going on.

"The trouble is, madam, that this foolish young man has left a happy home and now is sorry for it." Then addressing Joseph, she continued, "I tell you again that after what I've heard, I can and will do nothing for you. You are able to work; you must help yourself."

"But, madam, ..." answered Joseph.

"I don't want to hear any thing more," she cried raising her voice. "You can go."

Joseph bowed to the ground with a mock and insolent humility. "I thank the Countess," he said, "for all her kindness to me." With these words, he turned upon his heel and moved rapidly away, as Mme. D'Ornis said to her daughter-in-law, "You are very harsh, my dear."

"Do you think so, madam?"

"I am often struck by countenances; that young man's is very interesting."

"It expressed great insolence just now," replied Marguerite coldly; so saying, she regained her room.

Before returning to his employer, Joseph stopped a few moments before the castle gate, and looked about to discover the orangery which was to be the place of meeting. He saw it in one corner of an inclosed garden, situated on the side of the castle opposite the park. It seemed to him that it would be easy enough to reach it by climbing the wall; crumbling and broken, it offered an easy passage. The orangery, which stood near this wall, was an old-fashioned Chinese green-house, which contained two or three sickly-looking orange trees set in boxes. A few steps from it was a rustic gate, which communicated by a spiral staircase with Marguerite's room, the windows of which looked out on this sad garden. It had not been cultivated for several years, and there was no need of guarding it, as there was nothing in it to tempt a thief. Joseph approached the spot as night came on, and found in the wall a breach that could easily be scaled. Having finished this reconnoissance, he returned to Rousset, where he found M. Bertrand indulging in a bottle of wine. It was always his custom to drink freely before engaging in any serious undertaking.

At half-past eight, M. Bertrand and his workman arrived in

sight of Castle D'Ornis. They left the road, climbed the hill, and crossed a lawn planted with lindens ; on the other side of this lawn, they found the breach which Joseph had deemed practicable. The moon shone brightly from a cloudless sky, and the snow in the garden sparkled in its light. Fortunately, the thick branches of the lindens cast a dark shadow about the orangery. " It is understood," said M. Bertrand to his workman, " that you are to remain here and keep watch, and if you see any thing suspicious you are to hoot like an owl."

" All right," said Joseph.

" After what you've told me, I'm not afraid. It's very evident that our young Countess has let no one into her secret. Do you really believe in those three big fellows you told me about this morning ?"

" M. D'Ornis has only one servant, and he's a little chap. But let the three come on ! I don't know what's the matter with me to-night, but I feel as though I could fight ten men."

" Don't be a fool," said M. Bertrand. " Your duty is to fight with nobody. If contrary to what we expect, any one should come this way, you must hold him at bay long enough to let me escape ; you can fight a little to save appearances, and finally give yourself up. They will find no arms about you ; you can make up a story for them, tell them you're in love with Margot, and that you were prowling beneath her windows to catch a glimpse of her. They won't lock you up for that ; you'll get off with a few blows, and as soon as you return to Lyons, I'll put an ointment on your wounds that will heal them right away. You know what I mean."

" Very well," answered Joseph ; " only don't stay too long in the orangery. It's very cold, and I haven't a fur cloak like you."

" You ought not to be cold. You've got your bottle and your hopes to keep you warm."

The castle clock struck nine. " It's the lovers' hour," said M. Bertrand ; and as he saw Joseph press a paper to his lips, he added, " What are you doing there ?"

"I was kissing the note you signed for me this morning," he answered.

"It's astonishing," thought M. Bertrand, "that such a simpleton can repair cabinets so well." Then climbing through the breach, he gained the green-house door, which he entered with a stealthy step, casting a searching glance about him in the mysterious gloom.

CHAPTER XXXV.

THE FATAL PAPER.

Ten minutes passed. Joseph waited with trembling heart and bated breath, keeping his eyes fixed on the rustic door. Finally, he heard the faint creaking of a hinge, and saw a hooded shadow suddenly appear. It seemed to hesitate before trusting itself on a patch of snow lighted by the moon; then it ran forward, stopped a moment, started on again, and disappeared within the orangery. Joseph immediately left his post. He climbed into the garden, and walked on tip-toe along the narrow passage between the green-house and the wall. Having moved with great precaution toward a corner whence the low murmur of voices came, he hid himself behind a shutter which was leaning against the glass, and which hid him from the view of those inside. He could see nothing; but a broken pane permitted him to hear.

On perceiving M. Bertrand in the orangery, Marguerite trembled violently. The worthy merchant bowed with a respectful, almost gallant air. "You seem agitated, Countess; don't be afraid," he said. She threw her head back proudly. "Afraid of what?" she asked. "You had a proposition to make to me. What is it?"

"Let's commence right," he answered. "You expressed a desire to see me, and a desire expressed by such a charming mouth is sacred. I have no proposition to make; but you have something to ask me, I think."

She gave him a look of scorn. "There's no need of further quibbling," she answered in a voice that was low, but firm. "You took the trouble to send me word that you had a paper which compromised M. D'Ornis's safety, and that perhaps I would like to buy this paper of you. I must find out in the first place what it's worth. Let me know as soon as possible. I should be sorry to remain here two seconds longer than is absolutely necessary."

"You are in a great hurry, madam. I must explain in the first place how this paper came into my possession. It's a security which I took, and while it remains in my hands, it will endanger no one."

"Dear me!" she interrupted, "why are you wasting so much time?"

"Because I want to make you understand....We are all mortal. If I should have an apoplectic fit to-morrow, and that terrible paper should be discovered in my bureau—ah! madam, that discovery would have terrible consequences for M. D'Ornis and yourself. You understand, I don't intend to use it; but I am thinking of the future. Who can promise that my heirs will be as scrupulous as I?"

"It would be too much to ask of them," she said with increased impatience. "What does this talk amount to? I believe you're trying to cheat me, and that your paper isn't worth a farthing."

She felt a little reassured by M. Bertrand's digressions and by his embarrassed air. She forgot that it is equally embarrassing to have nothing to say, or to have too much to say. As she turned toward the door, he put out his arm to stop her. "Don't touch me!" she cried, shaking her sleeve as though to efface the imprint of that hand and arm.

M. Bertrand's anger was easily excited; although he cared little what others thought of him, he could not bear to have his wares depreciated, and in this case he had some reason for this feeling; the paper in his pocket was more authentic than his Peruginos. "My little paper not worth a farthing!" he cried rolling his eyes about...."Hear this, madam! Three years ago I wanted fifty thousand francs; I had a note to pay and my safe was empty. I said to myself, I'll go and see M. D'Ornis; he will advance me part of the amount, if not the whole. He knows me, and can be sure of getting his money back.... M. D'Ornis rose that day under an evil star. He refused me flatly, madam, and to tell the truth, he was a little rude. A few hours later, he offered me the fifty thousand francs upon his knees, and begged me to accept them.... Countess, in a few minutes, you'll offer not fifty thousand, but four hundred thousand francs for my little paper."

She shrugged her shoulders, and, folding her arms, stood silently before him. Although she tried to conceal the fact, she had lost something of her assurance; her uneasiness kept increasing. "I will tell you how it happened," he continued, "and why your husband changed his mind. Greatly mortified by his refusal, I turned my steps another way. I was denied everywhere and scarcely knew what to do. At last I concluded to drown my cares; at night I entered a tavern. It was half-past eleven when, on my return to Ornis, I was passing along a lonely path. I was in the little wood, ...the little wood, you know, on the border of your park....Suddenly I heard a cry, followed by a dull heavy sound. The cry was like a night-hawk's, but the sound was that of a falling body....I hastened my steps, and saw at the end of the little bridge two men, one upon the other. The one underneath was dead; the other was lying flat upon him, and looking with horror at his victim. He still held in his right hand the handle of a hunting knife; the blade could not be seen, and that for a good reason....I thought, at first, that he too was dead, he was so still. I approached and caught him by the arm. He sprang suddenly to his feet and bounded from the ground; then he looked at me with a madman's glare....He still held the knife, which he raised in the air, and I must acknowledge, madam, that he tried to stab himself. I was there, however, and succeeded in wrenching the knife away from him, receiving a cut upon my hand in the attempt....When any one tries to kill himself, madam, he must succeed at first; otherwise, he will reflect and reason and decide to live. This is exactly what happened to the man of whom I speak. Twenty minutes later, I was with him in his room. To tell the truth, I was the one who led him there; he could scarcely walk himself. No one saw us enter. He was in the habit of playing and drinking with a friend in a room that could be entered from the park, and all his people used to retire at eleven o'clock.... By the way, I ought to tell you that the man he had just killed was this friend.... Then he begged me to accept the fifty thousand francs he had refused me the same morning. On my side, note this point, I insisted on his giving me a little certificate which should protect me against any mistakes of justice. Justice is so suspicious! I had been seen, on leaving the tavern, going toward the wood, and then I was cut upon the hand. It would require less than that to convict an innocent man; virtue attracts misfortune as honey attracts flies.... Madam, it was to protect himself, that this madman, who had just killed his friend, gave me the note which I demanded of him. And now see what a good fellow I am! If the law had accused me of the murder, I believe I would have risked my life before making use of my certificate; but I was spared so great a struggle with my conscience. It seems there was a certain vagabond, who passed through the wood an hour or two after the crime had been committed. This idiot rifled the body lying in the path, and took its watch, its jewels, and its money. That was a very unfortunate accident for him; for the next day the poor devil...."

The words died upon his lips. He had told his story with his face turned toward the wall; finally he became curious to know what effect it had produced. He turned toward Marguerite and fell back a step. It seemed to him that it was no longer a woman, but a marble statue, that stood before him; and this statue seemed the more strange, because it held riveted upon him two large eyes, which appeared to look upon the world with great astonishment, as though they had been far away. Marguerite had experienced a thrill of horror; like a surging wave, this horror had mounted to her brain, and for the moment her reason left her. She was listening, she lost nothing of what was said; but her terror-stricken soul had fled—she could not call it back again. Suddenly she found herself at Mon-Plaisir. It was morning; the woods resounded with the songs of spring; she was walking in the garden, and Aunt Amaranth was saying, "Stoop down, darling, and let me put this rose in your hair." Some one called her; she raised her head and saw Uncle Benjamin, who was crying from his window, "Oh! the handsome girl! and she's so happy too." "Be still," she answered, "you don't know all." As she said this, she discovered that she was not at Mon-Plaisir, but that she had been shut up in a dark, damp cave, the gloomy silence of which was relieved only by the dropping of muddy water, which oozed from the low roof and fell drop by drop upon her head. Then M. Bertrand having ceased to speak, she suddenly awoke, and discovered that she had before her a garden covered with snow, on which the moon was shining, that she was in a green-house, that she was not alone, that a man was talking with her, and that this man had just revealed the fact that Count D'Ornis was a murderer.

She threw her hood back on her shoulders and, running her fingers through her hair, she fiercely cried, "It's false! You're a miserable impostor! There's not a word of truth in what you say. You think, perhaps, that I'll believe you. What a poor story you've made up! Don't you know that the Marquis De Raoux was Count D'Ornis's dearest and best friend?"

"What passed between them," answered M. Bertrand, "I never knew. I'm a discreet man, I have not questioned M. D'Ornis. But what do you think now of my little paper, Countess? Your husband would give his right arm to get it back again; should he receive it from your fair hand, he would be your slave for the rest of life; you could do whatever you pleased with him."

"Oh! yes, the paper!" she cried. "I don't believe there is such a paper. You can't show it to me.... I dare you to show it to me.... You're afraid to do it, you know I'm acquainted with his writing."

Then changing her voice and manner, she said in a plaintive, coaxing tone, like a child begging for a toy, "You must let me see it. You can't refuse me.... Please show it to me."

"Tell me first what you think it's worth," he answered with a triumphant air.

"How do I know? a million, a whole fortune.... But you

know very well he didn't write it. Show it to me, or I'll tell every one it's forged, and that you're a forger."

As she said this, she caught by the arm this man, whose touch had heretofore seemed loathsome to her. She had but one thought, one passion, one feverish desire, to see and know all, to make sure of her horrible misfortune.

He seized both her hands with a vice-like grasp, and drew her toward a window, through which the moonlight shone. She made no resistance, she would have followed him to the end of the world. Without loosing his hold, he leaned forward, plunged his left hand inside of one of his riding boots, and from a pocket in the lining, drew forth a paper, which he held up in the air. She bent her head forward, her eyes were fastened on the paper. He unfolded it with his thumb and finger, and she read the following words, written in a trembling hand: "*It was I who, on the night of the 26th of February*, 1867, *killed the Marquis De Raoux.—Roger, Count D'Ornis.*"

At this moment, M. Bertrand heard a rustling outside the orangery, which seemed suspicious to him. He started, let Marguerite's hands fall, and thrust the paper quickly into its hiding place; then he looked about him in the darkness, listening intently, with his right hand in the pocket of his cloak, and his thumb on the hammer of a pistol which he had taken with him. He soon recovered his composure. "It was a false alarm," he whispered.

He saw that he was talking to the air; Marguerite had vanished like a phantom. He waited a few minutes. "What isn't spoken, can be written," he thought. "It appears that she prefers to write." Then cautiously leaving the orangery, he directed his steps toward the breach, where he found, straight and motionless like a man on guard, the king of Josons, who held out his hand to help him over the wall. When he had reached the other side, he said, "Give me the bottle, my boy, I'm very dry." He nearly emptied it at a single draught. "Come, let's go on," he added. "I know a path that is shorter than the road by half an hour, and in it we won't run any risk of meeting Count D'Ornis returning from his visit to the Marquis."

CHAPTER XXXVI.

M. BERTRAND MEETS WITH AN ACCIDENT.

Ten minutes later, the master and his workman were moving along an ascending pathway which wound through a thick growth of underbrush. They could only pass through it in single file ; the master walked in front swinging his stick, Joseph was whistling as he followed him. If M. Bertrand had known what this whistling meant, he would not have felt so comfortable. He was far from dreaming of the thoughts that were passing through his companion's brain.

They walked on for some time without speaking. Joseph first broke the silence. "Well, master, are you satisfied with your little talk?" he asked. "Will Marguerite Mirion pay? She can afford to do it."

"Why will you renew my griefs?" answered M. Bertrand in the same tone that Eneas used when replying to the Queen of Carthage. "You see before you a man who has been robbed, and, what is worse, a man who has robbed himself."

"What is the matter, M. Bertrand? Wouldn't Marguerite believe you?"

"Alas! my boy, I warned you that I had a tender heart; my sympathies have ruined me. When I saw that poor girl cry, I was so affected that I acted like a fool, and gave her the paper without asking any pay for it."

"That story may do for some people," answered Joseph. "Do you think I believe in your crocodile's tears?"

"I don't know whether crocodiles have tears or not; but I have often cried a bucketful, myself, when something has come upon me unexpectedly. As I've heard in some opera or other,

'Le ciel fait un présent bien cher, bien dangereux,
Quand il donne un cœur trop sensible.'

I came to make a good bargain, and I've ended with a good action. The devil take Margot and her handsome eyes!"

"Well! that's your own affair," answered Joseph, "and as long as I get my two thousand francs...."

M. Bertrand stopped short. "Are you joking?" he said. "If I get nothing, you get nothing of course. When there's nothing made, the devil loses his rights."

"I don't understand it so," answered Joseph raising his voice. "You promised me two thousand francs; I've got nothing to do with your tender heart, I want my money."

"Shall I take it out of my own pocket? What is there to pay you for? You've only spent half an hour near an old wall, looking at the moon. Haven't you any poetry about you? You ought to pay me for the little treat I've given you."

"Thank heaven, you signed a note for me," said Joseph.

"Your note will do you lots of good. I promised to pay two thousand francs to Joseph Noirel, when he had faithfully performed the work committed to him. What is this work, I'd like to know? The note don't say any thing about it. I order you to restore immediately a hundred cabinets and fifty tables; after that I'll see about paying you."

Joseph was seeking a quarrel; he did not have far to look for it. "I'll show you that you can't act so with me," he cried as he raised his stick.

M. Bertrand looked at him with a compassionate air. He contrasted his own bulky frame with the slender form and narrow shoulders of his young companion. "Look at the little chap!" he said. "Poor Joson! I won't make more than a mouthful of you."

And, in a playful way, he placed himself on guard and aimed a blow at him. Joseph, however, received it on his stick, and with a dexterous movement disarmed his adversary, sending his cane flying into the thicket. "The little fellow fences well," thought M. Bertrand, surprised at his mishap.

Then with the paternal air of a hippopotamus which has been mastered and decides to wait for a better opportunity, he added, "Go and pick up my cane, son. You have a hard heart. You see me troubled because I gave up my paper, and instead of pitying me, you abuse me. Do you think that I would try to cheat you? We'll talk this over again at Lyons, and I promise that you shall be satisfied."

After a moment's hesitation, Joseph picked up the cane and gave it to him. His victory had been too easy; he could not follow it up. They started on again without exchanging another word, and soon reached the top of the hill, where the road ended and was followed by a large stony pasture ground, bristling here and there with clumps of bushes which cast dark shadows on the snow. In the midst of this pasture stood a stone cross. The place was wild and solitary; there was no habitation within a radius of a mile. A short distance from them, on the top of a little hillock, a deserted windmill spread out its great arms against the sky, and seemed pointing toward something on the horizon, or perhaps complaining to the stars of its inactivity and weariness. Behind the mill could be seen the undulating outlines of the hills, on which the moon shed its mysterious and silent light.

On arriving at the foot of the cross, M. Bertrand, who had been walking fast, stopped a moment to take breath. He wiped the perspiration from his forehead with his handkerchief. If he had turned his head, he would have been terrified by the look which his workman had fixed upon him. This look was as wild as the place about them, as fierce as the savage gesture of the mill which was talking with the stars. A cold breeze was blowing. The bushes shuddered and let fall some of those mysterious words which the wind caused them to utter to the night. There are moments when inanimate things seem to be alive; they look and listen. These slumbering witnesses awake; they gaze on man, and wonder at this strange creature who is so little like them, who has passions and volitions, who moves about and changes his ideas. Joseph raised his eyes toward the cross, and thought he saw it tremble; he cast a glance upon the mill, and it seemed to him that this mill was a living being, and was asking what Joseph Noirel was about to do. The mill, the cross, the wind, the bushes, the stars, the moon, all were spectators who expected him to furnish them a spectacle. Such indeed was his design; but he was looking for a beginning and could not find it. Chance came to his aid and served him as a prompter. The best opportunities are those which fortune proffers without consulting us.

After wiping his brow, M. Bertrand looked forward for the path. "This is the way," he said, and started on. The dimly-marked pathway, which he had to follow, ran along the crest of the hill and formed a narrow passage between two steep declivities. A few steps beyond the cross, it was obstructed by a fallen tree; to the left of this was a kind of ditch caused by the sinking of a portion of the ground. Perhaps M. Bertrand had made too violent an assault on Joseph's bottle, and his limbs had lost their usual steadiness. His foot caught in one of the branches of the tree, and sliding over the crusted snow, he fell at full length into the ditch. Fortunately, it was not deep, and the bed of snow which received him softened his fall; but his head struck an exposed root and the shock stunned him. He had come off well, however; he had neither bruise, nor sprain, nor fracture, nor serious injury of any kind; with the exception of a slight scratch upon the face, he had arrived at the bottom of the ditch sound in body, if not in mind.

CHAPTER XXXVII.

JOSEPH BECOMES MASTER OF THE SITUATION.

M. Bertrand, for a few minutes, entirely lost his consciousness; on coming to himself, his surprise was great. The first thing he noticed was the moon, which was directly over him. Turning his eyes, he saw the upper portion of the cross, which seemed to have a singular appearance; then looking to the left, he perceived the arms of the windmill, which he thought were rising up to gaze at him. He again glanced at the moon; that pale face also expressed a sly curiosity, and from it he concluded that something was going on. Whether it was comedy or tragedy, he did not know, but perhaps he was the hero of it?

His ideas began to grow more distinct and his memory to return to him. "Ah! yes," he thought; "I stumbled against a tree, and fell into a ditch; but when I fell, I was not alone. Where is Joseph?" Then he saw that Joseph was seated at the edge of the ditch above him, with his arms crossed and his feet swinging, and that he was looking coldly and fixedly upon him, as if he were a stick or stone.

"What are you doing there?" he cried. "Why don't you help me up?"

Joseph did not stir or speak. It seemed as though he was deaf and dumb. "What's the matter with him?" thought M. Bertrand, and as Joseph refused to help him, he attempted to get up himself. He tried to move his legs, but did not succeed; he found that they were tied together by a cord. He tried to move his arms, but found that his wrists were bound. He thought that he was dreaming; but the fact was evident enough, and he began to guess what the moon was looking at, and what gave it that appearance of mocking curiosity.

Meanwhile, his thoughts became clearer every minute, being aided by the snow which had been melted by the warmth of his body, and which, in spite of his fur cloak with its turned-up collar, had begun to penetrate his neck, and to run in a cold stream down his back. This disagreeable but effective sensation caused him to regain his power of reasoning, and he concluded that the real cause of the strange situation in which he found himself was that same Joseph who was silently regarding him. He remembered that the said Joseph had brought from Lyons, in his pocket, a small coil of rope, saying that there were a great many walls at Ornis, and that in climbing a wall nothing was more useful than a rope. It might also serve to prevent an honest man, who had fallen down, from getting on his feet again. Joseph's hands were not clumsy; on the contrary, he possessed a marvelous dexterity in his fingers, and M. Bertrand very justly inferred that a few minutes had sufficed to place him in the condition in which he found himself. But what had he done it for? His mind was not yet clear enough to understand this, and his first outburst of anger was not against Joseph, but against the tree which had tripped him up, and had thus been the first cause of his mishap. "That damned tree!" he muttered, after which he remained silent for a time. An idea had come to him. If a knot can be tied, it can also be untied; he tried to unloose the one that bound his hands. The attempt was vain; his hands were covered with fur gloves, which Joseph had not taken off, and these gloves were firmly fastened to his wrists. He looked mournfully upon his captive fingers which could render him no service. "That cursed tree!" he muttered the second time. Then he added, "But what is Joseph trying to do?" Three or four different suppositions passed through his mind.

A coarse smile crossed his lips. "What's the joke?" he cried to Joseph.

"The joke!" answered the latter gravely. "I don't see any joke."

"Oh! you've found your voice again. Will you be kind enough to tell me...."

"Silence!" answered Joseph; "don't you see that I am busy?" He held in his hands a pocket-book which he was carefully examining. M. Bertrand recognized it as his own and stared at him. "Are you going to rob me?" he asked.

"By no means," answered Joseph. "There are two notes of two hundred francs each which I won't take away from you. I'm not a petty thief; I like to do something grand while I'm about it....I was looking for that paper we were talking of. For once in your life you didn't lie, and Marguerite has really got it...."

He angrily threw the pocket-book into the ditch, then leaping down, he picked it up, and put it back in M. Bertrand's pocket. Happiness is a relative thing; M. Bertrand proved that a bound man is capable of being happy. His eyes sparkled with joy at seeing Joseph's discomfiture. His little paper was saved.

"Didn't I tell you," he said in a good-natured tone, "that I couldn't resist those handsome eyes? I'm a fool, I know; but you must own that you're a curious and unfriendly fellow. Now, let's make up; but first untie these knots as soon as you can, for I am a freezing."

"You ought to be comfortable," answered Joseph. "You're sheltered from the wind."

And regaining the border of the ditch, he sat down again upon it. His face bore no trace of anger; it was calm and sinister. This time M. Bertrand was frightened. "Hasn't this joke lasted long enough?" he said. "What are you waiting for? What are you trying to do?"

"You are a murderer!" cried Joseph in a terrible voice; "and the man you killed has, to-night, found an avenger."

"You are mad," stammered the other.

"Silence! I'm the one that's speaking here....When you were talking in the orangery just now, I became curious, and listened at a broken window. Unfortunately, from fear of being surprised, I didn't stay until you'd finished; but I heard a certain story that I shall not forget....You are a murderer.

Your conscience whispers it to you, at night, like a coward as it is. It's time that you were told of it aloud."

"Did I kill the Marquis De Raoux?"

"If you had killed him, I shouldn't care. What are all the counts and marquises on earth to me? Let them tear each other up like wolves! But you, by your silence, have killed a vagabond, a beggar, whose only crime consisted in having passed near the murdered man. I'm in a strange humor to-night, and this little incident interests me. These vagabonds and beggars are relatives of mine, and I have a great deal of family pride, you know.... I will avenge this innocent man."

"Innocent!" said M. Bertrand whose voice was almost choked with fear. "He robbed the body."

"If my father in his day," cried Joseph, "had found a dead man in the woods, he would have stolen his watch, perhaps. You see that this man was a relative of mine." Then stretching out his arm, he added, "How pale the moon is! it looks like a dead man's face."

M. Bertrand closed his eyes. The moon terrified him almost as much as Joseph. It was clear that it knew all, and its silence was more awful than any words.

"Seriously, what do you mean to do?" he asked.

"A very simple thing," answered Joseph with great coolness; "I'm going to bury you in the snow."

A great mass of snow had accumulated about this hollow. The north wind, which had blown fiercely for a day or two, had drifted it in that direction; held by the slope and by the tree lying across the ridge, it had piled up like a mountain. Joseph rolled up his sleeves, and with feverish haste began to transport huge masses of this mountain to the border of the ditch. M. Bertrand was now overcome by terror, and collecting all his strength, he gave a cry which was heard afar off in the woods, for an owl answered him. "Silence," said Joseph. "You know that the place is deserted, and if you should cry until to-morrow, no one would hear you. I'm working and don't want to be disturbed. If you don't keep quiet, I'll have to gag you."

He went to work again. M. Bertrand did not yet despair; he could not cry, he tried to think, and after much reflection said to himself, "That infernal Joseph, whom I should like to cut in pieces or burn alive, is playing a comedy for some particular purpose. It isn't likely that he would want to bury me under the snow, because I had something to do with the death of a vagabond whom he has never seen. I don't believe in such virtuous vengeance. He wants his money, and he's going to make me pay in turn. If that's all, it can easily be arranged."

"Joseph!" he cried, "my good Joseph!".... And as Joseph leaned toward him, he added, "You want your money, don't you? There, tell me how much, and let's have done with this."

Joseph raised both hands toward heaven, and his face lighted up like that of a man whose lawyer tells him he has gained his case. "O yes, it's money I want," he said. "How long you've been in making the discovery!.... But I'll be easy with you. All I ask is the two thousand francs you promised me this morning and refused this evening."

"You shall have three thousand," quickly answered M. Bertrand.

"You are too generous. I only ask what's due me; but I won't take off a cent, and as you've compelled me to distrust you, I must have security."

"Take the notes in my pocket-book on account."

"I don't take any thing on account. To-morrow you'll swear that you have paid me all. I intend to profit by your lessons. I want a note better than the one I took this morning, ...a little note in which you acknowledge that you allowed an innocent man to suffer death. This time I'll be sure to hold you."

"What an idea!" said M. Bertrand. "When I promise you...."

"Your promises are nice security. I want your signature. You don't like to write; so much the worse for you, for your writing I must have."

"Never!" cried M. Bertrand.

"You ought not to say never," answered Joseph. "It's a bad word for a citizen as well as for a statesman."

And he began to move the snow again.

A white and glistening wall had already risen beside the ditch; it kept constantly increasing. At intervals, Joseph looked over this wall at his master, and finally said, "Think of Brazil and your black harem! Have you changed your mind? Will you write the note?" "Never!" repeated M. Bertrand, whose voice appeared to stick in his throat. Suddenly Joseph threw part of the wall upon him; falling like an avalanche, it entirely covered his lower limbs.

M. Bertrand yielded; his teeth were chattering, he felt a chill run through his veins and gradually approach his heart, and that sleep from which one never wakes weighed heavily upon his eyelids. He moved his head and stammered, "I will write." With one bound, Joseph stood beside him, and raising his head, poured into his mouth the remainder of his bottle. Brandy is one of those friends that can always be depended on; it produced a magical effect on M. Bertrand, who immediately felt warmth and life returning to him.

"If you want me to write," he said, "untie my hands."

"You can use your right hand as it is," answered the inexorable Joseph. "I can manage to get off your glove. Here's a pencil and some paper. My left arm will answer for a rest. Your fingers are a little stiff; I will get them warm by rubbing them.... There, that's all right; now I'll dictate the note to you. The moon makes a splendid candle; it's almost as light as day."

He then dictated the following: "On the night of the 26th of February, 1867, I saw Count D'Ornis murder the Marquis De Raoux, and was paid by him for my silence, which caused the death of an innocent person.—LOUIS BERTRAND."

"Will you give me back this paper when you receive your two thousand francs?" asked the master as he wrote.

"Of course I will," said Joseph, "or I'll burn it before your eyes."

As soon as he had placed the paper in his pocket-book, he took out his knife, and a second sufficed to cut the cords. He even went so far as to help his master to rise and to draw him from the ditch; then moving away a little and leaning against the cross, he cried, "Monsieur Bertrand, will you be kind enough to feel in your boot, and see that your treasure has not dropped out."

M. Bertrand hastily placed his hand inside his boot; the pocket was empty. He started forward as though to throw himself on Joseph; but he was stiff with cold, and moreover was a prudent man. He ended by seizing his hair with both his hands as though he would tear it from his head.

"I'm a dealer in little papers now," said Joseph with a proud gesture; "I've got the heads of a count and a bourgeois in my pocket."....Then he added, "Would you like to take those papers from me? Let's fight for them? You forget you have a pistol in your pocket. I've got my knife."

M. Bertrand quickly seized his pistol, cocked it, and, with his finger on the trigger, took good aim; but he thought again a moment, changed his mind, and softly let the hammer down.

"If my knife frightens you, I'll only use my stick!" again cried Joseph, whose savage joy could no longer be controlled.

M. Bertrand stood motionless and gazed at him a moment. It seemed to him that this little fellow, leaning against a cross, was six feet high, that he was proof against all bullets, that the moon protected him, and that flames shot from his eyes. He made a gesture of despair and rage, returned his pistol to his pocket, and slowly moved away.

Joseph looked after him for some time, as he painfully descended the slope of the hill; then he threw a last glance on the bushes, the windmill, the stone cross, the fallen tree, and the moon; he seemed to say to them, "What a treat I've given you!" After which, retaking the path by which he came, he rapidly returned to Ornis.

CHAPTER XXXVIII.

MARGUERITE'S FLIGHT.

If Doctor Crotet had seen Marguerite leave the orangery and fly across the garden, he would have changed his diagnostic and have said, "She is not a lypemaniac, she is mad." Certain it is that at that moment Marguerite Mirion, Countess D'Ornis, had lost her reason; her ideas flew and danced about her brain as the dead leaves are whirled before the blast. Marguerite's mind had again deserted her, and her body had now a double duty to perform. This body hastened from the orangery, because the orangery terrified it. It unconsciously crossed a garden covered with snow, because, although it was possessed of eyes, these eyes could no longer see. It did not notice the movement which Joseph made to intercept it, because it did not know that there was such a person as Joseph Noirel in the world. It knew its road, however; it sprang toward a little door, pushed it open, closed it again, ran up a stairway, entered a bedroom, and dropped into an arm-chair, an inert mass. There, Marguerite regained her reason; her mind returned to her body, thought to her brain, and sight to her eyes.

With bowed head and folded hands, she gazed for a long time at her fate. It seemed like an abyss before her. Her eyes plunged to its lowest depths and found nothing but horror there. She could say like the poet who visited hell, "I was not dead, and yet I no longer lived." Her maid knocked at her door. She answered, "I don't want you now." She would not, for any consideration, have let her see her face; it seemed to her that her face revealed her secret, that strange lines were written on her brow.

As soon as Fanny had retired, she rose from her chair and said, "I can not remain longer in this house." Her good sense presented some objections; she thrust them at once aside. She was filled with horror and with fear, and, in spite of all that could be said, she wanted to go away. What answer could there be to that? All that her reason obtained from her was that she should write a few lines in lead-pencil on the first scrap of paper she came across, and place it in an envelope addressed to M. D'Ornis. These lines read as follows: "I am not happy here, and I do not make you happy. I am going to spend a few weeks with my parents. I do not ask your permission, because you would refuse to give it to me. I will write you from Geneva, and try to make you understand that it will be better for you as well as for me, not to see each other for some time."

She placed the note upon her dressing-table, and took a few gold pieces from her desk. The last thing she did was to unlock her door; she did not wish to have the locksmith called to open it after she was gone. This being done, she could give herself up entirely to her passion. She wanted to fly, to place leagues and hours, plains and mountains between Marguerite Mirion and the face that terrified her.

How she found strength to escape from the garden she never knew. She twice tried to climb the wall without success; she finally had the courage to re-enter the orangery, and to search there for a stool which served her as a ladder. At last she was without the grounds. She did not take the path which M. Bertrand and Joseph had followed; she was afraid of losing her way in the woods. At the risk of meeting some one that she knew, she took the high-road to Arnay-le-Duc. She had been walking about ten minutes, when she saw a carriage that she recognized moving rapidly toward her on its way to Ornis. She threw herself behind a tree, and the carriage passed. Then she began to run over the slippery snow, or, I should rather say, she flew; she felt as though her feet had wings, and she moved with that strange facility which we sometimes experience in our dreams. Most of the time, she did not look ahead at all; she saw nothing but her trouble and her fear which went before her and pointed out the way. At intervals she would awake and cast a glance over the fields of snow. As she did so, a shudder would run through her frame; she thought she saw in the snow large pools of blood. When she was about half-way to Arnay, she saw two men who had stopped to look at her. One said to the other, the words coming to her upon the wind, "Either I'm blind, or that is Countess D'Ornis." "No, it's not Countess D'Ornis," she thought; "I'm only Marguerite Mirion now."

She reached Arnay just at midnight. The express train from Paris to Geneva was due at Beaune between three and four o'clock. She had just time to get there. She knocked at the door of an inn, where she was known from having stopped there with her husband. Every body was fast asleep; she rang and knocked as loudly as she could. The landlord finally came to the door, with his nightcap in his hand.

"A carriage!" she cried, "a carriage! I'll pay whatever you ask."

"At this time of night? Impossible," he answered.

"I want it, I must have it!" she said stamping her foot. "Ask any price you please."

Her demands were so urgent that they triumphed over the landlord's doubts; he awoke his men and ordered them to harness up. Marguerite watched these preparations leaning against a post. She knew that all present were attentively observing her, and that even from the windows she was being looked at with astonishment and curiosity. She made an effort, and invented some story which bore witness to the sterility of her imagination; a tree struck by lightning can not yield fruit. Her explanations did not seem satisfactory; but the mouth that gave them was one of those that we love to believe; its accent was so pure. Then the glances that accompanied her voice at once disarmed all suspicion; they were the most honest glances in the world. This fact, however, did not prevent the landlord from more than once shaking his head in doubt.

If M. Bertrand had an instant of happiness in his ditch, Marguerite leaning against her post experienced a feeling of joy:

it was at the moment when the horses that were to carry her to Beaune came from their stable and their bells rung out on the stillness of the night. Never had music sounded so sweetly to her ear. She was constantly in dread, however, lest some accident should happen, lest a trace or axletree should break, or one of the horses should drop dead in the snow. She complained of the slowness of the hostler who was harnessing; it seemed to her that the number of straps and buckles in a harness was much too great. How much time was lost! how much useless labor! And why should Ornis be so near Arnay-le-Duc, and Beaune so far away?

She was not entirely reassured until she was seated in the carriage, and the driver having whipped his horses, the wheels rolled rapidly over the road. "Make haste," she cried to him, "or we shall lose the train." He honestly earned the fee she gave him; he drove his horses at full speed. Notwithstanding, she was uneasy and impatient. Every minute she would thrust her head out of the window and look back on the road; it seemed as though she was pursued, as though a man, or rather a crime, was running after her at full speed, crying, "You are mine, you married me!" Then she would cry to the driver in a voice of anguish, "Faster! faster! for Heaven's sake!" At this he would lash his horses with the whip, although they were doing their very best.

CHAPTER XXXIX.

ARRIVAL AT MON-PLAISIR.

It was Sunday. Toward three o'clock in the afternoon, the weather being too cold for the usual walk, the inmates of Mon-Plaisir were gathered in the blue room. M. Mirion was playing a game of chess with the timid Mlle. Grillet, who changed her mind a dozen times before each play. "It's touch and move," her cousin said to her. Seated near them, with his eye upon the board, Uncle Benjamin criticised the play, or, starting off on a tangent, spoke at length on the balance of power in Europe and the Eastern question. "Benjamin Pacha, keep quiet with your Grand Turk," M. Mirion said in an impatient tone. Aunt Amaranth, more be-ribboned and be-pinned than ever, was working by the window at her everlasting embroidery. Reclining in an arm-chair, with her chin uplifted, Mme. Mirion was learning by heart her paper, which she had exhibited an intense affection for ever since she had read in it the notice of her daughter's marriage.

They had received, an hour before, a call from Mme. Patet, that envious woman, who took it so to heart that Marguerite Mirion had become a countess, and who went about saying, "Those Mirions are trying to reach too high; they'll get enough of it before they're through." She had heard of Marguerite's sickness, and had come to ask about her. Mme. Mirion had at once informed her that her dear Countess had entirely recovered; that her mother-in-law and husband had watched over her like two angels. "My son-in-law wrote us every day," she added. "Such letters I never saw! they brought tears to our eyes." As soon as Mme. Patet had gone, she cried, "The poor woman! our good luck will kill her."

After finishing his game of chess, from which he came off

conqueror, M. Mirion turned his arm-chair toward the fireplace, and placing his feet on the andirons, gazed silently at the blue flames dancing on the logs. Uncle Benjamin was trying to prove to him that he had made mistake after mistake, and that he really ought to have lost the game. M. Mirion let him talk; he had been melancholy for some weeks past, since the most skillful and most ungrateful of his workmen had so suddenly deserted him. This departure had become a sad, almost a tragic incident in his life. It seemed to him, at times, as though he had lost an arm, and he felt troubled that it could not grow again. He had been in a revery for a quarter of an hour, when his wife said, "What are you thinking about, Mirion?"

"His Joseph, of course," said Uncle Benjamin.

"I wish the devil had him," cried M. Mirion.

"I couldn't ask any thing better than that," replied his wife.

"O yes; it's easy enough for you to talk," said M. Mirion, who, in this complicated matter, blew hot and cold at the same time. "That confounded boy was mighty useful to me, and I haven't been able to find another like him since."

"That could easily have been foreseen," replied Uncle Benjamin with a wise look, "and if you had taken my advice...."

"O yes; you're always right," interrupted M. Mirion in a vexed tone, and he began to inveigh against the new workmen whom he had brought from Paris to replace Joseph. One made more shavings than any thing else; the other was skillful enough, but whether business was pressing or not, he would scarcely work two days together, without running to the tavern. In fact, they disgusted him both with themselves and with the trade.

Mme. Mirion listened attentively. When he had finished speaking, she approached him, and blushing deeply, as she always did when a bold idea came to her, she said, "Haven't you worked enough, Mirion, and made money enough? Give up your business. You have a right to live on your income like a gentleman."

"So you've brought it out at last!" cried her brother-in-law with a sarcastic laugh. "It's a long time since you first wanted to say that. It's all right, of course. Your husband will die for want of something to do ; but the Burgundian castles will not be able to say, as Countess D'Ornis passes, 'Her father keeps a shop.' "

"I don't know where you pick up such nonsense," angrily answered Mme. Mirion, furious at having her thoughts thus exposed. Such mishaps are generally disagreeable to the ladies.

Uncle Benjamin was opening his mouth to answer, when the sound of a hurried step was heard in the vestibule, and the door, swinging wide open, gave admission to the Countess Marguerite, who sprang into the room with her arms outstretched before her. She seemed like a shipwrecked sailor who had at last arrived at port. The five persons in the room gave an astonished cry, after which a cross-fire of questions began ; then all were silent, for they now saw that Marguerite was very pale, and that there was a strange fire in her glance.

"O yes, it's me," she said. "I know you're all astonished; but nevertheless, it's me."

"I understand," cried Mme. Mirion. "Your doctor decided that you needed a change of air in order to get your strength again. Have I guessed right ?"

"Yes, that's it, that's it."

"And your husband ?"

"My husband.... Oh ! he's very well."

"Are you going to make us a long visit ? Have you brought all your trunks with you ?"

"They were lost on the road.... I will write about them."

Mme. Mirion drew her toward a window, and looking in her face, said in an angry tone, "Dear me ! what have you done to get so thin ?"

"It's not my fault altogether," she answered.

"Don't scold her," said Aunt Amaranth. "Her cheeks were too full before ; I think she looks better as she is."

"I think so too," said Cousin Grillet, who was always glad to agree with an already expressed opinion.

"I think so too," said Uncle Benjamin, who was willing to coincide with any opinion, provided it was not that of his sister-in-law.

"Of course," answered Mme. Mirion, "any body is liable to be sick; but she might have taken better care of herself. There's no need of growing thin, unless one chooses to."

"I love you, whether you're thin or not," said her father holding out his arms. Throwing herself on his neck, she burst into tears. He put his arms about her, and said in a surprised tone, "What's the matter, Margot? what's the matter?" She only wished that those arms which held her now, and which had so often tossed her when a little girl, could never unclasp again; she only wished that her head could always rest there, that no one could ever seek her out, and that her name could be forgotten by all the world.

After weeping a long time, she felt somewhat stronger. They attributed her deep emotion to the weak condition in which her sickness had left her. They drew their chairs in a circle about the fire, and tried to talk; but the conversation flagged and finally ceased altogether. Mme. Mirion was the first to grow uneasy and to suspect that there was something that had not yet been told. She rose, saying to her daughter, "You must be tired. Go and lie down a little while." Then she motioned to her husband, who also rose. They went out, and Marguerite followed them to their room. Mme. Mirion quickly shut the door, and seizing her daughter by both arms, said in a trembling voice, "Has any thing happened?"

"Yes," she answered; "he don't love me and I don't love him; it's a hell on earth for us to live together, and I won't return to him again. I will not do it.....No, I will not do it!"

This was a terrible blow to Mme. Mirion. She gave a cry and dropped upon the floor. She had a violent hysterical attack; her husband and daughter with great difficulty succeeded in bringing her to herself again. Her first words, on coming to her senses, were, "What would Mme. Patet say, if she should know it?"

She began to question Marguerite, who answered, "We will talk when you are better, and I have had a little rest."

Marguerite went up to her former room, which remained just as she had left it. Her furniture, her little vases and other ornaments were all in place. She took from her table a small box made of shells, which one of her boarding-school friends had given her, and a bronze statuette which her father had once brought her from Paris. Holding the box in her right hand and the statuette in her left, and pressing them both upon her heart, she lay down on the bed, and soon was fast asleep.

She was awakened by the dinner-bell. She felt calmer and acted naturally during the meal. Uncle Benjamin was in a talkative and laughing mood. Mme. Mirion did not open her mouth. Her lips were compressed, her eyes were swollen, there were red spots upon her cheeks; from time to time, she cast a harsh and gloomy glance upon her daughter.

When they had left the table and returned to the drawing-room, when Aunt Amaranth, sitting in her usual place, had taken up her work, when M. Mirion, in order to conceal his disappointment, had commenced a game of backgammon with his brother, and when Mlle. Grillet, with her glasses on her nose, had drawn from her work-basket, on which the word *souvenir* appeared in large blue letters, her embroidery, which the good old lady never brought out except on holidays and Sundays, Marguerite experienced, for the second time since leaving Ornis, a feeling which resembled joy. Her eyes filled with happy tears as she saw Aunt Amaranth at work, she listened with delight to the rattling of the dice in the cups and on the board, and to the blows which Uncle Benjamin struck upon the table as he cried, "Attention! now I'm going to take my turn." It seemed to her that she had awakened after a horrible dream, and had just returned from visions to realities. She promised herself that she would dream no more, that she would not again believe that there was a Castle D'Ornis, whose great walls chilled her heart, a castle haunted by peddlers who told strange stories, in which one felt more solitary than if alone, and in which one passed terrible nights, divided between incurable curiosity and hopeless fear—to say nothing of the fact that at the door of this castle was a garden full of snow, and in one corner of this garden an orangery.... No, all that was false. The truth was what she now saw and heard—the table, the dice-boxes, the dice; the floor divided into squares, which were not perfectly regular according to a certain critic; the simple lamp which flared sometimes, but which had never lighted any but honest faces; the footstool on which her feet were resting and which recognized them as old acquaintances—the real truth was these people before her, who had nothing on their consciences and nothing to conceal, this drawing-room whose inmates loved Margot, and were willing to devote themselves to her, and to throw themselves between her and misfortune. She went about the room, passing from chair to chair, softly pulling her aunt's hair, pinching her cousin's cheek, tickling her uncle's ear, placing her hand on her father's shoulder and saying to herself, "I knew it well enough; these are real forms and faces, the others were only phantoms." She finally took from Mlle. Grillet's work-basket a new handkerchief, which she began to hem. At intervals, she raised her eyes and gazed with confidence on the four walls of the room. They seemed to say, "She has returned to us, she belongs to us, they shall not take her from us; we will keep her and defend her."

CHAPTER XL.

EXPLANATIONS.

Mme. Mirion passed the evening in an arm-chair, with her back turned upon her daughter, her eyes half-closed, and her body trembling with convulsive motions. At ten o'clock, the entire company, according to their usual custom, put up their work, and as Uncle Benjamin said, each one regained his *chacunière.* As soon as Mme. Mirion found herself alone with her husband and daughter, she rose suddenly, and in a harsh voice said to Marguerite, "Confess that it's not serious !"

"Alas ! my poor mother, it's only too serious," she answered.

"Impossible !"

"Impossible ? I used to think so too ; I have now learned that nothing is impossible."

"Tell us what you complain about.... Can it be that your husband.... Can your husband have what bad novels call a mistress ?.... What things you make me say !" she added, covering her face with her handkerchief to hide her blushes.

"No, mamma. Count D'Ornis has no mistress to my knowledge. I wish it were nothing more than that ! I should then have borne my sorrows patiently, and should not now be here."

"You hear her, Mirion !" she cried to her husband who was resting his elbows on his knees. "Didn't I tell you that our son-in-law was incapable of such trifling, and that his habits were above reproach ?" Then turning toward her daughter, she continued, "You complain that he doesn't love you any more. You're a spoiled child. The honeymoon can't last forever.... He can't spend his whole life at your feet, and pass the whole blessed day in telling you that he worships you."

"He never worshiped me, and I have never complained of

it. I would have been satisfied with bread made of rye or oats. Even if I had found a great deal of chaff and straw in it, no one would have been the wiser; I would have eaten it as wheat-bread every day of my life.... But if they give me poison.... You don't want me to die, I hope. You know that I'm not difficult to please; a little respect and esteem would have satisfied me. He hates me; he despises me, I tell you, and God knows which of us has a right to despise the other..... Oh! I beg you, do not question me; I have too much to tell; I will tell nothing."

"Again I ask you to mention a single fact. I've heard nothing so far but big words and hollow phrases," continued Mme. Mirion with increasing bitterness.

"A fact! You want facts?.... I have been sick, have I not? sick almost unto death.... Shall I tell you why?.... We had a scene together, he and I.... A horrible scene.... He pushed me so rudely that I fell.... My face was covered with blood, and yet I smiled and held out my hand to him.... His own hung by his side.... He would not raise me up."

"Impossible!" said Mme. Mirion. "You're dreaming. You're not in your senses."

"You are right; I'm mad. That's what he says. How can you doubt it?.... Give him time and he'll make every one believe it.... Yes, I'm mad, for I've been unfortunate enough to discover.... Have pity on me! Don't you see that my secret must die with me?"

Mme. Mirion wrung her hands, and cried, "Oh! dear, what will become of us?" It was not her daughter's misfortune that troubled her. She thought of the unpleasant things that would be said; how all Geneva would talk of the affair; how the envious would be filled with malignant joy. "You want to compel me, then," she said, "to keep my room for the remainder of my life? I should no longer dare to appear in the streets. Every one would point their fingers at me.... Oh! I shall die. You can boast that you have killed me." Such was her conclusion. Marguerite looked at her in bewilderment. She had believed that she had a mother—vanity is a savage beast.

"So you don't believe me?" she asked after a moment's silence.

"I don't know whether I believe you or not; I only know that you want to kill us.... If I must speak frankly, no, I don't believe you. It's all very childish what you've said. Young girls often let their imaginations run away with them. You've had a quarrel with your husband, and it's possible that he's a little quick-tempered.... What of it all? You ought to remember that you owe him a great deal. Perfect happiness is not of this world; you must learn to bear such little troubles.... Where is your religion? You are guilty of ingratitude toward Providence, in despising his gifts because he brings them to you through care and sorrow. It is wicked to break your glass because you find a drop of absinthe in it. I will have your pastor talk to you. I'm sure that you don't read your Bible any more.... If your husband has done wrong, I'll guarantee he'll be the first to make amends. Let me arrange it.... Before a week has passed he shall come here for you, and lead in triumph to Ornis the happiest and best beloved of wives."

Marguerite shuddered from head to foot. "Condemn me to any torture you please," she cried, "to pass the rest of my days in a dungeon, if you will, but to see him again!.... Oh! I can not, I will not...."

Mme. Mirion paid no attention to these entreaties. Marguerite turned to her father, who, weighed down with his sorrow, gave no sign of life. "Dear father," she said, "speak for me, take my part. You know that my nature is sincere and honest, it's the nature you have given me.... Do you remember, you said once that I had never told a lie? I swear to you that, if I have broken my chain, it's because there are some things one can not bear without losing all self-respect. If you knew all.... Speak, speak; tell me that you believe me, that you'll defend me, that you will not permit that man to take away your daughter, and make her die of despair and shame."

At these words, M. Mirion drew her to his breast. "Yes, my child," he answered, "I know what you are, and I believe you. I thought I had had some trouble in my life. It all seems as nothing now. No matter, you have my word, you can count upon your father. I'll fight any battle for you.... Let the world blame, insult, or scorn us! It all weighs as nothing in the balance, when my child's life and honor are in the other scale."

"That's right," cried Mme. Mirion rising like a fury. "Take her part, persuade her that she has good cause to hate her husband, that Count D'Ornis is an incendiary or a murderer...."

Marguerite trembled. She thought as she looked upon her mother, "If I should tell her that my husband was a murderer, she would none the less send me back to Ornis, and bind me forever to him. Her chief end in life is to keep Mme. Patet from talking."

"I don't hate M. D'Ornis," she answered. "I only ask that I may never see him again, and so forget him....I will write to him. I want you simply to support me in what I say. Let him know that I am acting with the advice and consent of my family, and he, himself, will finally agree to every thing."

"I have no daughter," cried Mme. Mirion as she hurried to the door.

"Be comforted," said her husband, who was revolted by her cruel words, "you have a son-in-law at all events."

CHAPTER XLI.

FATHER AND DAUGHTER.

Marguerite's father trusted her. This reflection soothed her to sleep, and in the morning brightened her first waking thoughts. The weather had suddenly grown warmer; a ray of sunshine, gliding between the blinds, entered her room at an early hour, and began to play on the coverlet of her bed. This bright ray awoke her youth, which had remained within this room, and which now began to buzz like a fly in winter, warmed into life by an illusive semblance of the spring. Marguerite talked for some time with her former gayety, which endeavored to console her. There are some souls born with a natural vocation for happiness; in vain does it escape them, its denials can not overcome their perseverance; they always look and wait for its return.

Desiring to avoid a *tête-à-tête* with her mother, Marguerite had notified M. Mirion that she would accompany him to town. When they were in the carriage, he said, "Your mother has been pretty hard on me this morning; she opened fire before light."

"She evidently doesn't believe me."

"Alas! no. She pretends that the whole trouble is, that you were foolish enough to fall sick and lose your color, and that your husband lost his love for you. To hear her, you'd think it was only a question of being plump and well."

"You believe me, don't you?"

"Of course!.... I'm only sorry.... Are there really things that you can't tell us conscientiously?"

She placed her hand upon her heart, "Though it kill me, my secret must not escape," she said.

"That's bad. Your father will trust you, but other people will not, my poor dear Countess."

"Ah! if you knew how little I cared about the others," she answered. "But don't call me Countess, I beg of you. I don't want to be any thing but your daughter; I'm only Marguerite Mirion now."

"It's all very sad," he said with a deep sigh. "Who could have foreseen such misfortunes? Ah! why didn't you marry a good bourgeois like your father? There's nothing sure in this world but the bourgeoisie and the bourgeois. We are men of principle, you see; add property to this, and you have happiness. To tell the truth, neither property nor principles are worth much, when taken separately.... Ah! cursed be the day when that Count D'Ornis.... We were careless, we were in too great a hurry, and it's been proved that your uncle Benjamin was right, which provokes your mother very much. And Joseph Noirel, too, was right when he said on his return from Ornis, 'Don't be in too great haste, learn all you can about him.' Why should such a good counselor turn out to be a knave? If he had not been so heartless, he would have insisted on delay, and all this would not have happened: but he never loved any body but himself. He is infatuated with his ingratitude. Heaven help him and his mistress."

It was thus that, unavoidably returning to this unhappy subject, M. Mirion included his workman in his complaints against his son-in-law. It is a consolation to be able to put all one's sorrows in the same sack; it greatly simplifies misfortune. Marguerite did not continue this conversation. The name of Joseph Noirel, so unexpectedly introduced, had made her thoughtful. He had scarcely been in her thoughts before for thirty-six hours. "I am the one who is ungrateful," she said to herself. "That dear boy! what a faithful and devoted friend he is! He has done every thing he could. Thanks to him, I now know all I wanted to, and all I have to do is to get possession of that hateful paper, which I will use to obtain my freedom.... Or rather I will write to M. D'Ornis, 'Keep my dowry, and buy that paper with it; I only ask one thing in return, a promise that you will spare my family that scandal which it dreads more than death. We will separate quietly on the ground of incompatibility.' I have confidence in myself, I feel that I can begin life again. There are yet sunshine and flowers in the world.... My brave Joseph, it is to you I owe my safety, I ought to have written to you before this. He has doubtless returned to Lyons, where he awaits my orders.... I know well what I'll do to reward him for his care and trouble. I will reinstate him in this house, which he left for me and by my order. He shall be treated henceforth as he deserves, not as a dependent, but as a friend. My father is kind and reasonable; he will give him an interest in the business, and every body will be satisfied. Ah! how much better it would be for society, if all understood what was for their interest!"

Thus thought and reasoned Marguerite Mirion, although she had learned, when a child, the fable of *Perrette and the Pot of Milk;* they used to make her recite it, dressed in pink and standing on a chair, every Sunday afternoon, when there was company at Mon-Plaisir. M. Mirion had fallen into a mournful silence; he was ruminating over his sorrows.

Just as the carriage was entering the city and crossing the *Place-Neuve*, Marguerite said to her father, "Isn't there any way of making up with that poor Joseph? I should be very glad to use my influence with him."

"I only know too well, now," he answered, "how useful that abominable boy was to me; but he shall not enter my house again, until he has promised to do better and begged my pardon on his knees."

"I don't think his pride will allow him to do that," she answered.

"His pride! his insolence rather. He's a perfect monster."

Marguerite said no more, determining to wait for a more favorable opportunity to pursue the subject.

"However," added her father, "that is nothing in comparison with the sorrow that you cause us."

"That I cause you?" she said in a reproachful tone.

"I beg your pardon, Margot. I meant to say, that our amiable son-in-law causes us."

"Don't be discouraged. It isn't a question of being plump and well, as mamma says; you will find that it will reduce itself at last to a question of money, and that will not kill you, will it?"

He gazed on her tenderly as he said, "I would gladly give up both my hands, and all the wealth that they have gained, to hear you laugh as you used to do."

Marguerite left her father to make a few necessary purchases, she having arrived at Geneva without trunk or valise. She rejoined him in the shop, at the door of which the carriage was to call for them. She was deeply moved on seeing again this shop, which recalled to her the happiest hours of her childhood. At that time, they had not yet purchased Mon-Plaisir; they lived in a gloomy suite of rooms on the fifth story, and Margot's chief amusement was to noiselessly descend into the shop, to stand before a bench, to look at the rapid movement of the plane, to listen to the saw as it cut smoothly through the wood, to gather in her little pink hands, which she joined together like a cup, the saw-dust which rained upon them, tickling them as it fell, to touch and examine every thing, to roll herself in the shavings, to pass her fingers over the twisted columns of the old cabinets, or to look at the old oak boards, the shining knots in which resembled faces and told her stories. Oh! what a happy time, and what merry games of hide and seek she had played at dusk in that store below, so full of corners and of hiding places! There was not one of those corners that had not heard her call or laugh; they knew all her songs and at that moment were repeating them to this poor Marguerite, who no longer knew how to sing. Alas! there also had first appeared to her that dark stranger, who had become her master. Hidden by the furniture, he had suddenly emerged into the light, and fixed upon her beauty the burning glance of a bird of prey. She had not been able to defend herself, she had trusted to the chances of an inexorable fate, as the swallow to the wind that carries it away. Now she knew that stranger; she had succeeded in reading the secret of his gloomy glance, she had seen upon his hands a stain of blood that could never be washed away.

Quickly crossing the store, she sought her father in his office, near which stood a bench, where he still worked at times. She profited by a moment when his back was turned to stoop to the floor, to run her fingers over the boards, and to cover them with dust; then passing in review the saws, the chisels, and the planes, she impetuously carried them, one after another, to her lips.

"What's that performance?" asked her father, who turned around as she was honoring with her caresses a large chisel. "Take care! some of those tools belonged to that unlucky Joseph."

"You ought to have told me sooner," she answered with a blush.

CHAPTER XLII.

CAPTURE AND RETURN TO ORNIS.

The carriage in which the father and daughter returned to Mon-Plaisir entered the paved court, on which the windows of the drawing-room looked out, at noon precisely. A hired vehicle had preceded them, and had left the tracks of its wheels upon the snow. M. Mirion had just stepped to the ground, and was helping his daughter out, when, turning suddenly toward the house, he said, " What's going on in there ? Somebody is talking very loud."

She listened also, and heard a voice she recognized too well. She grew very pale, and turned about as though to fly. "Come," he said, taking her by the arm. "Take courage ! I am with you."

He drew her into the house more dead than alive. When he had opened the drawing-room door, she saw on the left, in the recess of the window, her aunt and cousin, who, with troubled faces, were gazing, the one at the floor, the other at the ceiling; at their right, her uncle, red as a beet, was leaning against a table ; in front of them, with her face buried in the cushions of a sofa, was Mme. Mirion, who seemed a prey to the most violent despair; and leaning against the mantelpiece, gloomy, terrible, with a menacing air, stood the man whom she had determined never to see again.

On learning of his wife's departure, M. D'Ornis had had a furious fit of passion, and had started in hot haste in pursuit of her. In vain did the old Countess, who was secretly delighted with what had taken place, use every endeavor to retain him ; she was ignorant of his reasons for not loving his wife and, at the same time, determining never to be separated from her. He had answered her remonstrances very curtly, and had just fallen like a bomb-shell at Mon-Plaisir, in the midst of the family assembled for the noon-day meal. Without losing any time in asking questions, he had at once assumed the offensive, as might have been expected from his natural audacity. The strange accusations which he had just made had caused Mme. Mirion, with sobs and cries, to hide her face within the cushions.

She raised her head as she heard the door open, and seeing her daughter, cried to her, "Marguerite, is it true that you love,....that you love....Ah! I can never pronounce that name."

Marguerite had advanced to the centre of the room. She had looked fixedly upon her husband; their eyes had met like two flashing swords. "Go on, finish your question," she said to her mother.

"Yes, finish your question," cried M. Mirion. "Count, Marguerite is our daughter. She has never loved any thing but her duty...."

"And one of your workmen, named Joseph Noirel!" answered M. D'Ornis, twisting his hat with his trembling fingers.

Then turning toward Marguerite, he continued, "I am not an accommodating husband, madam. I want my rights, and I am jealous,....so jealous that I've trampled my pride beneath my feet to come here and claim you from my fortunate rival. ....What a noble rival! he's one of those that you can flog, but can not kill."

Marguerite could not say a word. She could not believe her ears; such audacity bewildered her. Remorse and innocence have sometimes the same way of clasping the hands and casting down the eyes. M. Mirion attentively observed his daughter; her silence and embarrassment terrified him. He bowed his head as though overwhelmed with sorrow. This, then, was Marguerite's secret! Had she not just asked for Joseph Noirel's pardon, saying, "You ought to make up with Joseph; I'll gladly use my influence with him." He groaned aloud, and dropped into an arm-chair. "Speak, madam," continued M. D'Ornis, who thenceforth felt himself master of the situation. "What makes you hang your head? Is it so hard for women to lie? Deny boldly that that young man whom I'll not name again—once is quite enough—resolved to leave this house the day after your marriage, because he could not bear to stay here, with you away. Deny that a few weeks later you had a private interview with him, and that since then you've kept up a correspondence with each other. Deny that he kept hanging about Ornis in the hope of seeing you, and that I surprised you both one day, alone together in the snow, and not seeming to feel the cold at all, so great was the charm of the conversation which I had the misfortune to interrupt. Deny that he returned, day before yesterday, to Ornis, and that he enacted a little comedy in the court in order to bring you out to him....Can my mother be mistaken? She says that she saw him whisper in your ear, and, by a strange coincidence, that same evening Countess D'Ornis flies from a castle, which she has taken a dislike to because her movements there are too well watched, because her rendezvous are too well known, and because she thinks she can taste here the sweetest of liberties, the liberty of the heart....Deny all, madam, that you are here, that you have compelled me to come after you to save your honor and my own, that I am looking at you, and that you are filled with fear!"

At these words, as though by some magic spell, Marguerite regained her voice. She advanced toward M. D'Ornis, saying, "Ah! sir, I thought I knew you pretty well, but you've succeeded in astonishing me."

"Marguerite," cried her mother, "there's nothing in these stories, is there? It's all a mistake, a misunderstanding.... Explain it to him; but don't speak in that way. Ask his pardon for the trouble you have caused him, ask his pardon on your knees."

She raised herself to her full height. "On my knees to him!" she cried. "I did kneel to him once; but now!.... Confess yourself, sir, that it would be a shame."

"Since you refuse to speak, I'll speak for you," said Mme. Mirion, grasping her son-in-law's hands and pressing them to her lips in an attitude of supplication. ....."Have mercy, pardon her," she cried; "I promise you that she is still worthy of your love. Her head has led her astray; but her heart is right. My daughter love that scoundrel! She doesn't love him; she respects herself too much. If you knew the principles in which she has been educated! She has never read a bad book; no novel has ever been allowed within this house. .. It's possible that the wretched fellow may have forgotten himself so far as to fall in love with her. He may have made use of some strange pretext to approach her; she ought to have driven him off, to have shown to him the slough in which he was born. She is too kind-hearted; she is afraid of hurting people's feelings; I've often scolded her for it; but believe me, she never could have cared for a workman whose father died in a hospital....I repeat that she is innocent. Just think, the poor child has been sick. She is not yet well, her mind has not entirely recovered; she has been guilty of great folly. She will explain it all to you, and you will find that she is less culpable than you think....Ah! Count, she knows what she owes you—the honor you have done her in letting her bear your name; her heart is full of your kindness to her, and only yesterday she spoke of you with a respect—an affection.....Isn't what I say true, my child?...."

M. D'Ornis stemmed this flood of words by saying, "I wish I could believe you, madam; but, after all, I am not an exacting judge. While awaiting the explanations which she owes me, I ask only one thing of your daughter, that she will return with me at once. You shall see that she will not consent."

"You misjudge her!" cried Mme. Mirion. "I should like to see...."

"Return to Ornis!" interrupted Marguerite; "return with him! Never."

"You hear her, madam," said M. D'Ornis coldly.

Marguerite's exclamation produced a disastrous effect on those who heard her. Mme. Mirion gave a despairing cry, and her husband raised his arms as though to curse his daughter. Aunt Amaranth fastened on her niece eyes as terrible as were those of the four-and-twenty elders of the *Apoca-*

lypse, when they looked upon the wicked one. Mlle. Grillet placed her head in her lap and stopped her ears; her affrighted virtue could hear no more. At this, Marguerite fell on her knees, her frame quivering, her hands trembling. She cried, "Mercy! pity! If you love me, do not condemn me to this frightful torture!....There are things that I can not tell. Oh, you don't know that man, he is deceiving you."....Then turning to him, she continued, "Sir, have mercy on me! I will tell nothing, I swear to you that I'll tell nothing; you know that we can not live together....I will try to forget you; but I beg you, do not let me see your face again!" While thus speaking, she approached her mother, fastened on her dress, and tried to take her hands; those harsh hands pushed her away, and she fell forward upon the floor. "You want to dishonor us," cried her doting mother. "Is it not written in the Gospel, 'Woe to him by whom the offence cometh?'" Her father also repulsed her, saying, "You've been trying to deceive me. Where is that Joseph? Where is the villain, that I may kill him before your eyes?"

Among the witnesses of this scene, there was one, however, who, more clear-sighted or more disinterested than the rest, understood the whole affair, and spoke out for the right. This was Uncle Benjamin, who, not being able to control his indignation any longer, suddenly left the table against which he had been leaning, and stepping forward, cried, "Brother! sister! what has become of your good sense and your affection for your daughter? What! that dear child, whom we all know as an angel of goodness, purity, and truth, can not succeed in moving you? Don't you see that, if she is silent, it's because she has too much to say, and can not defend herself without accusing some one else?"....Then turning to M. D'Ornis, he continued, "Glare at me all you please, Count, you can't prevent my speaking. I'm only an humble teacher at your service; but I have nothing on my conscience. Are you sure that you can say the same? In my opinion, the accusations you make against this poor girl are false; they remind one of a man whose case is bad, and who tries to stir up the water, so that no one can see the mud below. Besides, I tell you plainly, your face never pleased me, and if I had had any thing to say about it, my niece would not have been your wife to-day. Alas! they would not believe me. No one is a prophet in his own family, and vanity will never listen to reason."

"Monsieur Mirion," said M. D'Ornis in a haughty tone, "has this house changed its master?"

M. Mirion started as though his son-in-law had struck him with a whip; turning toward his brother, he addressed him in a manner which was very unusual for him. "You're going too far, Benjamin," he said. "Who asked for your opinion! We have listened to your impudence too long. Be quiet, or leave at once."

"You'll never have an opportunity to say that to me again," answered Uncle Benjamin. "I leave you never to return." So saying, he rushed from the room, pushing the door to violently behind him.

Marguerite had remained upon her knees. She cast once more a terrified glance about her, and felt that she was deserted and alone. There were with her only eyes that did not believe her, hard hearts that refused to hear, souls at the doors of which her misfortune knocked, but could not enter. Then came the temptation to take her revenge, to tell all she knew. A terrible struggle took place within her. Her secret rose to her lips; she was on the point of crying out, "That man who accuses me is a murderer, and he has permitted an innocent person to bear the penalty of his crime!" But as the fatal words were about to escape her, she made a desperate effort, and they found a wall of silence before them which they could not pass. Her lips moved convulsively, cold drops of sweat stood on her forehead. Thrice her mouth opened as though she were about to speak; thrice she thrust back her secret, which fell heavily upon her heart. Suddenly, by an heroic effort of her will, rising to her feet, with flashing eyes, passing her feverish hand over her burning cheeks, like a wounded lioness who has fought her last fight and knows that she must die, she staggered toward Count D'Ornis, and, in a hoarse voice, uttered these words, which were understood by no one but himself, "Take me away at once! Your life depends upon it."

A few minutes afterward she was in the carriage. M. and Mme. Mirion stood at the doors on either side, and, moved by a sudden change of feeling, lavished their caresses on her. She did not seem to see or hear them. Only one thing occupied her thoughts; throwing herself back in one corner of the carriage, she watched to see that her dress did not touch M. D'Ornis, who had seated himself on her right. The carriage started. Then she leaned forward and gave a last look at the walls of that house which had promised to defend her, and had failed to keep its word. That look seemed like a last adieu. Then she closed her eyes, and, with her head bowed down, buried herself in her destiny.

It took a long time for that house, which had refused to defend Marguerite Mirion, to recover from its fright; it seemed as though a tempest had passed over it. Mme. Mirion was the first one to regain her usual demeanor. "There's a great deal of mystery about it all," she said. "There are three things, however, as clear as daylight to me: Joseph is a villain; my daughter is innocent, but imprudent; and her husband, by his jealousy, has shown how he adores her."

M. Mirion had more difficulty in recovering his composure. He was uneasy and full of doubt. In the evening, he went out to walk upon the terrace; a new surprise was there in store for him. He had not moved more than ten steps, when he thought he saw a dark figure appear at one of the angles of the house, and disappear immediately behind a bush. He cautiously approached it. The figure endeavored to escape; contrary to its expectation, however, a gate through which it tried to effect its retreat proved to be shut and padlocked. The gate was high and difficult to scale. The nocturnal marauder turned and faced the enemy.

"Ah! it's you, you rascal!" cried M. Mirion.

After leaving M. Bertrand, Joseph had returned to Ornis with his two papers in his pocket. He had passed the morning in prowling about the castle, at the door of which he did not dare present himself. No Marguerite was to be seen. At noon, he went to the *White Horse Inn* to dine; he entered the drinking-room as a peasant was telling Mme. Guibaud how, the night before, the young Countess D'Ornis had been seen on the road to Arnay, running at full speed, and how her husband had started in pursuit of her. Joseph rightly guessed that, being overwhelmed by the discovery she had made, Marguerite had taken refuge with her parents. He went at once to Beaune, and, concluding that M. D'Ornis would take the first train, he prudently waited for the next one, which entered the station at Geneva an hour after the husband and wife had started on their return. At nightfall, he went to Mon-Plaisir to find out whether Marguerite was there, impatient to see her and talk with her; there are unlucky days, however, when even the shrewdest men are caught.

"It's you, you rascal!" repeated M. Mirion, stretching out his arm to seize Joseph by the collar. The latter quickly stepped aside saying, "I'm not going to run away."

"Is it true," continued M. Mirion, "that in return for all the favors we've conferred on you, you have dared to raise your eyes upon our daughter? Can Joseph Noirel so far forget himself as to fall in love with Marguerite Mirion? Fortunately, Providence has thwarted your vile plans. I don't know what you have said to my daughter to irritate her against her husband; but just now they met here, had an explanation with each other, and went away together.... Do you imagine that Marguerite could really love you? Do you forget the distance there is between you?.... You villain, what have you said to her? how have you managed to deceive her? what black falsehoods have you told her?"

Then suddenly overcome by his feelings, he changed his tone, bursting into tears. "Joseph, my good Joseph!" he cried, stretching both his hands toward him, "remember the past, remember what I have done for you, and what you have done for me. I am so unhappy! Tell me all, and I will forgive you all."

Joseph looked at him in silence for a moment; then slightly shrugging his shoulders, he rudely answered, "Your daughter's secrets are her own, and mine belong to me; I have nothing to tell you."

He had not finished speaking, when M. Mirion, furious with indignation, gave him a terrible blow, the consequences of which were to be more terrible still. Joseph gave an angry cry and raised his stick as though to strike his old employer; he soon mastered his rage, however, and as though proud to show that plebeian souls have their hours of royalty, with a gesture worthy of Louis XIV., he lowered his stick until one end touched the ground, and, breaking it with his foot, threw the pieces far behind him.

"Henceforth I owe you nothing!" he cried in a threatening tone.

And before M. Mirion, who was astounded by his action, had time to stop him, he had fled across the terrace and the court, bearing with him his blow, his wounded love, and his bleeding pride which cried for vengeance.

CHAPTER XLIII.

COUNT D'ORNIS TELLS HIS STORY.

Count D'Ornis was not a malicious man; he had never in his life been guilty of useless cruelty; but his character exhibited a formidable combination of calculation and passion; and, although it often happens that a passionate temperament is at times exceedingly generous, he was never known to have performed an act of self-sacrificing generosity. He was the most selfish of men. Why had his brother been born with a club-foot, and why had this brother, held in aversion by his mother, been constantly sacrificed to him? The Benjamins are a terrible race. When they are in a violent mood, they kill Raoux, and Raoux being dead, having a crime to conceal and heir life to defend, woe to Marguerite Mirion, if she ever cease to be a source of pleasure to them, or if they ever suspect that she may become a source of danger.

M. D'Ornis's triumph was complete. He was taking home his prisoner, and he flattered himself, not without reason, that she would not try to escape from him a second time. Whither could she go? He had closed the doors of Mon-Plaisir to her, he reigned there as he did at Ornis. He could not feel entirely at ease, however. After having lived for forty-eight hours in a storm, his mind had become calm again; he had recovered his reflective powers, and his thoughts troubled him. Marguerite's words, "Take me away at once; your life depends upon it!" tormented him. Did she suspect the truth, or had she really learned the facts? What had occurred between her and Joseph? He wanted to know immediately. Several times, while on the road, he tried to engage his wife in conversation. She did not seem to see or hear him; sometimes she closed her eyes, sometimes she let them wander vaguely about. "I hope," said M. D'Ornis, "that we shall at least keep up appearances; it's more for your interest than for mine."

It was only on seeing the roofs of Castle D'Ornis, the vanes on which shone brightly in the sun, that Marguerite felt the full horror of her situation, and the terrors of this prison, the doors of which were so soon to close upon her. As the carriage approached the village, she made a desperate call upon her courage. She sat erect and firm. She bore without flinching the glances of derision and curiosity which those passing cast upon her. She looked without a shudder on the orangery and the garden, where she thought she still saw her foot-prints in the now half-melted snow. She passed through the arched gateway, and heard the ringing of the horses' hoofs on the stone pavement of the court. When she reached the steps, she descended from the carriage without assistance, and, bowing to the servants, ran to her room and shut the door.

At midnight, worn out with fatigue, she felt the need of rest. She reflected, however, that M. D'Ornis was peculiar in his choice of times and places, and that he would be very likely to surprise her in her sleep. She thought of bolting the door, but her numerous failures had disgusted her with all precautions; and, besides, why should she try to avoid the inevitable? She did not leave her arm-chair. A few minutes later, her door opened, and M. D'Ornis appeared.

He seemed surprised to find his wife still up, and remained motionless for a moment. Finally, resolving on his course of action, he approached her, saying in a low tone, "Will you be kind enough to explain to me why you left this house?"

She looked him in the eyes, and answered in a steady voice, "Because I discovered that you murdered the Marquis De Raoux."

He staggered as though a ball had pierced his heart. He would have fallen, if his hand had not been resting on a chair. His face grew livid, his features were no longer under his control. He thought he saw the room turning around him, carrying Marguerite with it, and it seemed to him that in every corner of this room sat a woman crying, "You are the murderer of the Marquis De Raoux !" He whispered in a hoarse voice, "Speak lower, for God's sake !" Then recovering from his dizziness, he found that there was but one woman present, and that woman was his wife. He raised his arm with a threatening gesture. Despair knows no fear. Marguerite was calmly looking at him, and her glance restored him to himself.

He walked about the room, cautiously opening and shutting all the doors, in order to assure himself that no one had been listening ; then he again approached her, and his first words were, "I am very sorry for you, madam, for you must understand that after this we never again can separate."

For a few minutes both were silent. At last he said, "Speak ! Who gave you this information ? You must speak," he continued in a low voice. "This is a time for explanations. In our common misfortune, we must save each other the trouble of trying to discover any thing more. Do you want me to commence ? It's so long since your curiosity has been at work. I knew very well that this would be the end of it....Have you any thing to ask me, madam ?"

She shook her head. "You are mistaken," he said. "You are dying to know how and why....You will have no rest until you know. I prefer to tell you all myself."

He stopped a moment to wipe his forehead with his handkerchief; great beads of sweat stood on his brow. In a still lower voice he continued, "The quarrel was about a horse. Raoux had sworn to own it. Unbeknown to him, I offered a higher price, and the horse was mine. From that day a coldness arose between us. He begged so hard that I finally agreed to play a game of chess with him for the horse. We drank a great deal of wine that night, we almost lost our heads. Since then I have never drunk any thing but red wine, and you know the next day I killed the horse ; I did not wish to see it, or ride it, or have any one else ride it....Where was I ? You want to know all, you shall know all....He said to me, 'You see that you're checkmated !' With that he went to the other end of the room and took a glass of water, which he emptied at a draught; he was very thirsty. When he returned, I answered, 'You're mistaken; don't you see, I can move my king?'....Then he declared that I had moved his knight while he was away. I felt myself turn pale; I proved to him that he was mistaken. He upset the chess-board, repeating again and again, 'You are a cheat!' Then he added, 'To-morrow the world shall know what you are.'....I swear to you that I was patient with him. I begged him to be still; I told him that I should do some desperate thing. He continued to repeat, 'To-morrow the world shall know!' I lost my reason, I seized a knife. He fled across the park; I caught him near the bridge....Did they tell you that I tried to kill myself? Some one was there and prevented me. When a man does not succeed in killing himself, he defends himself; I will defend myself, I will save my life!...."

He stopped again; then, in an almost inaudible voice, he whispered, "Have you any thing more to ask me?"

"Yes," she answered; "I want to know the name of that man, that vagabond...."

He made a terrible gesture. "Be still," he cried; "I don't want that man here."....And, by a mechanical movement, his eyes turned toward the window and the door, as though to make sure that they were still closed; then he hid his face within his hands. Marguerite began to sob.

"That's right, madam, follow your trade," he said starting to his feet again. "Women always weep as though their tears were going to do some good. You know nothing of the world or of men. You imagine that, coolly and deliberately, I said to myself, I'll let that beggar die. Don't deceive yourself in that way. Every night, before going to sleep, when I did sleep, I thought, 'To-morrow, I will confess.' The morrow came, I thought of my name and honor, and was silent; the days passed, the head fell. What was the use of saying any thing after that?....You don't know what a gambler is, nor what a fierce desire he always has to win. What will he do when his life is the stake for which he plays?"

He succeeded in mastering his emotion, and added in a dry

one, "Don't weep, madam; after all, the head that fell wasn' worth a crown."

Marguerite ceased to sob. She cried, "Enough, sir! not another word, I beg of you!" He seemed a monster to her. She was mistaken; he was only a spoiled child who had lost his conscience in the game of life.

At that moment, M. D'Ornis thought he heard a noise without. He ran to the window that faced the garden, opened it, raised the blind, looked out, and listened. He saw nothing but a dark and cloudy sky; he heard nothing but the moaning of a warm wind, which blew in gusts and was melting the snow. He let the blind fall again, but only half closed the window; he was very glad to have a little air in the room, he was suffocating. Approaching his wife, he said, "It is your turn to explain now. I flattered myself that only one man possessed my secret. He was interested in keeping it; he made a revenue of his discretion. Did he tell it to you; or did some one else?"

He awaited her reply in an agony of expectation. He gave a sigh of relief as she answered, "Be comforted, it was himself."

"He came here? You saw him?"

"You refused to tell me what you were; I determined to find out."

"Confess, madam," he cried, "that I formed a just opinion of you."

"You ought to thank me," she answered; "I have good news for you. A certain paper that villain holds is for sale. You have my dowry; if that is not enough, you can call upon my father. You are well acquainted with Mon-Plaisir and its inmates now; they are at your service. Ah! sir, confess on your side that it is fortunate for a man like you to have married a bourgeois's daughter."

With these words she began to weep again; she had undertaken a part beyond her strength. He did not notice that she was weeping; he had not heard all she said; he only knew that a certain paper would soon be his, that he would burn it and cast its ashes to the wind, so that the wind itself could no longer read his name, that the past would be dead, that he could kill his memories and begin to live again. Suddenly his face grew dark and frowning. "You are imposing on me, madam," he said. "M. Bertrand is very suspicious. You have laid a trap for him, and the faithful agent who has served you in this affair is undoubtedly that workman....Good God! madam, does he too possess my secrets?"

"He only knows," she quickly answered, "what I was able to tell him when I as yet knew nothing. Would I ever have spoken, if I could have guessed how terrible your secrets were?"

"If ever I come to an unhappy end," he violently cried, "it will be your work, madam!"

She clasped her hands together. "I will answer for that young man," she said; "I can depend on him."

"Can I frighten him? or must he be bought?"

"I only know that he's my friend, the only one I have on earth."

"I should be glad to believe that he was nothing more," he answered. "To-morrow you must write to this young man a letter that I will dictate, and bring him here. You must find some means to rid me of him forever. Think it over, form some plan. You can send him to America, or anywhere else you please. The main thing is that I shall never see him, and that we shall never have occasion to speak of him again."

She was silent for a moment, and then said, "Very well, I submit. After that, what are you going to do with me? It seems to me that I have a right to make some conditions."

"Conditions!" he replied. "Do you forget that you were met the other night out on the road alone? Are you supposed to be mad or false? I don't know what they're saying about you to-day in Arnay-le-Duc and Ornis; to-morrow they'll say what I want them to....You'd better submit without conditions. I don't intend to abuse my power; you will only be my prisoner, a prisoner well watched."....Then he added, "Why haven't we a child? It would be a guarantee for me; it would answer for your silence."

These words seemed more terrible to Marguerite than all that she had heard before. "Ah! sir," she cried, "yesterday I was in my father's house; I knew only too well the future that awaited me here, and a single word would have saved me; why did I not speak that word?"

He answered with a bitter smile, "Do you want me to admire your generosity? If you did not speak, it was because I was there and you were afraid of me."

She hid her head within her hands. What she felt was neither anger nor fear; it was that horrible loathing of life and of men, which every one experiences who has a true and noble soul, and finds that it is of no use to him, such merchandise having no value in this world. When she uncovered her face, her husband was standing before her, looking at her with an expression that made her shudder. She rose in terror. He gazed at her in silence for a moment longer; then taking up other thoughts, he rudely turned his back upon her and retired to his room.

He walked there for a long time, absorbed in thought, looking carefully at his new position, passing in review his hopes and fears. He wanted air. Toward two o'clock, he opened one of his shutters, and leaned upon the window-sill. Suddenly a stone passed over his head and struck against a mirror, which was broken by the violence of the blow. M. D'Ornis leaned out and thought he saw a figure flying through the garden. He closed his blind and picked up the stone, about which was wrapped the following note:

"I have become possessor of the paper which you wrote on the night of the 26th of February, 1867. If to-morrow morning you have not left Ornis to return only at your wife's request, the next day the imperial attorney at Beaune shall receive my visit. JOSEPH NOIREL."

With a whirling brain, M. D'Ornis sank down upon a chair; he was still there when morning came. Like a tired swimmer who thinks he feels the ground beneath his feet, but whom the waves seize and carry back again, so scarcely had he seen his deliverance approaching, when it escaped him, leaving him a prey to dark despair. That terrible paper, which bore witness against him, had seemed for a moment to be within his grasp; now he had learned that it was in the hands of a man who could not be bought. What did this man want? He, himself, seemed to know too well; he evidently nourished within his breast a love and hate which he had determined to gratify at any cost. He could reason with Bertrand; he could not reason with Joseph, a madman and an amorous fool....

When M. D'Ornis had at last shaken off his gloomy stupor, the first idea that came to him was to run after Joseph, to take him by the throat, and kill him. The second was to kill Marguerite: was not she the one who had plunged him into this abyss? He did not tarry long over these mad thoughts: his reason overcame his rage, and prudence gained the day. He silenced his pride, and determined, after considering the question in all its bearings, to set out at once for Paris, not without the idea of returning, not without cherishing the hope of a speedy and terrible revenge. Joseph's note, which he read again and again, seemed to breathe a candor almost childish in its insolence; from it he augured favorably for the success of his plans. "Good!" he thought, "I will leave these imprudent lovers a clear field; then I will surprise them in my own good time, and hold them thereafter in my power."

He rang for his valet, sent him to pack his trunks and to order a carriage, left some money to settle a few open accounts, wrote two or three words to be given to his wife after his departure, and, at ten o'clock precisely, started for Blaizy-Bas, the nearest railway station on the road to Paris.

CHAPTER XLIV.

JOSEPH REVEALS HIS SECRET.

Joseph Noirel had returned in haste from Geneva to Ornis where he arrived at midnight, almost fainting from fatigue and hunger. As soon as he had swallowed a few morsels of bread, he glided into the little garden, whence he saw a light and heard a confused murmur of voices in Marguerite's room. He succeeded in climbing upon a shed near by. A few disconnected words and scattered phrases fell upon his ear ; he readily guessed the rest. Sliding to the ground, he picked up a stone, fastened a note to it, waited an opportunity, and at last his missive sped to its address.

The next morning, he was in the little wood when the carriage that contained Count D'Ornis passed over the road to Blaizy-Bas. Hidden behind some bushes, the branches of which he pushed aside, he cast a look of triumph on this carriage which had thus obeyed him. He experienced a transport of joy; his success exceeded his anticipations. He looked down upon his hands with proud complacence ; he had promised to make them rulers over fate, to place puppets under their control: he had kept his word.

Pushing his way into the wood, he cut off an ash branch, from which he made himself a stick to take the place of the one he had broken the night before. With this stick, which he kept whirling in his hand, he struck the bushes as he walked along, cutting down those branches which projected over the path. He thus moved on, whistling and singing, leaving behind him a pathway strewn with twigs and leaves. I do not know what he was thinking of, or what this slaughter meant to him. Perhaps he thought he saw certain heads at the ends of the branches which his stick struck down. History does not state of what use this carnage was, nor whether the bushes were the better for it.

When his murderous joy at length had ceased and his reason had returned to him, he suddenly grew thoughtful. He gained the most retired part of the wood, as though to surround with impenetrable silence the council which he was preparing to hold with himself. Finding an old stump lying on the ground, he sat down upon it and remained there more than an hour, leaning forward and digging into the ground with his cane, while his mind was working at a thought. What was he going to do? He did not yet know, himself, but he wanted to know at once. He questioned himself, he deliberated, he consulted. Two days before a man had said to him, "Can it be that Joseph Noirel has dared to raise his eyes on Marguerite Mirion?" And that man had given him a blow. As he thought of it, the blood mounted to his cheek, his eyes shot fire, a serpent was biting at his heart. In the great debate which his good and his evil genius held before him, the advocate of pride and vengeance, that advocate who is always pleading in evil causes, made terrible use of that cruel blow. He referred to it with touching eloquence, and unfortunately he addressed himself to one in love. It is an easy matter to pass from one folly to another. Nevertheless, when Joseph rose to go to Marguerite, he had not yet determined what to do.

He passed over the bridge, rapidly crossed the park, and, without the least precaution, went straight toward the room from which he had once been ordered away by the old Countess. As he entered it by one door, Marguerite came in by the other. She gave a cry on seeing him, and running toward him said, "Are you the one who has worked this miracle?"

Marguerite had passed the night in constant dread, fearing each moment that her door would open again. The morning had come, and her fears, more cruel than all her previous sufferings, had not been dissipated. What should she do? The most reasonable project she had formed was to fly, to go straight on, not knowing whither, and, if she could succeed in finding the end of the world, to engage herself as a servant to some laborer, on the sole condition that no one should ever call her by her name. This was her thought when a note from M. D'Ornis was handed her, which read as follows: "I have decided to go away; I shall proceed first to Paris. I will return whenever you express a desire to see me again. If you wish to write me, address your letter to the Grand-Hotel." She read a dozen times those two lines which informed her of this unexpected deliverance. It was her nature to give herself up entirely to the impressions of the moment. The good news which she had just received caused her, for some hours, to forget all her troubles, all the gloom and misery of her life. The poor child was like a gambler who seats himself before the table with his pockets full of gold and jewels; he has lost all and is ruined, when on going out, he sees an old copper in the road; he picks it up and carries it to his lips: that poor coin takes the place of hope and happiness. In fact, Marguerite felt herself thenceforth capable of loving that gloomy castle, where fate had placed her without hope of escape, for she could come and go in her prison without meeting the face that terrified her, without speaking to or answering it, without having to defend herself against it in her sleep.

As she entered the room, Joseph was astonished at her rosy cheeks and sparkling eyes; she seemed to have recovered her former beauty. This flower, which bent beneath the fierce glare of the sun, needed only a drop of dew to raise it up again. She made him sit down and talk with her, without for an instant thinking that they might be surprised. Her liberty had been restored to her; could she make a better use of it? Joseph told her all he had said and done during the last ten days. She was greatly confused and agitated on learning that he knew all; she quickly reassured herself, however, saying that he belonged to her, that she could depend on him as on herself.

When he had finished his recital, she scolded and thanked him at the same time for the risks that he had taken for her; then she cried, "What an abyss my destiny is! If any one had predicted, six months ago, that such a fate awaited me, how I should have ridiculed the story! It seems to me that I was born for an entirely different purpose, to lead an uneventful life, made up of days when I could sing and nights when I could sleep. God tempers the wind to the shorn lamb, they say. What am I, to be thus beaten by the storm? I believe that there is some mistake, that the Lord has taken me for some one else, and has sent afflictions which were never intended for me. Oh! that the world may never know the truth concerning this! They may say what they please of me; I will not defend myself, I will die before making any accusation. I should be filled with terror if any one but you possessed my secret; but what have I to fear from you? If called upon, you would help me to be silent."....Then she added, "Such trials as still await me, I shall bear with greater courage when I think of the friend who has been so kind and devoted to me. He would have healed all my wounds, if they had not been incurable. Alas! he is about to leave me; perhaps he still dreams of going to America....But now I think of it, you told me once that when we met again, you had certain plans to tell me of and to ask my advice about. My head is clear to-day; during the last two hours I have recovered the power of putting two ideas together. Profit by this opportunity to consult me. You also have a secret. I hope it's a happier one than mine!"

The supreme hour had come. Joseph's face grew pale. Two roads were open to him. Which should he take? At the end of one he saw a mournful, arid desert; the other conducted to a precipice. He covered his eyes with his hand. Like a judge upon the bench, he rapidly summed up the arguments of the opposing counsel whom he had listened to in the wood. His trouble constantly kept increasing. "Ah! I ought not to have seen her again," he thought.

Marguerite looked at him in astonishment. She began to grow uneasy. "Is it so hard to tell?" she asked.

He raised his head. "You promised me," he cried, "that whatever I might tell you, you would not be angry."

"I will keep my promise," she answered. "How can I be

angry with you? Still, if you think.... Yes, perhaps it would be better to say nothing...."

He rose and started as though to leave the room; then, falling back upon a chair, he said in a trembling voice, "This is my secret! My feelings toward you have never been those of friendship.... I have been mad enough to love you, I love you madly now."

Marguerite hid her face within her hands, and in her turn grew pale. "How terrible!" she murmured. They remained for some time motionless; they dared not look upon each other. "How terrible!" she repeated. He opened his eyes at length; what he saw recalled his courage. Marguerite's trembling lips expressed neither scorn nor anger; her face and attitude betrayed simply her confusion, the disorder of a mind surprised by an unforeseen event. A visitor who is not expected enters suddenly, and nothing is prepared for his reception. What shall be done with him? What room shall be allotted him? All is hurry and excitement, and confusion reigns supreme.

Joseph gave Marguerite no time to recover from her bewilderment. In a hurried voice, he told his story: the commencement of his love, all that he had suffered, all that he had dreamt, his illusions, his vain hopes, that ploughed field which he had crossed holding her in his arms, that little slipper which he had hidden in a drawer, the evenings which he had spent stretched out upon the floor talking with shadows, all that he had felt on learning that another had been bold enough to love her, and that her beauty was to become this robber's prey, his passion, his despair, the broken ring, the diamonds thrown into the stream.... She did not wish to hear him, and yet she listened. It was the first time she had heard the music of love, and when that strolling musician sings at the door, a young heart, that has never heard him, can not be kept back from the window. Marguerite could not understand herself. "I am listening without interrupting him," she thought. "What change has taken place in me?".... It seemed to her that within her was a double nature—a nature at the same time old and young; two souls, one of which had lived through centuries during the last few months, while the other had but just been born. Her former nature had been beaten by misfortune, which had ceaselessly struck upon it, night and day, as the blacksmith strikes upon his anvil; it was now bent and useless, and was astonished at finding by its side a new heart which had never yet been moved, and which felt all the curiosity and wonder of life's first hour. It had been awakened from its slumber by a serenade, and instinctively had run to listen to that harp which sung and wailed and moaned, mingling with the sweetness of its harmonies harsh and jarring notes, and strange and bitter cries. "You come too late," she said to it; "I am no longer gay. Why did you not awake me sooner?"....As Joseph hurried on, Marguerite moved her hand to stop the impetuous torrent of his words; but this motion, although begun, ceased of its own accord. Her conscience reproached her, being roused by her calm demeanor. She answered, "Why should I stop him? This will soon be over, and we will think no more about it."

Scarcely had he ceased to speak when, encouraged by her silence and the dreamy look he saw upon her face, he threw himself at her feet, and, looking wildly at her, caught one of her tresses in his hands and pressed it passionately to his lips, crying, "Oh! I love you! I love you!" This act and these words brought Marguerite to herself. Like those princesses in the fairy tales, who are enchanted by one genie, while another breaks the spell, she recovered her power of action, her reason, and her voice. She gently pushed him back, and, standing before him with a reproachful and commanding look, she motioned him to rise.

He obeyed, but with a frown. She saw gathering within his eyes one of those clouds which, growing as by miracle, herald the sudden explosion of a storm. "I have offended you!" he cried with bitterness.

"Offended?" she replied. "I promised you that I would not be angry; but I pity you and pity myself. I have suffered every trial. I had a friend, and I am about to lose him! I can not see him nor speak to him again. Why did they not cut off my hair? You would then have been cured of your passion, and I should possess your friendship. Or rather why did you not speak to me when I was free? My mother often said, when I was a little girl, that I never guessed or invented any thing, but that I readily received the ideas of others. You ought to have explained yourself, to have given me that idea, to have pointed out the way, saying, 'It is possible.' I should have followed you, and perhaps we should have surmounted every obstacle, and I should not be here, in this prison, in this solitude. To-day I am not free. Would you have me prove those slanders true? When M. D'Ornis accused me, and I reproached him for speaking falsely, was he telling the truth, and I a lie? Where is he now? We have driven him from his home, and are profiting by his absence....What has just occurred seems like treason to me, and I am pained that the walls about us should have seen and heard you. No, Marguerite Mirion will never forget that by a cruel decree of fate she has become Countess D'Ornis. Whether she loves or hates, the absent are always sacred to her."

He did not understand her: he thought that she was trying to recall to him the distance that there was between them. The storm-cloud burst. In a harsh and cruel voice he cried, "I'm a greater fool than I thought I was. I imagined that you were different from those who brought you up, and I laid at your feet my heart, my dreams, and my workman's blouse. Your father, the other day, treated me like a beggar. He gave me to understand that you also scorned me, and, as I seemed to doubt him, he struck me on the cheek; you have just struck the other. It's all right; the beggar has received his due."

With these words, in spite of her efforts to appease and detain him, he gained the door and hastened away, without turning his head to look at her again.

CHAPTER XLV.

THE LAST FRIEND PROVES FAITHLESS.

This scene threw Marguerite into a deep and settled melancholy. It was too much for her to bear. The man who had espoused her cause, the only living being who wished her well, had just broken with her, and had left her forever, wounded unto death, breathing forth threatenings and accusations. Each coming day taught her a new mode of suffering. It seemed to her that there was yet hidden in her life an abundance of misfortune, and that the cruel smith, multiplying his blows, would not cease to strike upon the anvil till she was quite destroyed. A thought which suddenly crossed her mind increased her perplexity. Joseph had departed without leaving her those dangerous papers which he had brought for her. He had kept them in his hands which were trembling with anger. What would he do with them ? She trembled as she thought of the evil counsel which despair might give to a wounded and savage soul. She tried to reassure herself by thinking that this soul was loyal, that after this transient storm it would grow calm and listen to the voice of reason. "Undoubtedly he will write to me," she said ; "I will answer him, and, while trying to console him, will ask for those two papers ; he will not refuse to give them to me." What did she propose to do with them ? She had determined to destroy them. Of what use could this arm be to her ? She did not intend to defend herself. Assailed by the wind on every side, her poor bark, leaking and dismantled, was drifting on to hopeless shipwreck. The oar was useless now. Nothing remained for her to do but to lie down quietly and let herself be driven by the storm.

The next day she received a letter from Mme. D'Ornis.

"What have you done with my son, madam?" her mother-in law wrote, "and what inexplicable power do you exert over him? Was I not right in objecting to his marriage? From the first day, I foresaw the consequences of that rash experiment. Matters are progressing faster than I expected, though. I do not understand what has occurred between you, and I never want to understand it. I can not help noticing, however, that my son voluntarily leaves his home in order to give you perfect freedom. Such an example of generosity stands by itself in the whole history of marriages. Henceforth the house belongs entirely to you; you receive visits there which are very strange and somewhat compromising; every one to their taste as regards their company and friendships. I did not know that Roger was so accommodating; but you seem able to work miracles. May Castle D'Ornis prove an agreeable place to you! I am much mistaken, or you will finally believe that you are there at home."

While reading this letter, which she tore in pieces as soon as she had finished it, Marguerite felt tears of indignation starting to her eyes; she held them back by an effort of her will. "Am I not to believe this house is mine?" she cried. "If I did not think so, where should I go?" The evening before she had walked to the end of the village for the sake of the exercise and change of scene. On every side she heard low whisperings; each one nudged his neighbor as she approached; even the little children, who were eating their porridge in the doorway, hid their faces in their bowls as she drew near, and quickly lifted them again as soon as her back was turned, to stare with wonder at this gray wolf, this great beast of the *Apocalypse.* Marguerite resolved never again to set her foot in Ornis, to walk nowhere excepting in her park. She owned this park in the same sense that a prisoner owns his prison, and an unhappy person his misfortune.

New sorrows kept coming to her poor heart, either small or great, ridiculous or tragic. A week after her husband had departed, she received from her parents a letter of at least ten pages. Her father informed her that his meeting with Joseph had made him ill, that for a week he had not left his bed. He now rose from it to reproach her in the strongest terms for her unpardonable imprudence and indiscretion. "It is absolutely necessary," he added, "that we should have an explanation of this mystery. If you wish to regain our affection, you must make a full confession, omitting nothing, and not trying to palliate your fault." Mme. Mirion then came to the charge, and addressed to her daughter a sermon in three parts, in which she called her attention to her duty toward her husband, her duty toward herself, and her duty toward her family and country, representing to her in the style of Mme. De Sotenville that she was a Genevese, that is to say, of a race too virtuous to ever permit itself to commit an act by which its honor might be wounded. The good lord came last; he did not lose any thing, however—a fair share of space was allotted him. Marguerite could not read this letter through; she could not bear these horrible commonplaces, with their heartless morality and asphyxiating catechism, which rained on her devoted head at a time when she was exerting all her strength to stand erect. Thenceforth Mon-Plaisir was no more to her than Ornis. Whither should she go? Whichever way she turned, she saw nothing but impossibilities, obstructed pathways, and forbidden doors.

But these miseries were nothing when compared with the torments which Joseph's letters caused her. After ten days of silence, he had begun to write her every day. He had found a lodging place in a suburb of Arnay-le-Duc, whither M. Bertrand, happy to get rid of him so cheaply, had sent at his request his workman's certificate, and the other articles which he had left at Lyons. Turning a deaf ear to every thing about him, Joseph was working for a wheelwright; his apprenticeship had been short, he already understood the trade. Unfortunately, he employed a portion of his nights in scribbling, and these scribblings made Marguerite despair. They were composed of complaints, tendernesses, adorations, and passionate entreaties, interspersed with objurgations no less pathetic, with irony, with bitter sayings, mingled with which were endless arguments on what he called the great injustice of society, anathemas against the spirit of caste and the narrow-minded bourgeois, lyric and wordy apostrophes to the people, to the proletary, to the workman, that eternal victim, that eternal pariah. These grand words and phrases served to cover here and there certain vailed threats, which appeared beneath this frothy rhetoric like the rocks beneath the surface of the wave.

Marguerite had the double misfortune of having to read these letters and to answer them; add to this her constant fear lest one of these missives should go astray or be intercepted. She endeavored to calm Joseph, to pacify him by every means which her tormented mind suggested; reduced to extremities like a besieged town, she had recourse to all manner of expedients. After having appealed in vain to the reason of her passionate solicitor, after having declared a hundred times that there was neither pride nor scorn in her refusal, that for her there were no pariahs, and that she loved him as a brother, she appealed to his generosity; she besought him, she adjured him, she begged for mercy. She wrote one morning: "I had a dream the other night. I was at Mon-Plaisir, I was just sixteen. You entered suddenly in my dream, and said to mother, 'I love her, I want her for my wife.' She immediately placed my hand in yours, and you kissed me, saying, 'We will live together in an attic, and we will work, she with her needle, I with my plane, for she is to be a workman's wife.'.... I thought I saw that attic, and I felt such a thrill of joy, that I awoke and wept." This recital and the comments which she added to it had a contrary effect to what she intended; she was throwing oil upon the fire. Clear and intelligent as was Joseph's mind, and though he had learned the wheelwright's trade at once, there was one thing he could never understand: he knew not what a scruple was, and, having but an intermittent conscience, he had little faith in the conscience of another.

Marguerite's chief thought and care was to obtain from him those two papers. Her uneasiness increasing day by day, she demanded them with tears and cries; he pretended not to notice this, and never referred to it in his replies. She wrote to him: "If you will send me those papers, I will write you that

I love you, and you can show my letter to the world." He still turned a deaf ear to her. She then began to comprehend that his determination was irrevocable, that she could not move him, that there was a bargain to be made, that all her reproaches and appeals were beating against a wall, and that in trying to save herself, she had simply changed her master and the form of her misfortune.

A new suspicion increased still more her cruel agony. She could no longer doubt that her maid was in the service of the enemy ; this girl was constantly at her side, always watching her, following her about, entering her room without permission. Suddenly, as though new instructions had been given her, she relaxed her vigilance and pretended to avoid her mistress. Marguerite inferred from this that they had determined no longer to keep a check upon her movements, but to leave her free to commit some indiscretion. She questioned Fanny ; her embarrassed answers not satisfying her, she dismissed her, and took in her place the daughter of the old paralytic whom she had cared for, and who had remained faithful to her. About the same time she made another observation. At the end of the park was a spot from which the old Countess's house was visible. Marguerite noticed that there were two windows in this house, the blinds of which were always closed. Was some one concealed behind those blinds ? How great was her emotion when in the midst of one of her sleepless nights, having heard footsteps in the garden and softly opened her blind, she thought she saw gliding along the orangery a man who, in form and manner, resembled M. D'Ornis ! The evening before Joseph had written her that he often escaped from Arnay after supper, and wandered during the night about the castle. At the mere thought that these two ramblers might meet each other, Marguerite felt her blood freeze in her veins. She feared lest one should kill the other, or, if he should fail, lest the other, released from his promise, should carry his terrible threats into execution. These two alternatives both filled her with alarm ; the second, which seemed most probable, terrified her most. Her husband's words, "If ever I come to an unhappy end, it will be your work," were constantly resounding in her ears; she repeated them again and again, by day and by night.

From that moment, she had not an hour's rest. At times, she shook and trembled like a leaf. Soon she felt moving in the deep confusion of her soul a thought, vague and obscure at first, but little by little taking consistency and shape. This thought or shape seemed like a monster to her. Her heart would not acknowledge this enormity; it cried out against it when it first appeared, but finally was silent. In certain situations, the soul soon becomes familiar with such monsters.

CHAPTER XLVI.

AN APPEAL FOR MERCY.

A few days later, Marguerite received from Joseph a sealed letter, which she turned for some time in her fingers before daring to open it; she had a presentiment that it contained her fate. Finally she broke the seal and read it. It was short, containing only the following words:

"My strength and reason are both exhausted; I have resolved to end my life. There is nothing to keep me longer in the world; my mother died two weeks ago, I received the news this morning. But I do not intend to die without being revenged, or rather without avenging that innocent man whom a criminal allowed to die in his place. I am working here; I shall be free in a few days, and will set out for Beaune, where I will see a certain person I need not name. I have a right to do this; if I can believe my eyes, the tacit promise which was made me has been broken. It is possible that you may have given your consent, but mine has not been asked. So justice shall be done before I die. My resolve is fixed, do not try to change it; you might as well reason with a stone. And yet, if you had wished it otherwise,....but you do not wish it. Henceforth I am only a judge and executioner."

Marguerite walked for some time up and down her room with this letter in her hand; then she sat down and leaned her head against the bed. She remained for two hours in that position, so motionless that it seemed doubtful whether she breathed at all. She held a last deliberation with herself. She looked at all those doors which were closed against her, she timidly tried those inexorable bolts which refused to give her passage. Death alone was possible; but could she quit the world and leave those papers there behind her? Must she not, at any price, carry them with her to the tomb? Her new maid twice entered the room while she was thus absorbed in thought, and twice approached to speak to her without securing her attention. Her silence and immobility filled the good girl with terror, and she retired on tip toe, as much startled as though she had seen a corpse.

At the end of two hours, Marguerite rose, and running to her desk, rapidly traced the following reply:

"I, also, have my folly, and you must make yours conform with it. I have made my decision; like you, I wish to bid farewell to life. This is my proposition: you must give up your plans of vengeance, and I will pass a day with you in some place which I shall indicate, and the evening of the same day we will die together. Do you accept?"

She ran her eyes over what she had written, and with a convulsive laugh, she cried, "That is the monster!" The letter remained for half a day upon her table. From time to time, she read it over, asking if it was really herself, if it was Marguerite Mirion who had written those four lines. Then she passed her whole life in review, in order to convince herself that the person who had been sitting by that table and who had dipped her pen into that inkstand was the same who, in former days, joyous and happy as a bird, had related to her dearest friend all the innocent secrets of her boarding-school, and who afterwards had, for three years, filled with her laughter a country-house called Mon-Plaisir. Improbable as it seemed, there was an identity between the two. "How could it be otherwise?" she said in a low tone. "We are at the mercy of events, events beget monsters, and misfortune is a horrible toothed wheel; if it catch you only by the finger, it will soon draw in your arms and head. Whose fault is it? I was a good girl, I asked only to be good, my intentions were the best, I did not know that good intentions were scourges and snares; one day, with the most honest purpose in the world, I committed an imprudent act, and this act led me to an abyss. Then I escaped as best I could, and now I am writing and sending letters, and there are carriers who bear them away without knowing that what they are holding in their hands contains the honor and the life of Margot." Such was her story; thus she had commenced, thus also she was about to finish, and it all was linked together, it could not have been otherwise. This letter was the necessary solution, the inevitable *dénoûment* of the tragedy. She sent it in the afternoon.

The next day she received an answer, which ran thus: "Yes, yes, a thousand times times yes. To die with you, what joy!"

She sent the following reply: "I have your promise and you have mine. I ask for four or five days in which to make necessary arrangements; at the end of that time I will write and make an appointment with you; but you must agree not to leave Arnay during these five days, and you also must not write to me. If you fail to keep these conditions, our agreement will be ended."

Why did she ask for this delay? Apparently because she was twenty-one, and because at that age one has the divine instinct of hope, because one insists in believing in the unforseen, in the miracles of chance, in the saving event which may come to-morrow; in order to give it time to come, one puts off the evil day. Marguerite usefully employed these days of grace which she had not been able to deny herself. A short time before she had been taken sick, in order to fill up the long solitary days, she had formed the plan of sending to the daughter of her father's farmer a complete Burgundian costume, which consisted of a tulle bonnet, gathered in behind and furnished with a ruche, a jacket of red silk, a black collar from which hung a silver cross, a short full skirt of black rep, and a pair of figured stockings and buckled shoes. She had already made the bonnet, and cut out the waist and skirt; but the brain-fever had interrupted her, and the unfinished garments had been laid away in a closet. Marguerite took them out and set to work to finish them, fitting them to her own form. This work kept her constantly employed.

A new alarm caused her to hasten her preparations. She had acquired that unnatural acuteness of hearing which is sometimes caused by uneasiness and fear. One night she thought she again heard footsteps in the garden, and this time, the moon shining brightly, she distinctly recognized M. D'Ornis, who was moving toward the orangery, where he remained concealed for about two hours. She rose early the next morning, put every thing in order, and burned all her letters and her papers; then she sat motionless for a long time in the corner of the room, her head bent forward and resting on her knees. She was talking in a low voice, she was saying, "Thou, who knowest all, wilt thou not pardon me? Thou knowest that I am doing the best I can, that I can not do otherwise. I have sought and have not found. What a life has mine been! Thou knowest my days and nights, my sorrows, my repentance, and my fears. Thou knowest that I can not remain here, and that no other place is open to me. That is nothing though. That man whose wife I am, who could accuse me of having sought his life, and could say, 'My blood be upon thee!' .... that is what terrifies me. Yes, I committed a fault, a serious fault; I ought to have kept my trouble and unhappiness to myself. I did wrong to trust in friendship. Why was I not taught to believe in nothing, to think that every thing on earth is false? Now I must expiate my fault. If any thing else is possible, tell me now, I pray thee, before it is too late. Dost thou not hear me? I know that thou dost hear, although I speak so low: this is a secret between me and thee, and no one else must hear us. If thou dost not answer, I will speak still louder; but my cry must reach thee, wherever thou mayst be. Thou knowest all things; thou knowest that, in my happy days, the beggars that I met had scarcely to move their lips. I understood them before they spoke." She stopped here, her voice was choked with sobs; a moment after, she again began to speak to the eternal silence.

Finally, she felt that this door, the last at which she had knocked, also refused to open; that He to whom she spoke would answer neither yes nor no, that He would leave her free, reserving the right to judge her. Then she took the final step. She sat down at her writing-table, and it seemed as though her pen ran over the paper of its own accord without the aid of hand or will.

"The time has come. I have a desire to die near Geneva, in a village built on the slope of a hill from which Mon-Plaisir is visible. We were there three years ago; you accompanied us in our walk. It was Easter-Sunday. I now and then helped you to carry the lunch basket. You passed your cane through the handles of the basket; you took hold of one end and I of the other. The cane broke, but the basket was not hurt. My memory fails me; I can not recall the name of the village; you surely will remember it. Go there and wait for me. You shall see me coming day after to-morrow morning, by a lovely road that runs in zig-zags, and passes through a certain hamlet..... My memory has entirely deserted me..... Yes, now I know, the hamlet is called Perly-Certoux. This name has come to me, but not the other."

Then, without letting the ink dry on her pen, she wrote the second letter as follows:

"I am going to Geneva. Do not be disturbed. I will speak of you to no one. I will see no one except a man who has promised to kill me, and afterwards kill himself. When you read these lines, you will have neither wife nor enemy; and, without its having cost you any thing, the paper you know of will have been destroyed. I swear it shall be so; for once in your life believe me."

She sealed these two notes; then ringing for her maid, whom she knew she could depend upon, she gave the letters to her, directing her to send the first one immediately to the post, and to give the other the next evening to Mme. D'Ornis. She then told her that she was going to Paris to be absent for some time, and ordered her to pack her trunk, naming piece by piece the various articles she wished to take. After that she kissed her, and slipped into her hand a box containing a bank-note for a thousand francs, requesting her not to open it till after she had left. It seemed to her that she could not recompense sufficiently this fidelity of the last hour.

About ten o'clock she was riding in a carriage on the road to

Blaizy-Bas. Her coachman leaned back to ask her where she wished to stop? "At Blaizy-Bas," she answered.

"My lady is going to Paris?"

"I said so once, I think," was her reply.

When she had reached the railway station, she ordered him to return as soon as his horses had had some oats. While they were eating, with their heads bent toward the trough, a singular thought came to her; she kissed each of them tenderly on the white star on their foreheads. These horses were hers, and had never caused her any trouble; such a miracle called for a reward. Then she entered an inn near the station, engaged a room, and, while waiting for the Paris train, opened her trunk, took out the tulle bonnet, the red jacket, the short rep skirt, the figured stockings, and the buckled shoes. She spent some time at her toilette, and was well satisfied with her appearance when it was finished. As soon as she had passed about her neck the black collar and the silver cross, she placed in her trunk the garments she had just taken off, and throwing a large cape over her shoulders, started for the waiting-room. The people at the inn who saw her pass gazed at her in astonishment; she paid no attention to them; she cared little for such gazing now.

She arrived at Lyons in the evening. She did not leave until the afternoon of the next day. It is probable that what she saw at the end of her journey terrified her, and that, by a last effort of nature, she sought to gain a little time. Besides, was it not necessary that she should allow time for that master of ceremonies, whom Death had chosen, and had sent before her to a village to prepare the feast? Marguerite reached Geneva toward midnight. She stopped at the hotel which was nearest to the station.

At daybreak she wrote a letter to her uncle, in which, without mentioning any facts or accusing any one, she told him of her supreme determination, and begged him to seek for her body the next day in the village of Confignon: this name had finally returned to her. She thanked him for having been the only one who had believed her innocent. She begged him to continue to believe that, notwithstanding appearances, she was more deserving of pity than of blame, and that the determination she had taken was the result of a terrible fatality. In a postscript, alluding to one of the favorite expressions of the worthy man, she added, "Life is a great *chosier* in which there are more things than young girls can understand. What I have found there has given me a horror of living. Fortunately this great sack is open at one end, and we can leave it when we will."

She slipped this letter into her pocket, and then left her baggage with the proprietor of the hotel, telling him that in a few days she would send for it. This being done, she took a carriage and started on her way. Her route took her past Mon-Plaisir, the inhabitants of which seemed to be asleep. She stopped at the entrance of the road leading to Perly-Certoux, and paid her driver, who afterward testified that he noticed at the time that she had a singular look. She made a mistake in counting her money, confusing the gold pieces with the silver. Finally, she became impatient, and gave the driver all the money in her hand.

CHAPTER XLVII.

A DISASTROUS TRIUMPH.

The road that Marguerite followed is bordered with oak-trees and quick-set hedges. After making several turns, it slopes gently toward a stone bridge thrown across a stream, which is called the Aire. On arriving at the bridge, you have before you a village built on the side of a hill, and surrounded by black walnut-trees. On either side runs the stream, its green waters bubbling over the pebbles which form its bed, while aspen-trees and willows line its banks. Marguerite saw neither the village nor the stream; she saw nothing but Joseph standing on the bridge. It was her destiny which there awaited her; she did not try to escape; she moved directly toward him. Joseph looked at her as she approached with some surprise, scarcely recognizing her in her disguise, which was displeasing to him. Doubtless the tulle bonnet and short dress enhanced her beauty; but it was not exactly the Marguerite whom he expected, the one whom he had seen in his dreams, and whom he had sworn to possess. His displeasure soon vanished, however; his mind was occupied with more serious thoughts.

He fell on his knees in the centre of the bridge, and cried with a voice which seemed to come from his inmost breast, "Your father is right; I am a villain. Spurn me from you as I deserve. I made an infamous proposition to you, and I have used violent means to obtain your consent. Here are the two papers; do what you please with them. I release you from your promise."

As he finished speaking, she shook her head, and a bitter smile crossed her lips. There was but one thing left for her to do, to choose the manner of her death. She preferred the knife, and determined soon to tell him so. In the mean time, she eagerly seized the papers, and, asking Joseph to give her a match, she lit them and threw the burning fragments into the air, the wind bearing their ashes to the stream. Leaning upon the parapet, she watched them as they disappeared. Now she could die, she had made reparation for her fault; there was nothing more for her to do.

The pathway which they entered follows the course of the Aire, and leads into a wild and desolate country. Since they last had met, an event had taken place, which, although the world has had plenty of time to become accustomed to it, always appears as wonderful as a miracle; I refer to the coming of the spring. It was now the latter part of April, and the first renewal of the face of nature, with all its uncompleted graces, had begun. Some trees were already covered with a light foliage which promised rather than gave a shade, and which allowed the eye to wander through the woods and to lose itself in the far distance. The hedges were white with the freshly opened hawthorn blossoms; in the orchards near the villages the peach-trees were covered with pink clouds. The willows bent their light green branches toward the stream, and newly springing plants were mingled with old mosses. The first verdure of the poplars could just be seen; these tardy ones, who were hurrying on, fearing to miss this happy time, seemed to reproach their sap for moving slowly. The black walnuts and the plane-trees had not yet begun to blossom; the oaks had not even shaken off their dead leaves, and gazed as in a dream at the bright fresh grass, the green bushes, the sudden appearance of the violets which were springing up at their feet, whose subtile perfume surprised them in their slumbers. Every where Life was defying Death, and Death itself experienced a secret desire to live again. These two children, who were about to die, did not think of greeting the eternal Cæsar, that omnipotent Nature, whose sovereign will sports with its creatures, brings them forth but to destroy them, and, warming again their cold ashes, causes a new progeny to spring forth. They walked beside the river, and, while absorbed in thought, passed by this festival without perceiving it. Sometimes, their eyes met, and then they shuddered. One was filled with grief, remorse, and expectation ; the other felt her destiny weighing heavily upon her, and thought she heard within the woods the frightened beating of a heart which was kept in motion only by its fears. God knows that there was nothing in the woods except the spring, which was now calling its orchestra together, and except the birds, who, knowing of its coming, hastened to try their voices and attune their instruments, without ever dreaming that misfortune was passing near them. What had these artists, in their divine abstraction, to do with such a stranger ?

At noon, Joseph left Marguerite in the retreat which they had chosen ; he went to the village for some food, for they had determined not to die of hunger. When he had reached the top of the hill, he stopped at a spot from which he could see the valley, on one side Geneva with the three towers of its cathedral, on the other Mon-Plaisir with its avenue of pear-trees. He remained for some time motionless, his hair streaming in the wind, his glance scanning the entire valley. He wished to exhibit the pride which sparkled in his eyes, the intoxication of his triumph, his cheek which had forgotten the blow it had received, his hands which seemed to grasp their prey. He flattered himself that he had conquered fate, that he had secured that happiness which had been so rudely denied him, and that this happiness would avenge him for all the scorn he had received. He had only one regret, which, however, was a serious one : no one seemed to know what he had done. He wanted to cry in clarion tones : 'She is mine !" He wanted to be heard at Mon-Plaisir and at Geneva, so that at the one place they should cry with rage, and at the other toss their caps in air, as a sign of joy and triumph ; he wanted the Jura and the Alps to be informed of his adventure. The truth is he persisted in believing that he had undertaken a great work, that he had begun a revolution, and that he had given the signal for the long-delayed revenge of the oppressed.

He finally reached the village inn, procured a loaf of fresh bread, a few slices of cold meat, a cake, a bottle of white wine, two forks, two plates, and a single glass, placed them all in a basket, and, with this basket on his arm, hastened back to the banks of the Aire, to the solitude where he had left Marguerite. He found her lying on the grass asleep. He sat down near her respecting her slumber. Now and then her lips moved, and her fingers nervously grasped the silver cross which was hanging from her neck. She was dreaming; it seemed to her that just as she was leaving Ornis, Death, moved with pity, had transported her, without a struggle and without pain, to a world where there were no castles, nor garrets, nor orangeries, where she saw no Bertrand, no Count D'Ornis, no Joseph, to a divine world where there was no thought nor care, where she could sleep in peace—for what she most desired was to have no one speak to her again, to recover from her weariness, to drown her memories and her fears in deep oblivion. Leaving the earth, her soul expanded, floating in an immense solitude and infinite silence, which was interrupted only by soft strains of mysterious music, sounding like the faint notes of an organ far away.

Joseph finally grew impatient, and noisily struck his hands together. She shuddered, opened her eyes, and found that she had not left the earth, that she was lying on the bank of a babbling stream, near a wood to which the wind was whispering her name, that she was not dead, that the knife still awaited her. She sat up suddenly with an angry look. She was still at the mercy of her illusions ; like Life, Death also had deceived her. Her anger embraced the entire universe, but fell chiefly upon Joseph. Why had he awakened her ? why had he not killed her in her sleep ? She must then begin to live again.

She answered his questions with dry monosyllables, only tasted of the food, and refused to drink the wine, perhaps because there was but one glass. When the meal was finished, she quenched her thirst at the stream, joining her hands together to form a cup.

Joseph mistook the cause of her irritation. He thought that on awakening a desire for life had come to her, that she had felt her resolution waver, that she desired to change her purpose, and that she was angry because she had to make the humiliating confession to him. He experienced a feeling of unutterable joy, and, when she had seated herself at his side again, he made known to her the hope which had been concealed within his breast. "This isn't such a serious matter," he said in a tender voice. "We will not die; life is too sweet."

As she was silent, he continued, "Ah! you might have known that I should never have accepted your proposition, if I had not thought that you would repent of it." Then, opening his heart, he besought her to fly with him; he painted in glowing colors the happiness in store for them beyond the sea, in America, in a house which he intended to build for her with his own hands—their daily joys, his adoration, his devotion, his tender love—how he would work for her, the wonders his ten fingers would perform, those fingers which were worth a fortune to him, and which would gain that fortune for her. "Do those die who love and whom happiness awaits?" he cried. "What is death that we should think of it?" As he spoke thus, he tore from the ground handfuls of fresh grass and held them toward her.

She let him finish; then looking fixedly upon him, she asked in a dry and abrupt tone, "Do you suppose that I am happier to-day than I was yesterday?"

These terrible words recalled him from the sky, and completely demolished the castle he had built; he began to re-build it again, however; he was not a man to yield so quickly.

She interrupted him, saying, "You may as well understand the truth: you hate the bourgeois, I owe you a confession; I feel that I am a bourgeoise in my entire nature. I have but little heart, I am narrow-minded; I was brought up in that way. The only happiness which tempts me is the happiness of a bourgeois, and, besides, I have the peculiar ideas of my class; what we care most for is to be thought well of. How can it be otherwise? We are so constituted that we must have the esteem of those about us. I would rather die a dozen times than to hear it said some day, 'People think that she's his wife, but she really is his mistress.' You will answer me that over there no one will know, that we can tell them what we please, and they will believe us. But there comes in another of my prejudices: I have a holy horror of a lie, and I could not be untruthful for three days in succession, without loathing myself and the man who forced me to it!"

He was filled with anger; the hot blood mounted to his face, and fierce threats rose to his lips. He gave himself up to the most violent passion. Perhaps he thought this would frighten Marguerite; what now had she to fear? She laughed aloud and said, "Good! take vengeance on this bourgeoise; kill her in your mad fury; that is the best thing for you to do. Where is your knife?"

Joseph felt his anger suddenly depart; he began to weep, to beg for mercy, to tear his hair, to kiss Marguerite's feet, to call her by her name again and again. She was inflexible, inexorable; she repeated the words which he had written: "You are talking to a stone." At last he understood that he could effect nothing, that his tears and cries could not change her resolution, that he had cruelly deceived himself, that his happiness was but a dream, and that his punishment had now begun. He fled into the woods, where he remained for more than an hour, walking about, out of his mind, stumbling over rocks and striking himself against the trees. His pride was dead; in his broken heart remained only an incurable grief, a nameless despair, a hopeless love which was terrified by the promise he had made and by the blood he was about to shed. He thought for a moment of killing himself then and there, in order to escape the horror of seeing her die; but his soul was strong even in its weakness—his promise must be kept. He submitted to his fate, his heart beat more calmly, and passing from the woods, he returned to Marguerite, whom he found motionless in the place where he had left her.

She received him kindly; her usual voice and manner had returned. She said as she held out her hand, "I do not reproach you; who are we that we should struggle against fate?

I have always had confidence in your courage and your promises. Otherwise I should not be here." She permitted him to again seat himself at her feet and to repeat all the tender thoughts with which her beauty and their unhappy fate inspired him. She listened to him indulgently, or, I should rather say, with the fixed attention of a person who desires to master something she can not understand; he spoke to her in a strange tongue, and in what he said there were many things which her good sense could not explain. She finally confessed this fact, but with so much tact and gentleness that he could not be offended. A moment afterward he became silent and thoughtful; he had learned since morning that he was under the influence of an illusion. He had thought himself alone with Marguerite; a third accompanied them; it was Death, who, standing near her, covered her with his dark shadow.

They rose and walked about the woods. At nightfall a shower came on. They began to run, and Joseph went ahead to prepare a fire. He did not notice that, on entering the village, Marguerite had met the postman who was taking the letters from the box to carry them to Geneva, and had quietly handed him the one which she had written in the morning.

CHAPTER XLVIII.

THE LAST ACT OF THE TRAGEDY

The night before, Joseph, not finding any rooms vacant at the inn, had applied to an old peasant who owned a very respectable house, two rooms of which he rented to city people who wished to spend the summer out of town. As it was early, the rooms had not yet been taken, and Joseph engaged them both, telling the good man that he had just been married, that his wife had gone to see some relatives in Savoy, that she would soon return to him, that he wished to pass the honeymoon like a gentleman, and, his means permitting it, to work no more till it was over.

As Marguerite appeared in the doorway, their host was throwing an armful of vine cuttings on the fire. How very familiar he was! "What a handsome girl!" he cried. Then he added as he drew two chairs before the fire, "The lovers must sit down and dry themselves." At these words Marguerite frowned; there are moments when false notes are very painful to the ear. She became nervous and somewhat cruel.

The old man, although he could not see very clearly, was struck by the whiteness of her hands. "Where did you find that girl?" he said to Joseph. "Those hands have never touched a frying-pan."

"Do you think so?" she replied. "Give me some eggs; I'll make an omelette for you."

He took her at her word. She cut her parsley very fine, beat her eggs up in an earthen dish, and melted her butter in the frying-pan. The omelette was ready in a trice, and strange to say it tasted well. During supper Marguerite kept up her part; she boasted to their host of her housekeeping abilities, explained to him how she would take care of her house, and described it in detail with all its furniture and cooking utensils. She was in haste to take possession of it; life is so sweet when love is in the heart. What happy parties they would have on holidays and Sundays! what dinners spread upon the grass! They would start at daylight, stop and drink cream at the cottages on the road, and in the evening return, tired with their journey, but cheerful, happy, and contented.

"How long will that last?" the peasant asked. "Youth passes quickly."

"Mine will not die before I do," she answered.

At that moment they heard the singing of a bird. "A nightingale!" she cried with a sudden start. The old man began to laugh, and told her that the nightingales never came before the middle of May. She insisted that she had just heard one, and, as he still contradicted her, she became excited.

"I will maintain to my last hour," she answered, "that I heard a nightingale to-day."

Joseph, with his head resting on the back of a chair, seemed absent from the world and did not speak a word. His silence was an abyss into which Marguerite's words dropped one by one, like stones whose fall is heard as they strike the bottom of a chasm.

She rose and, touching him on the shoulder, said, "The time has come, let's go up-stairs."

He rose mechanically to his feet, and, taking a candle, went up the stairs. He looked like a walking statue. Before following him, she turned toward their host and said, "We are two fools, who will give you a great deal of trouble, perhaps; I want to pay you for it in advance."

And, approaching him, she put three gold pieces in his hand. He looked at her with a bewildered air; but the gold pieces pleased him, and he took them from her.

When she reached the room, Joseph, who had just placed the candle on the table, fell on the floor like one dead. He remained there for a long time, biting his hands and sobbing bitterly. She sat down in a chair in front of him; she tried to comfort him, she chided him. He prayed for mercy, he no longer asked for years, he begged for days, for hours, for minutes. Then she told him that she had written two letters. "To-morrow a man, it may be two, will come for me," she said. "I want them to find me dead and cold."

At these terrible words, he rose upon his knees. A cold sweat poured from his face, his mouth was writhing, his agony was depicted on his brow. "After all," she said, "your misfortune is not so great. You may be sure that you would never have been satisfied with me. You are very romantic, my poor friend, and I am not so in the least. Strong passions and deep emotions were never meant for me. When you spoke of your love just now, I told you that I could scarcely understand you, I have loved many things, but I have never worshiped any one, I do not think it would be possible for me. I am simply a very quiet and very ordinary person, and, this time I say it without anger, I am a bourgeoise at heart; I was born to live, like nearly all the world, far away from adventures and from storms. The storms have come and have beaten upon me, and I have now an intense loathing of life. A little good sense and a great deal of gayety, that is what Marguerite Mirion was. What is left of it all, to-day?.... I have suffered so much that my heart has been slowly eaten away. There is no more oil in the lamp; it flickers and its flame is dying away; it is better to blow it out at once."

He was not in a condition to understand her; but her gentle accent and the music of her voice soothed his despair, which finally passed away. Seeing her so calm, so strong in courage, he was overcome with shame, and after remaining a few minutes motionless, with his face buried in his hands, he rose and said, "I am ready; I will do whatever you wish."

She thanked him earnestly, and then a last strange fancy took possession of her. In passing through the village, she had noticed an open barn, where the carpenters were at work. She asked Joseph to go there and get some shavings for her. He hastened to the spot, and soon returned with the shavings in his blouse. When she saw these friends of her early days entering the room, she smiled. She took off her hood, let her hair fall upon her shoulders, and, after tenderly kissing the shavings, wove them into a crown, which she placed upon her head. There was a broken mirror at the other end of the room; she walked over to it, looked at herself, and admired her new head-dress. Turning toward Joseph she said, "Is it not true that carpentry is the king of all the arts and trades, and that we will die faithful to our early love?"

He did not answer. He could no longer live except in silence; it seemed to him that his courage and his life were at the mercy of the first word that he spoke. She came back to him; changing her tone, she said, "I have been very harsh to you, to-day; I have given you much pain. Forgive me, as I forgive every one on earth."

Then, taking his head between her hands, she gently kissed his brow. Immediately afterward she bared her breast. "Now is the time!" she said. He opened his knife. He was white as a piece of marble, and before his eyes there floated a cloud of blood, through which he saw Marguerite very small and far away, as though he was looking at her through a telescope reversed. He felt that his arm could never reach her. He poured some water into a basin, plunged his head into it, and rubbed his eyes. The cloud vanished; when he stood up again, he saw clearly, his ideas were not confused. He knew that he was there, that she stood before him, and that he was about to kill her.

She spoke again. She was standing very straight, her back resting against the wall. She was thinking of an old dancing master, who had often tormented her at boarding-school. He always said, "Stand up straight, mademoiselle, and keep that left shoulder in, I beg of you." By a mechanical movement she drew in her left shoulder. Joseph raised his arm, but it refused to strike because she was looking at him. In a broken voice he begged her to close her eyes; her eyes prevented him from killing her. She did not close them, but she turned away her head, and the last thing that she saw was an immense Castle D'Ornis on the wall before her, which was spinning swiftly like a top. Then she gave a feeble cry; Joseph had stabbed her to the heart, and with such a blow that death was instantaneous, and not a drop of blood flowed from the wound. She sank down heavily; he caught her in his arms, gazed for a long time into her face, and assured himself that she was dead. Then he took her up and laid her on the bed, by the side of which he stood for a long time, arranging her hair, fastening her jacket, and smoothing out her dress. At intervals, he kissed her feet; but his eyes were dry, he could not shed a tear.

The remainder of the night he spent in scribbling; this had always been a mania of his. He wrote a letter of twenty pages to the workman with whom he had gone to Fossaz on the day of Marguerite's marriage. Faithful to his oath, in this rambling and incoherent letter, he spoke only of himself, sometimes to boast of what he had done as a great and noble act, sometimes to accuse and revile himself as a villain and a murderer; his epistle ended with a formal dissertation on the social question, in which a few sparks of good sense were dimly visible through dense clouds of smoke. The last line ran thus: "Workmen, when will come the day, in which you shall be the masters of your masters?"

His candle, which was nearly burnt away, suddenly went out. He waited for the dawn; he did not wish to die without seeing again his idol and his victim. As soon as a dim light began to fill the room, he approached the resting place of what had once been Marguerite. He opened her eyes again and asked himself what there was within them; then he pressed his lips on those cold lips which could not speak to him; he strove to draw a last breath from them, as though to make her say she loved him. The light increased. He wound his left hand in the bright tresses which had won his heart, and plunged the knife three times into his breast. When the room was entered, he was breathing still; a moment afterward, he was no more.

Uncle Benjamin arrived two hours later. On entering the blood-stained room, his surprise was as great as his despair. M. D'Ornis had preceded him, and, leaning over the bodies, had just finished searching their pockets which were turned inside out. It appears that he had met the driver of the carriage which Marguerite had taken. Some also pretend to say that he had followed her without her knowledge, and that, if he had wished, he might have intercepted her the day before ; but this has not been proved. Since that time he has not been seen ; it is impossible to discover what has become of him, or whether he has had the pleasure of learning that M. Bertrand, after selling all his property, had departed suddenly for Brazil. The adventure at the ditch and Joseph's face and form as he leaned against the cross had left an indelible impression on the mind of this mediocre rascal. On his arrival at Rio Janeiro, he told some one that an accident had happened which had disgusted him with Europe.

At Mon-Plaisir, they are disgusted not only with Europe, but with every thing ; they still gather pears in autumn, but there are no more roses to be seen in spring. Mlle. Baillet, who has become very devout, pretends that Marguerite had read some novels without her mother's knowledge. Cousin Grillet is more than ever convinced that the world is full of thorns ; she scarcely dares to take a step. Mme. Mirion has not been able to bear her sorrows. For six months she did not pronounce her daughter's name ; on her death-bed, she felt her mother's heart awakening again ; she said to her pastor, who was at her bedside during her last moments, "My pastor, I am sure that in her heart she was innocent, and that that villain laid a trap for her ; I am going to meet in heaven that poor dear Countess." Since M. Mirion has become a widower, Uncle Benjamin has returned to live with him. He is proud of having been chosen by Marguerite to receive her last farewells ; but he is wrong in sometimes saying, "Didn't I tell you so?"

Marguerite Mirion's story, the mystery surrounding which has never yet been cleared away, caused a prodigious sensation at Geneva. For some weeks it was the chief topic of conversation—in fact, they talk about it still. Some are without pity for M. and Mme. Mirion, whom they accuse of being the real authors of the calamity. "That is what you might expect," they say, "from the spirit of intrigue and ambition." In other circles, Marguerite is blamed, the most virulent anathemas are hurled against her, and she is reproached as being destitute of principle and religion. Those who are more thoughtful or better informed consider, on the contrary, that there are in this world, as Marguerite wrote one day, terrible fatalities, and that it is a wise man's part sometimes to suspend his judgment. Among the workmen there are many who look upon Joseph as a hero: he might have been a hero, but he failed; he belonged to a very dangerous race.

www.ingramcontent.com/pod-product-compliance
Lightning Source LLC
LaVergne TN
LVHW020221110826
845151LV00003B/784

* 9 7 8 1 4 2 5 5 3 2 7 0 3 *